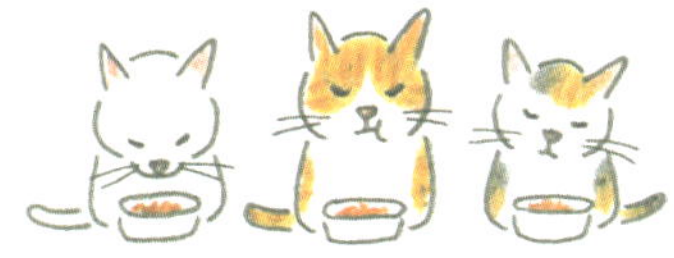

How to Draw
KAWAII CATS

Sayo Koizumi

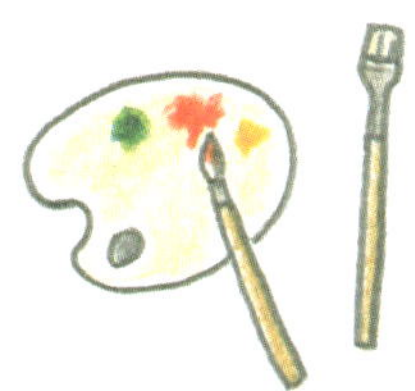

TUTTLE Publishing

Tokyo | Rutland, Vermont | Singapore

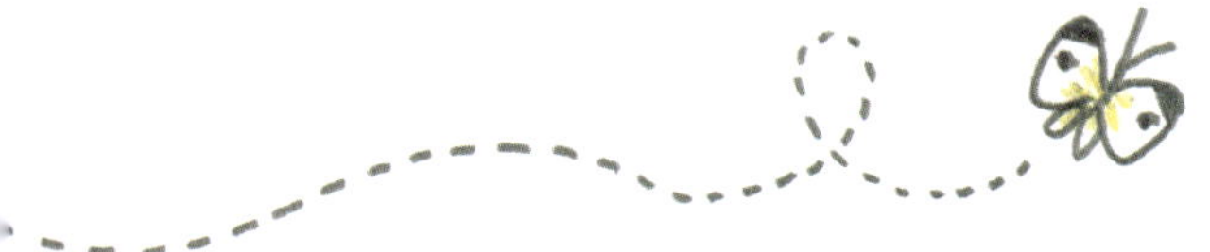

Table of Contents

PART 1

Start Drawing Cats

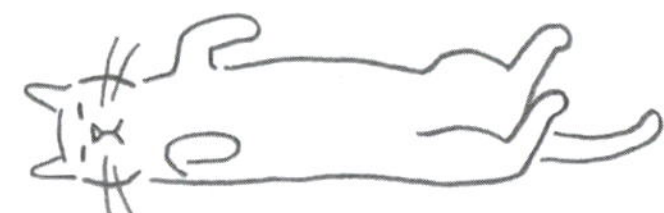

PART 2

Understanding Cat Shapes

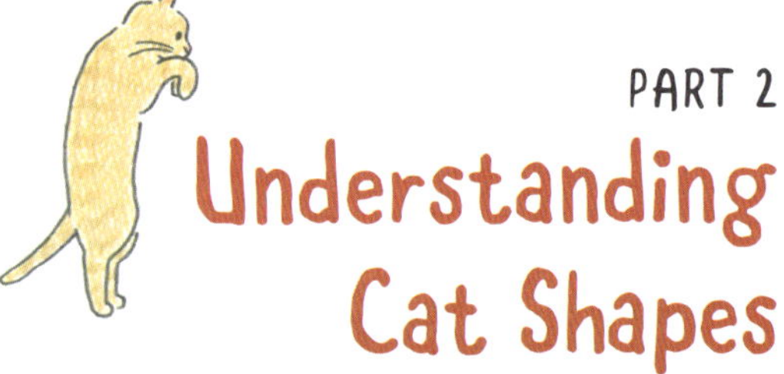

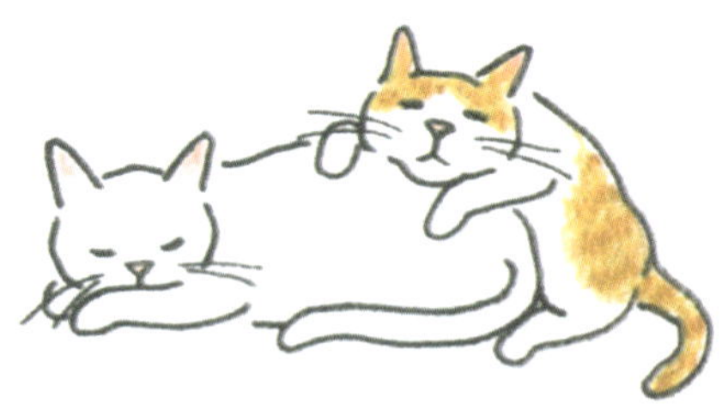

PART 3

Drawing Techniques by Medium

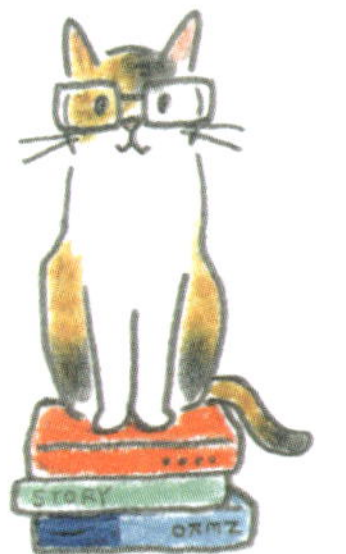

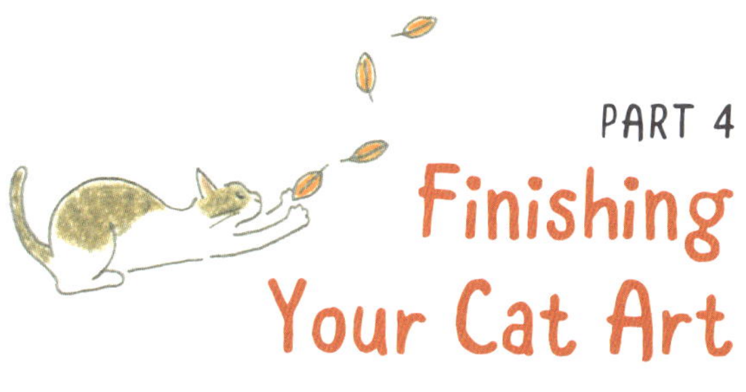

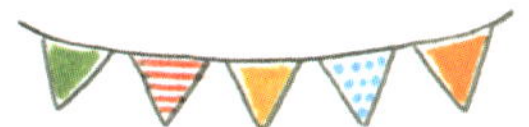

SPECIAL FEATURES

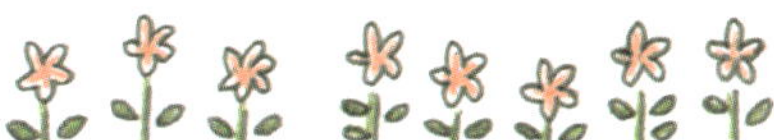

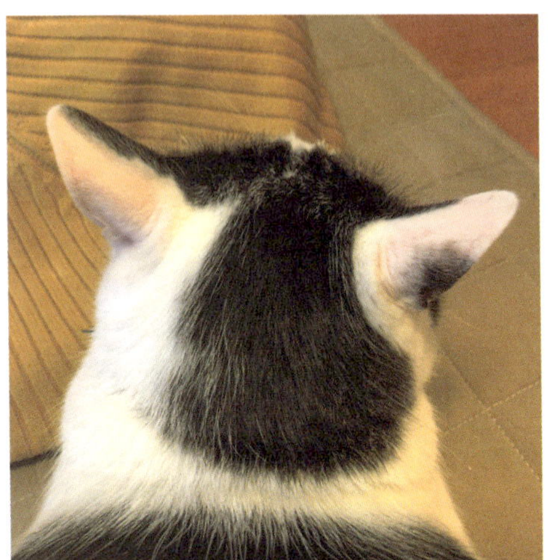

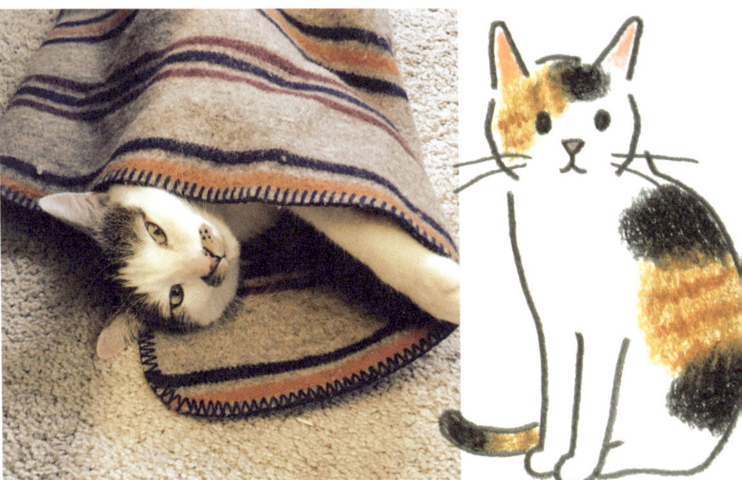

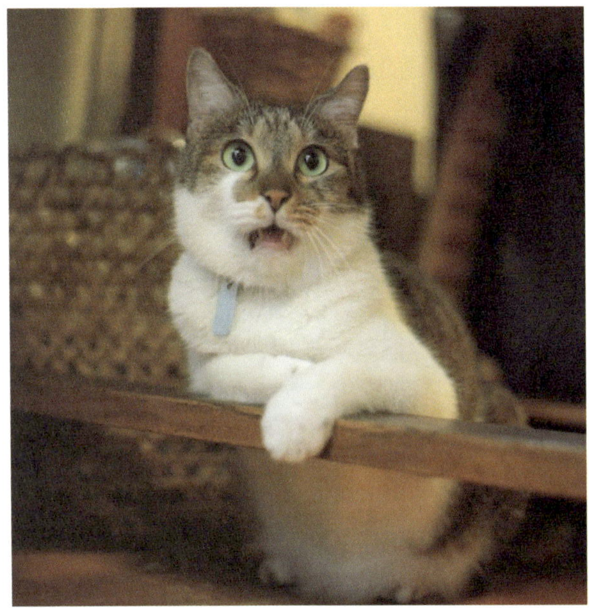

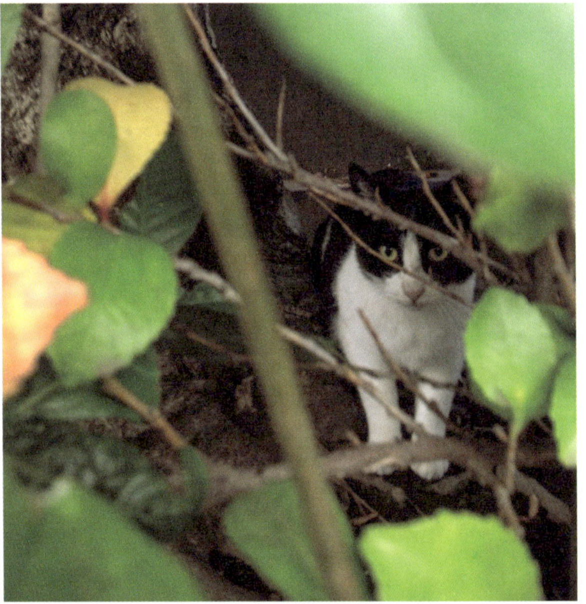

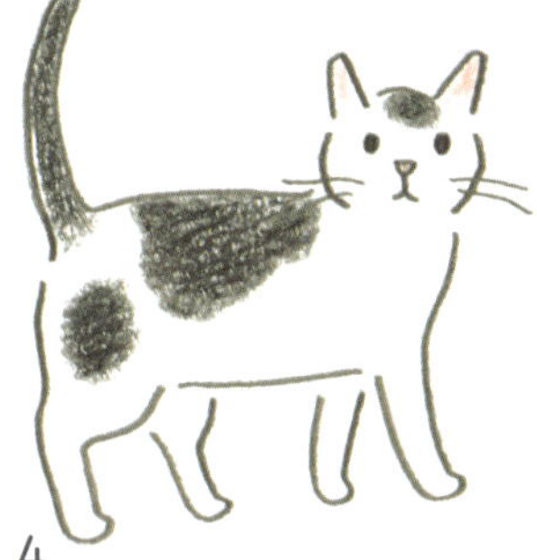

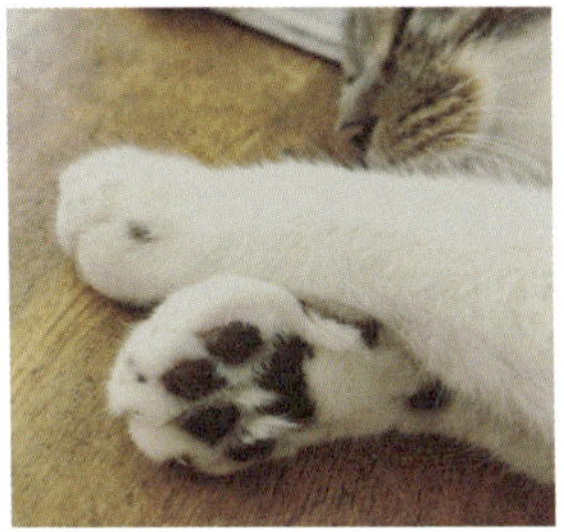

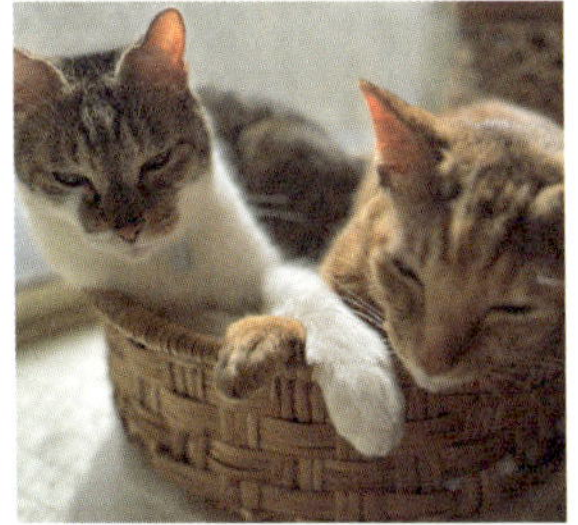

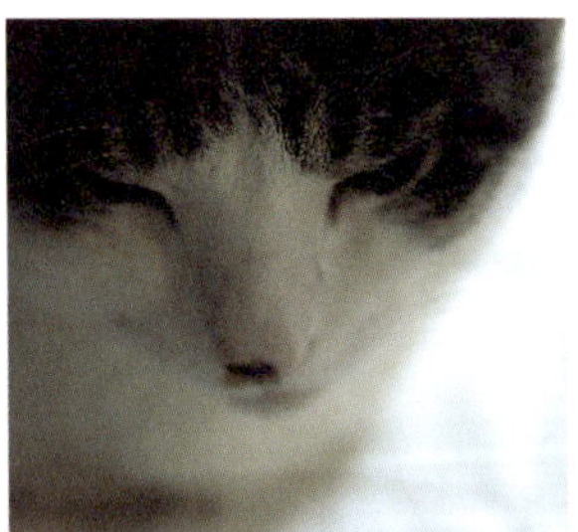

Why I wrote this book

Do you like cats? I love them! Their fluffy, supple bodies and irresistibly charming expressions are all just too cute. They're free-spirited, independent and go at their own pace—always treating you the same no matter what, always giving you the comforting feeling that "everything's okay." To me, they've become beloved life companions.

Many people capture their cats in photos, but why not take it a step further and try drawing them? Whether you live with a cat or not, whether you love drawing or don't feel very skilled—as long as you love cats, that's enough!

In this book, you'll find plenty of tips and tricks—so go ahead and start making your very own cat drawings!

—Sayo Koizumi

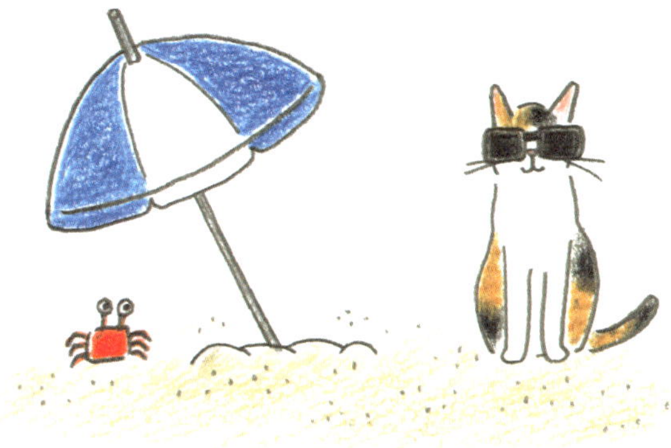

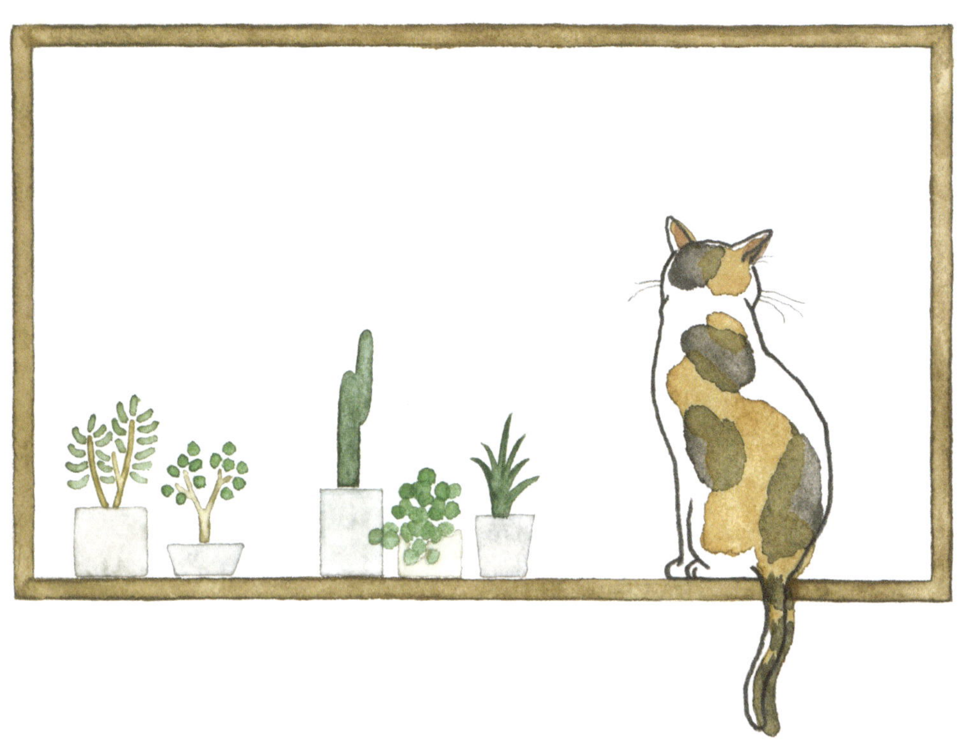

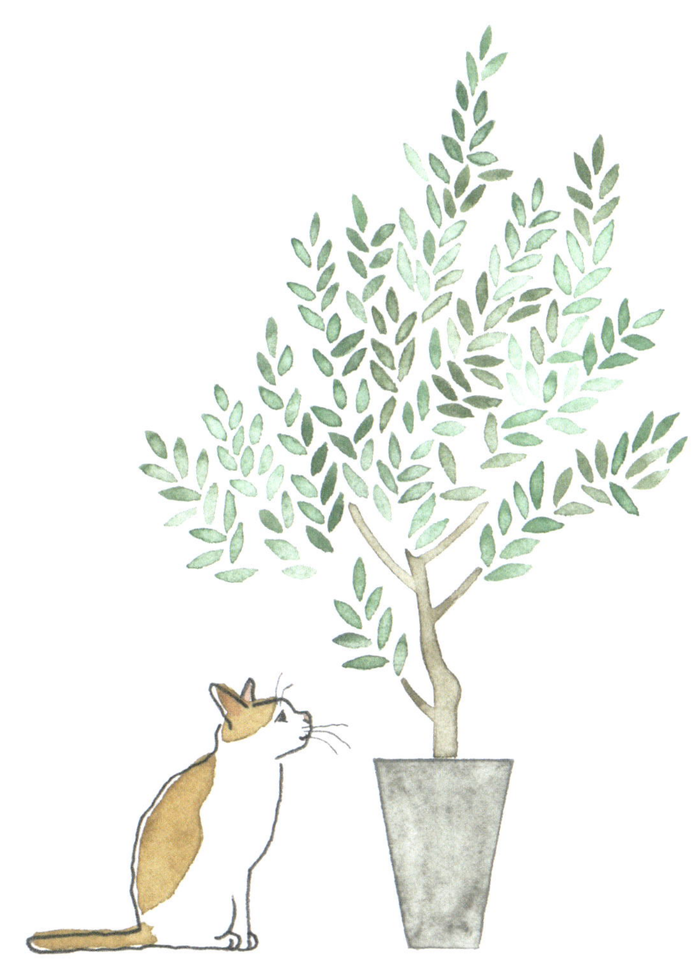

From *Eleven Things I Want to Tell People Who Are About to Get a Cat*
(by Satoshi Nio; published by Tatsumi Publishing) • Media: pencil and transparent watercolor paint

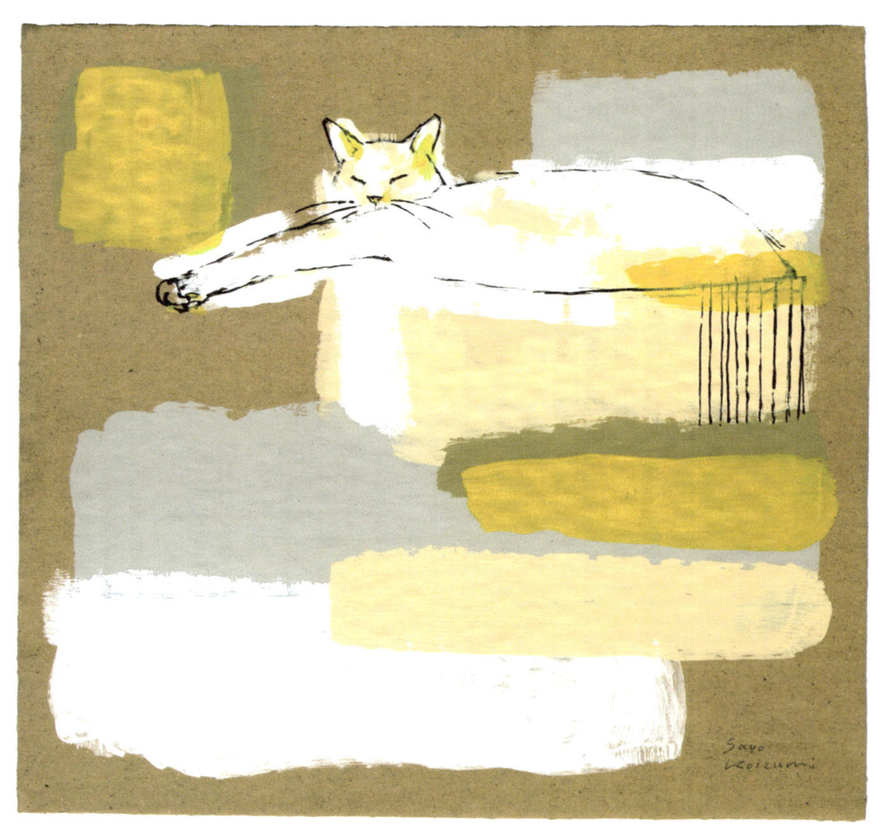

Sayo
Koizumi

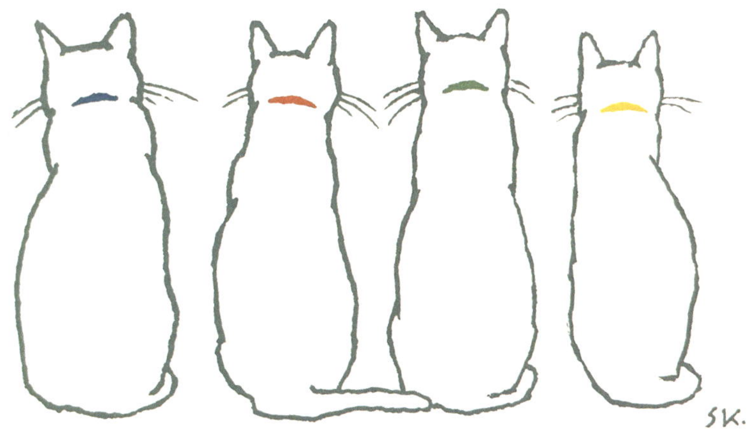

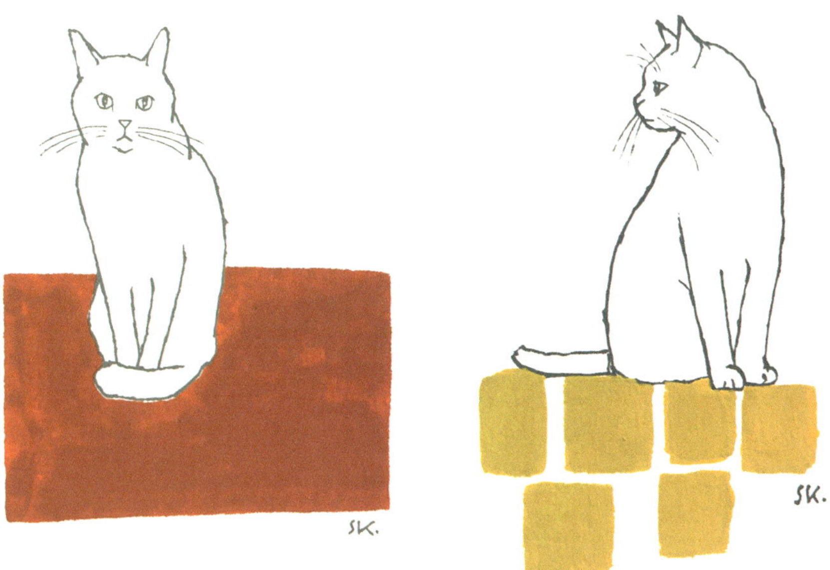

Facing page: *Cat in the Sun* • Media: cardboard, acrylic paint
Above: *Drawings* • Medium: acrylic paint

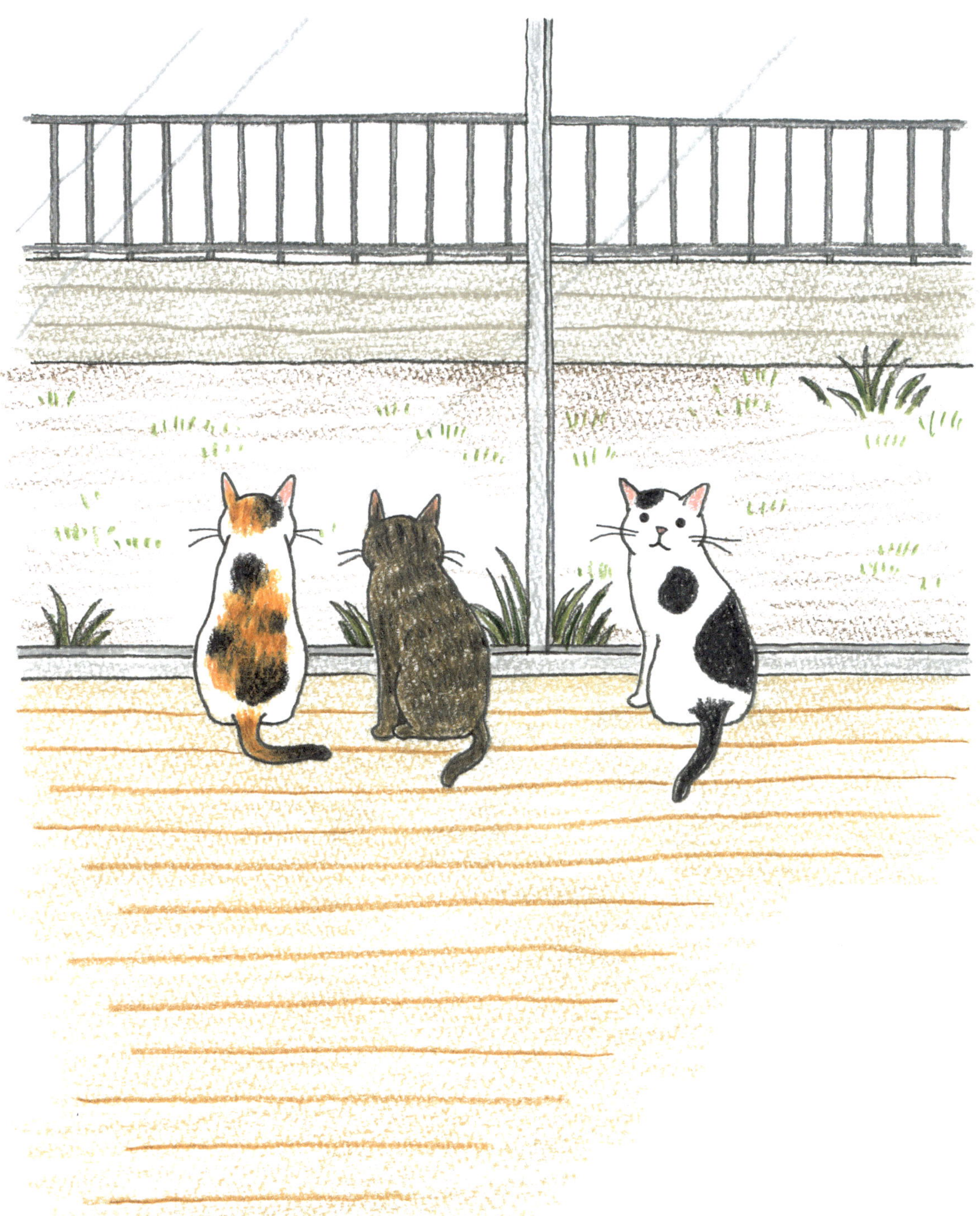

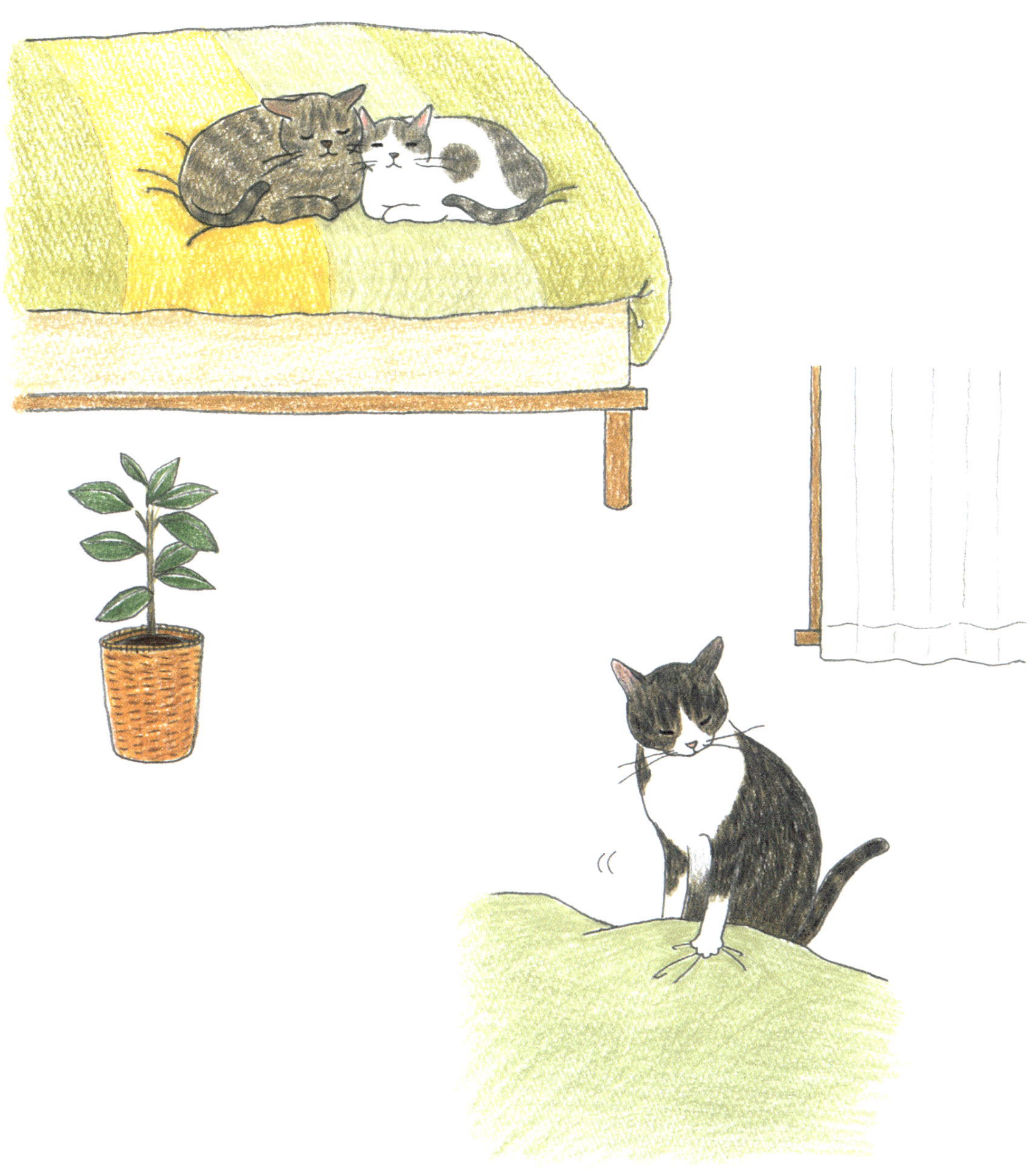

From *I Want to Go Home to a House with Cats* (by Satoshi Nio; published by Tatsumi Publishing)
Media: pencil and colored pencil

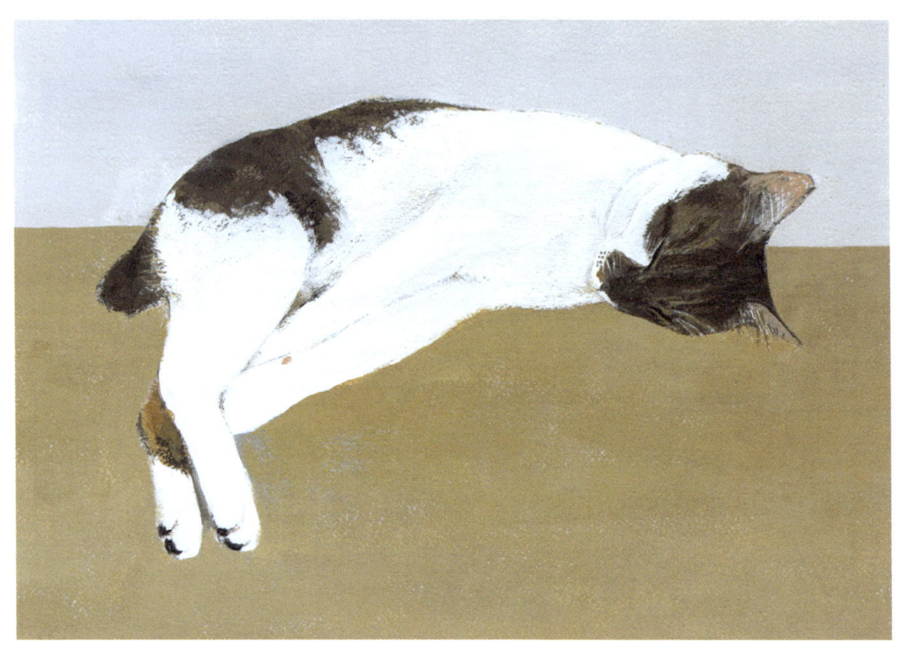

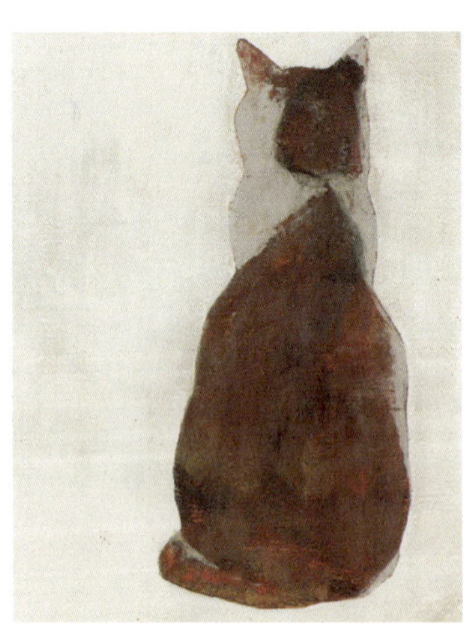

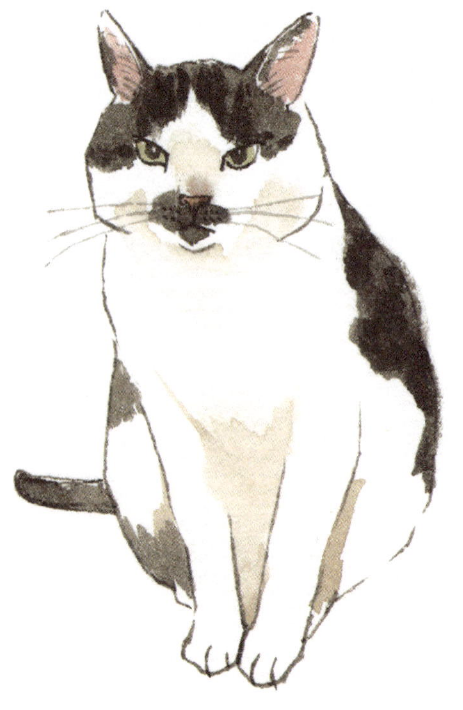

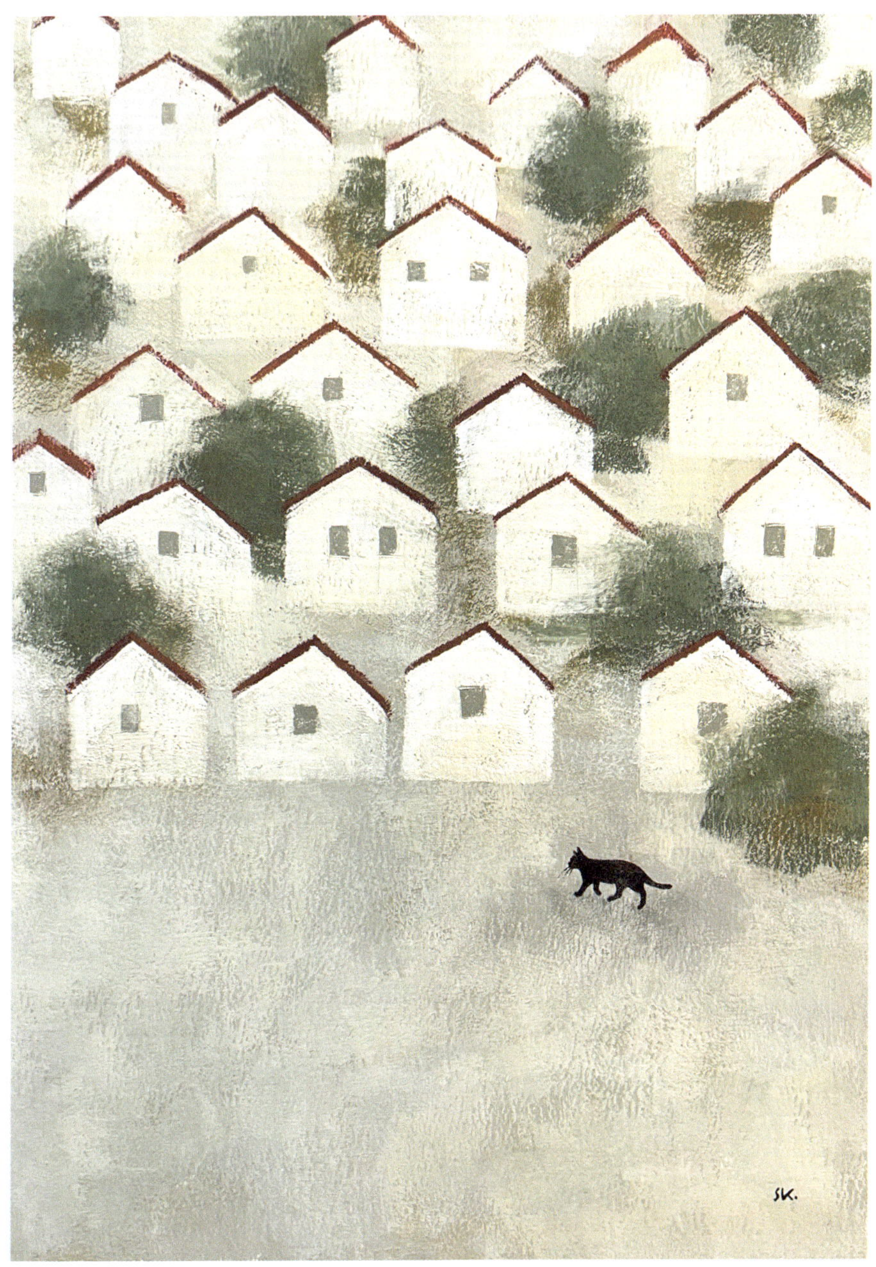

Facing page, top: *Cat, Sound Asleep* • Medium: acrylic paint

Facing page, bottom left: *Back* • Medium: acrylic paint

Facing page, bottom right: *Sitting Cat* • Medium: transparent watercolor

Above: *Walk in a Dream* • Medium: acrylic paint

PART 1

Start Drawing Cats

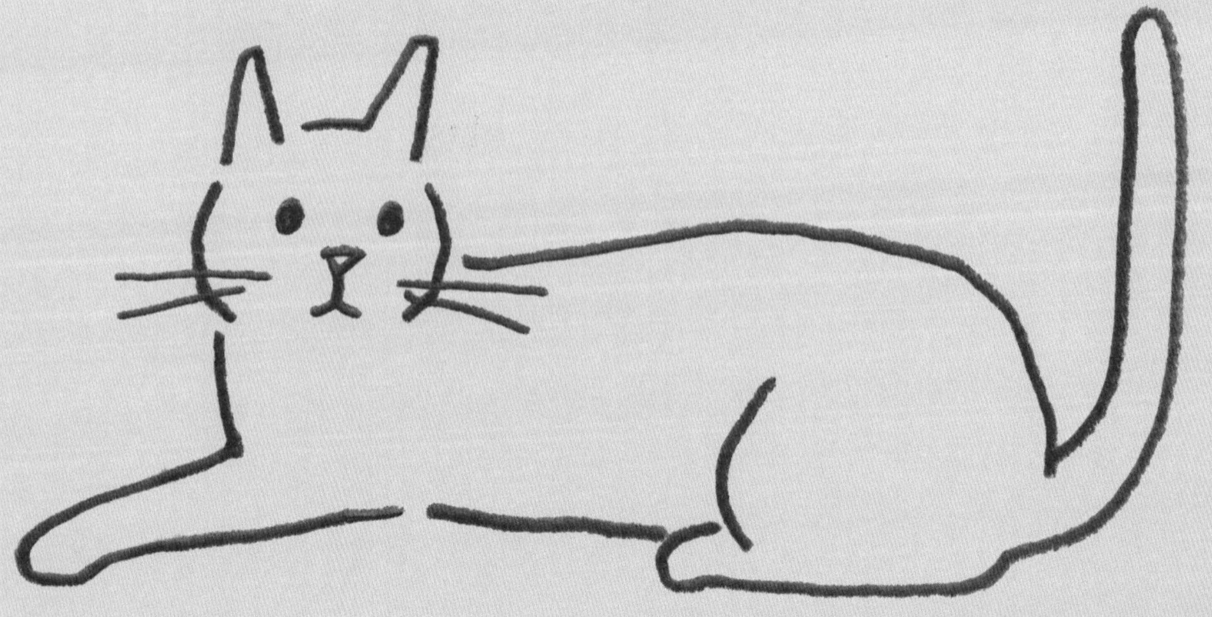

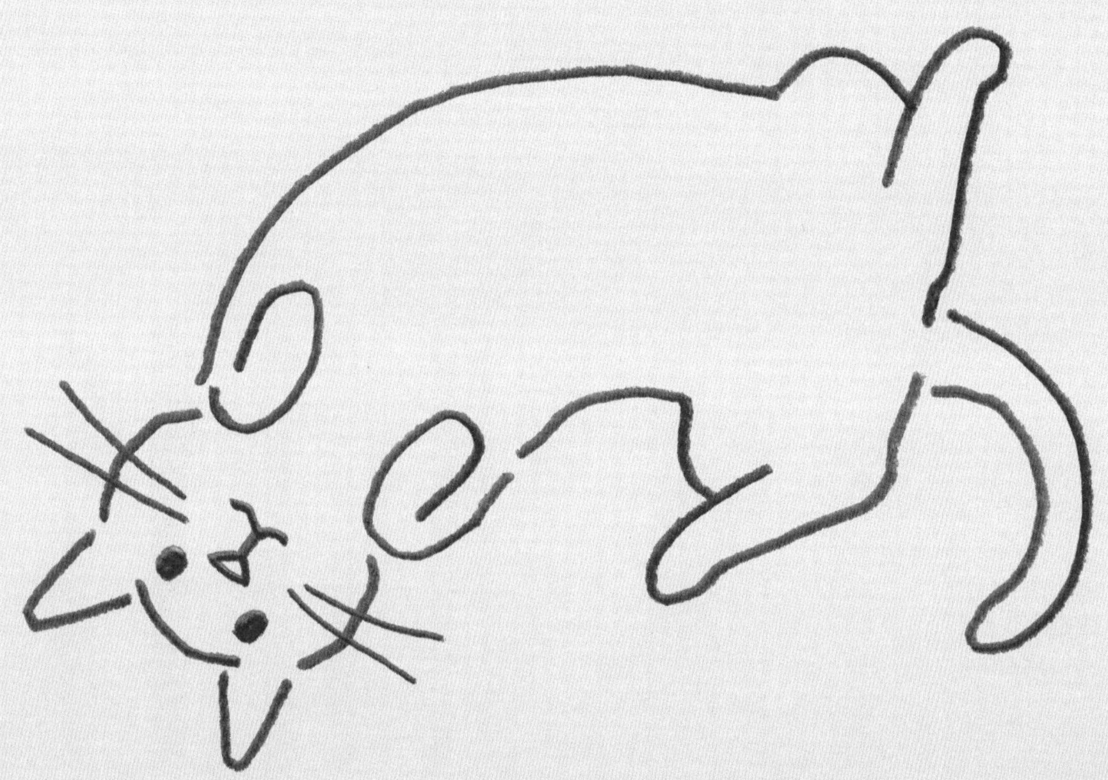

 # It's fun to draw and paint with these tools

Let's start with an introduction to some basic, easy-to-use tools and art materials. Most of them are easily available or items you may already have at home. It's best to start with materials that are easy to get your hands on. Visit a stationery or art supply store and gather the basics. Even just browsing the selection of drawing tools can be a lot of fun!

Pencils • Water-based pens

Drawing starts with the basics—pencils. If you already have drawing pencils at home, it's easy to begin. If possible, go for 2B or 3B hardness—they're easier to handle and draw with. Once you're used to it, try exploring different pencils until you find one that suit you. Water-based pens are also convenient and recommended. Try different types like water-based ballpoint pens or felt-tip pens—you can also choose different nib thicknesses.

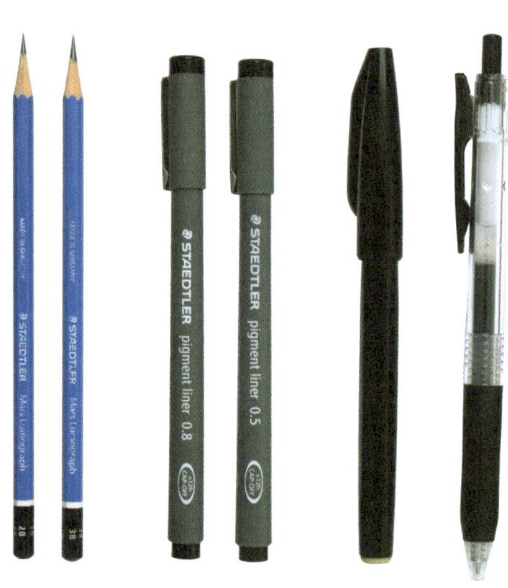

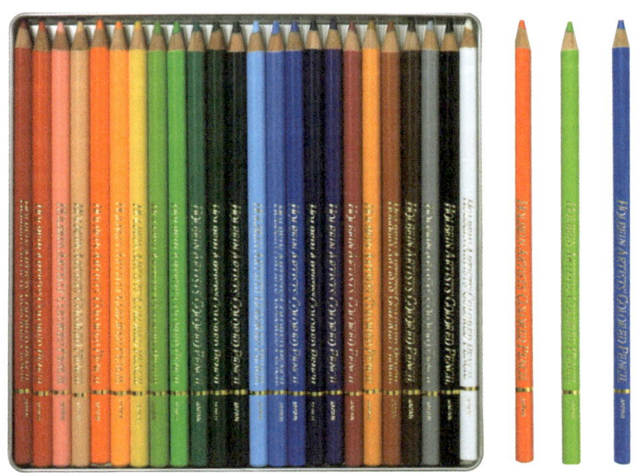

Holbein Artists' Colored Pencils—24-color set

Colored pencils

If you're a beginner and want to try coloring, colored pencils are a great place to start. They won't get your hands dirty, and you don't need water. Investing in a 24-color set is a good idea. You can also buy individual colors you like or will use often, like shades for cat fur. I often use Holbein Artists' Colored Pencils. They're on the softer side and easy to apply.

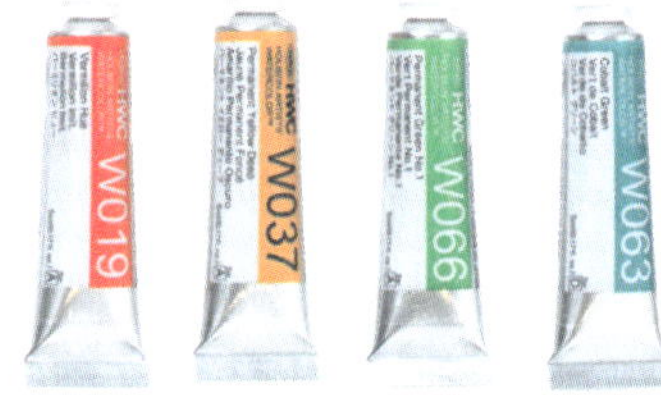

Watercolor paints • Acrylic paints

There are two types of watercolor paints: transparent and opaque. You can choose based on preference, but I recommend transparent watercolors because layering and mixing colors results in beautiful textures. Acrylic paint is opaque; it hardens when dry and doesn't wash off. The dried paint is matte and the colors are strong. While layering hides the colors underneath, the appeal is that you can quickly cover an area with uniform color.

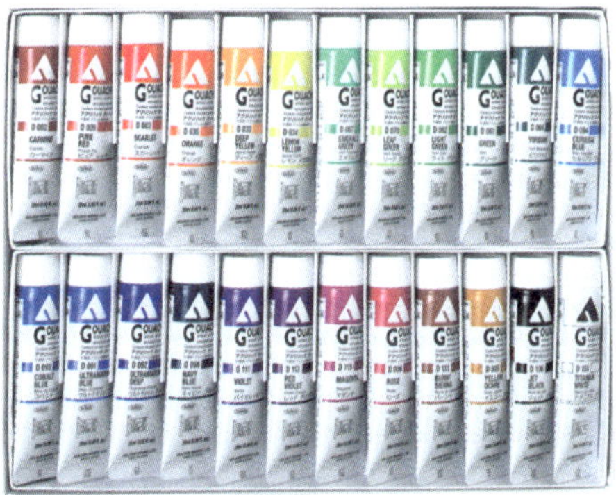

Holbein Acrylic Gouache—24-color set

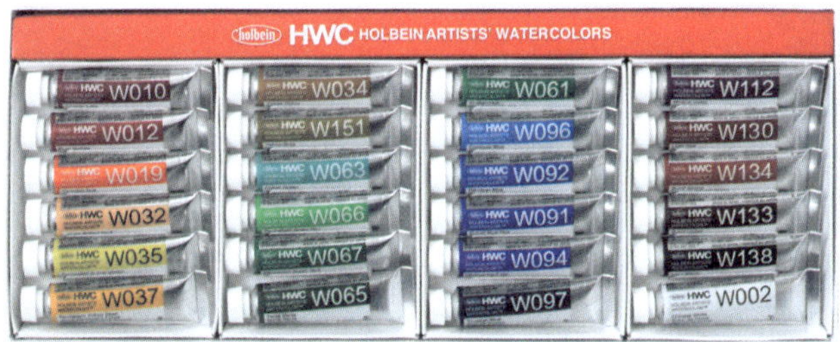

Holbein Acrylic Gouache—24-color set

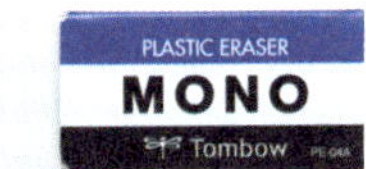

Plastic eraser • Kneaded eraser

A regular pink eraser you already have at home will do just fine, but a plastic eraser will work best. If possible, get a kneaded eraser too—they're flexible and handy. You can find them in art supply stores.

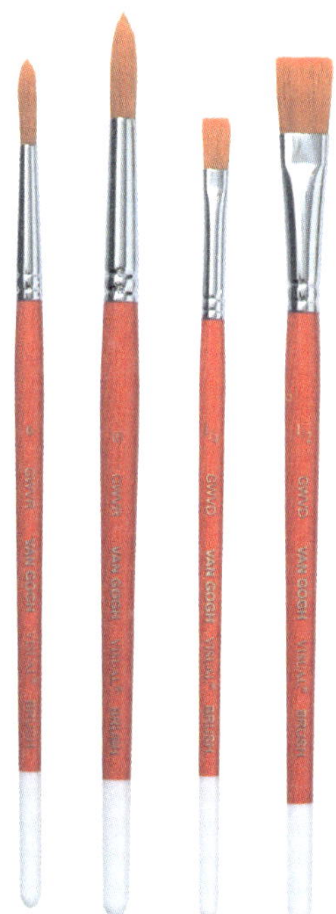

Brushes

Round brushes are good for beginners, but flat brushes are useful for covering larger areas. It's even better if you have a variety of sizes, but to start, having two thick and two thin brushes is fine. If you want to paint fine details later, add fine-tipped brushes to your toolkit.

 # Ideal materials to draw and paint on

Let's explore some beginner-friendly materials that are easy to work with. Drawing paper and sketchbooks are common, but there are various other types of paper products available. You can buy fine materials to create serious artwork, or simply add little drawings to memos or planners.

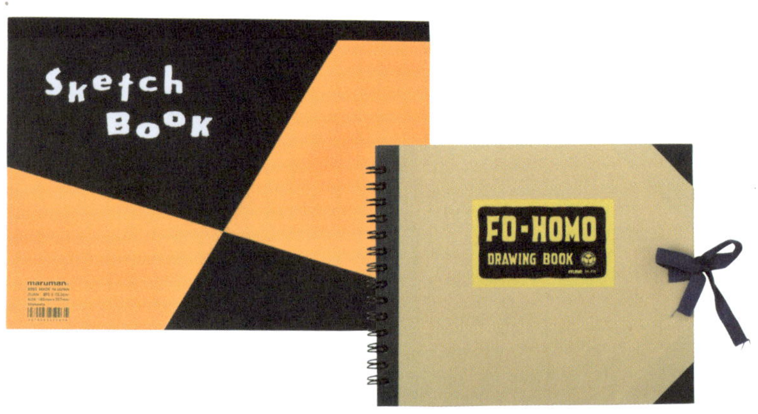

Sketchbooks

Sketchbooks are the easiest to get at stationery or art supply stores. There's a wide variety of paper thicknesses and textures. Try starting with something not too thick and of medium grain. Even those from dollar stores are fine.

Loose papers

There are various types of papers, like traditional drawing paper, toned drawing paper and copy paper. White is standard, but picking your favorite color is fun too.

Illustration boards

These are dense cardboard bases with drawing paper mounted on them—thick and sturdy.

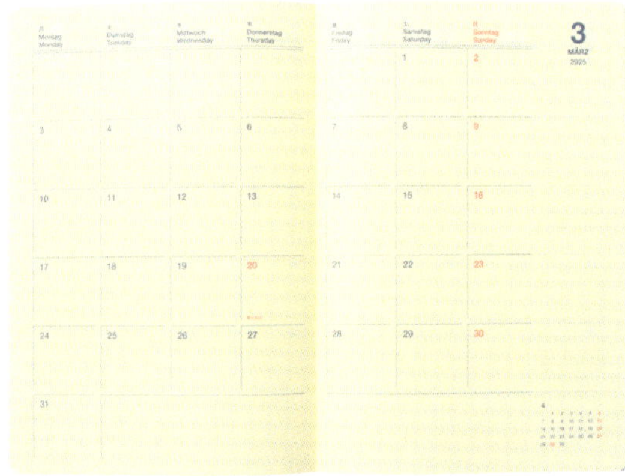

Planner pages

This topic comes up later in the book too, but drawing little icons and doodles into your schedule or boldly decorating to create a custom illustrated planner is also a wonderful way to express your creativity.

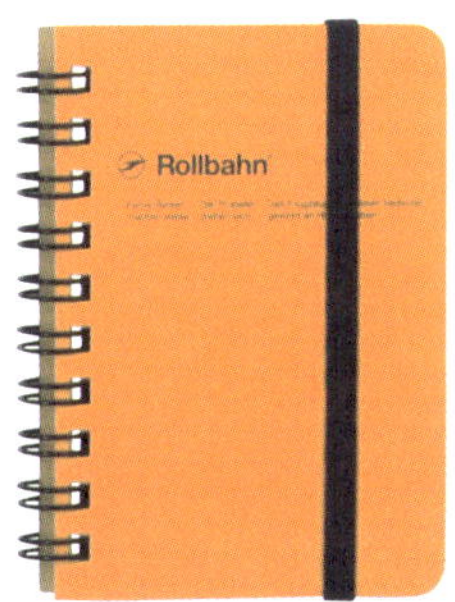

Memo pads

Add illustrations to a small note pad. Carry it with you so you can draw whenever inspiration strikes.

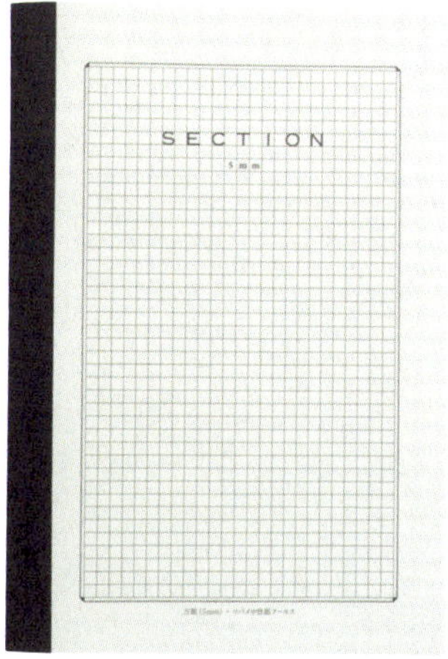

Notebooks

Make study notes or recipes easier to understand—and more fun to look at—with illustrations. Drawing flipbook-style doodles in the margins is also fun.

Cardboard

It may be unconventional, but this is actually an excellent and easy-to-draw-on material. Instead of trimming neatly, roughly cut or tear to add charm.

Plain picture books

If you have access to books like these, you can draw illustrations on the plain white pages, creating your very own picture book.

 # Get the ball rolling by tracing

If there's an illustration or photo you like, try tracing it over it using a sheet of tracing paper! This is good practice, so trace lots of different pictures to get a feel for them! Buy tracing paper at stationery stores, art supply stores and dollar stores.

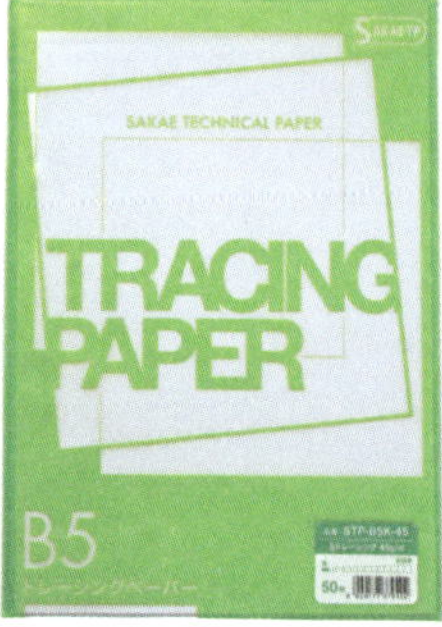

Tracing paper

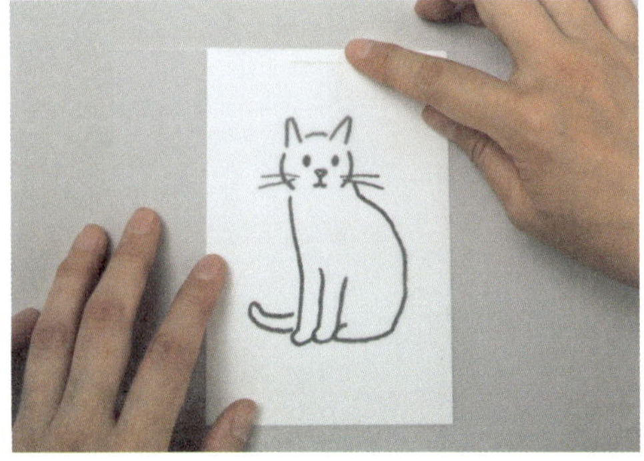

1 Place the original illustration or picture on a flat surface, lay the tracing paper on top, and lightly secure it with tape so it doesn't shift.

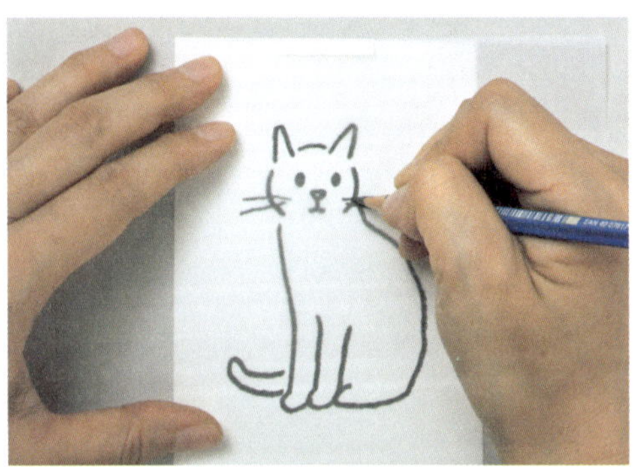

2 Trace the visible lines using a pencil or pen. Make sure that nothing is misaligned.

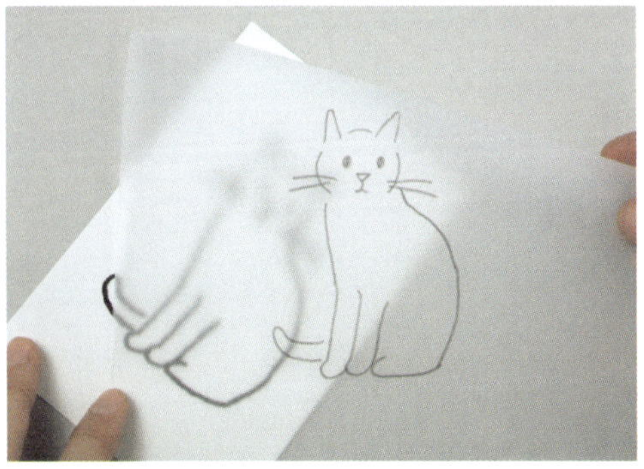

3 Once you finish tracing, you're done. Does your drawing capture the look of the original? Practice with many different images.

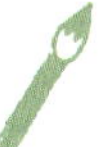 # Trace to capture the image

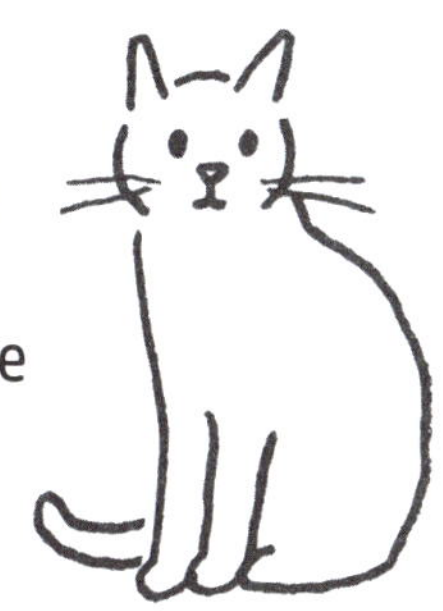

Pages 22–25 have illustrations for tracing practice, so you can use those to get started right away. Because you can actually draw directly on pages 24–25, you don't even need to hunt for tracing paper! You can also practice with other books that provide tracing exercises.

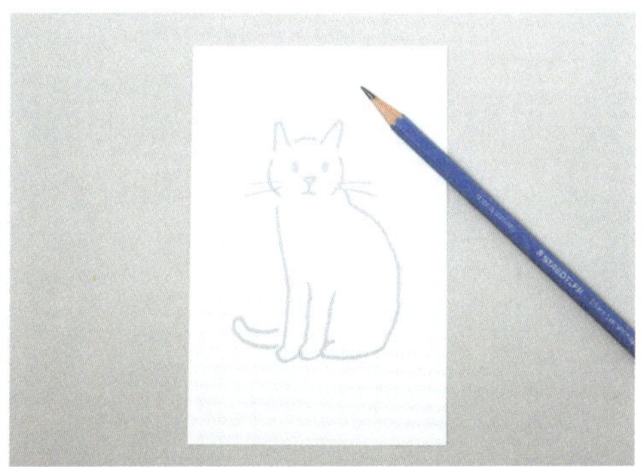

1 Use any materials you like, such as pencils or pens. There are no rules, so start with wherever feels easiest to use.

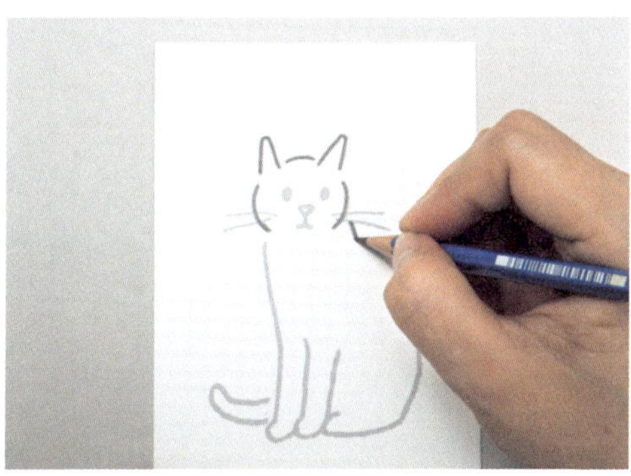

2 Draw boldly, as if you're the original artist of the illustration.

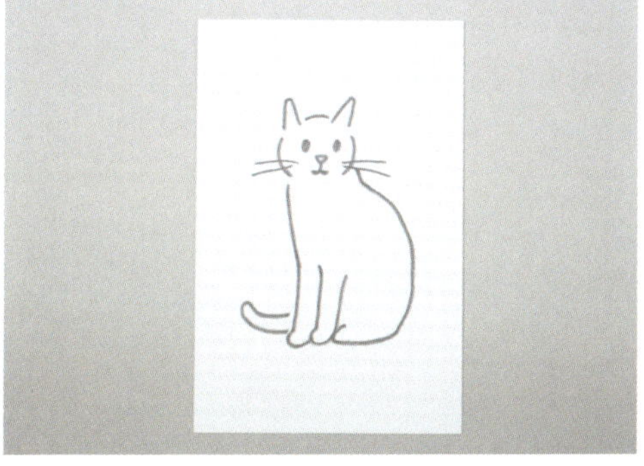

3 Once your tracing is completed, you can add interior detail lines or color it in to make your own unique version.

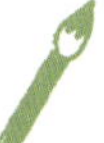 Tracing practice with tracing paper

Place tracing paper over the illustrations and try tracing them.

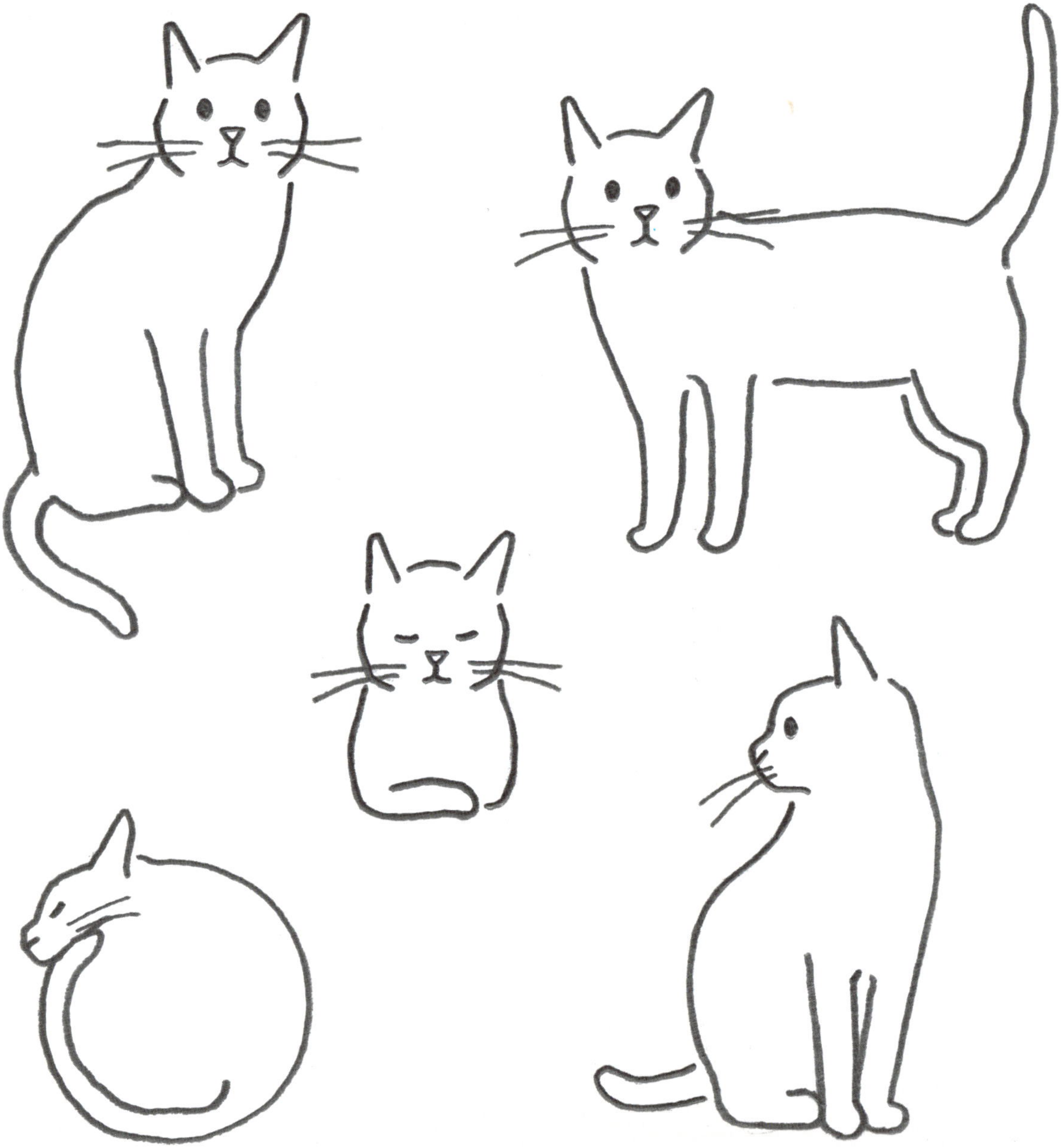

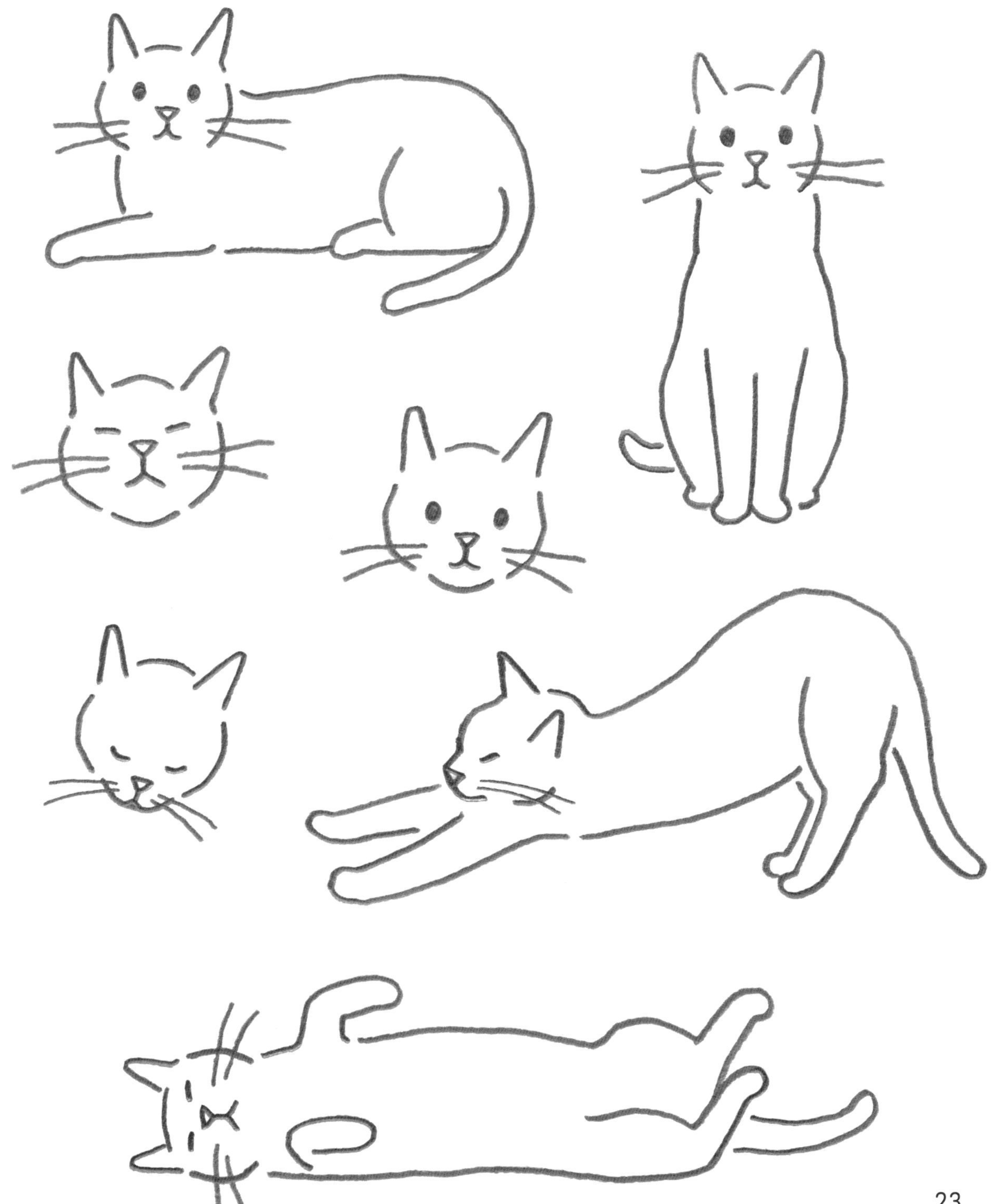

# Tracing practice directly in the book

Try tracing directly over the illustrations.

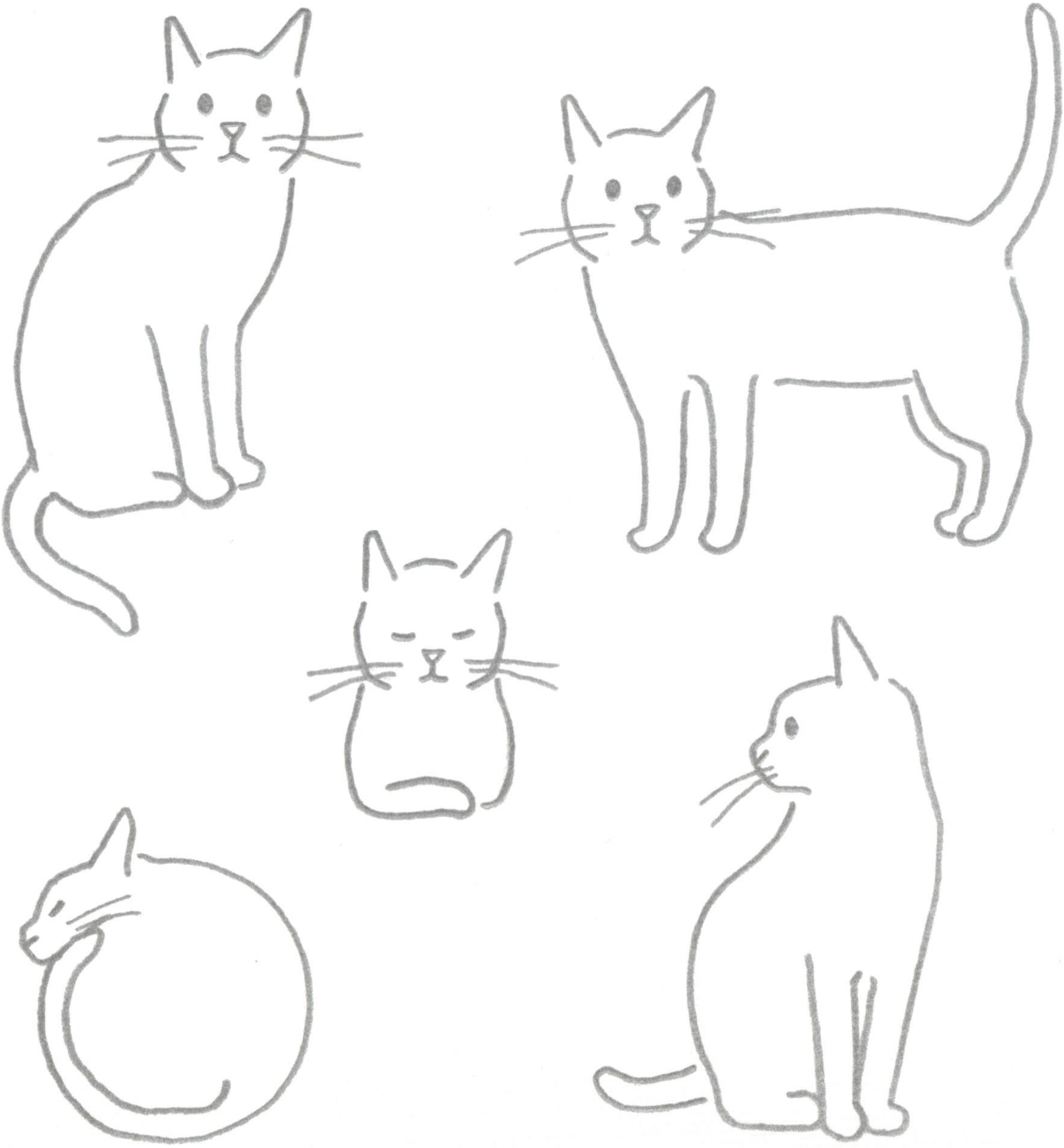

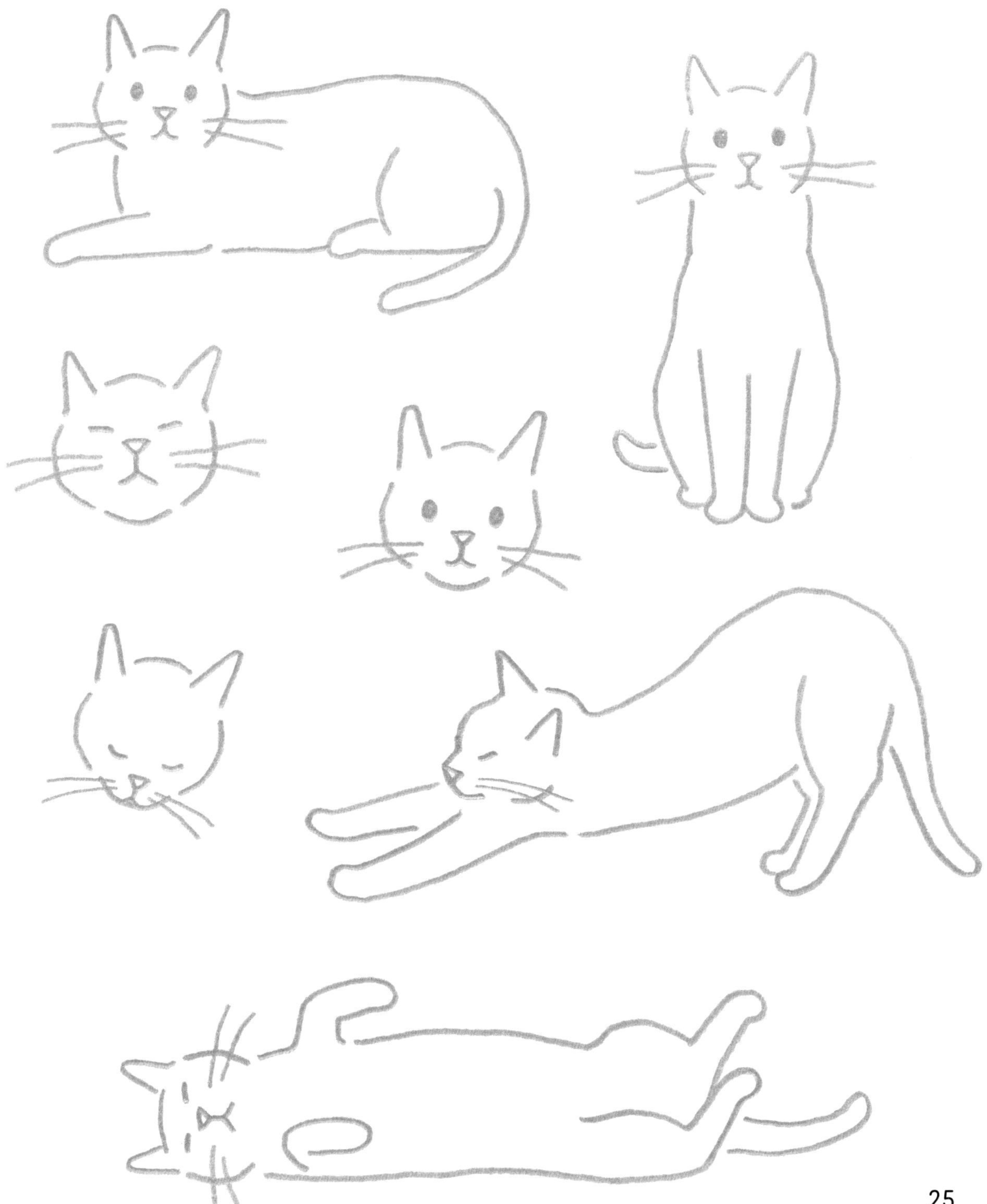

# Try your hand at croquis

Croquis (gesture drawings) are rough, expressive sketches that are drawn quickly. Unlike time-consuming sketches or fussy, detailed drawings, drawing freely in as short a time as possible helps hone your ability to capture the essence of your subjects. It's perfect practice for drawing cats that move around a lot. If you make this practice a daily exercise, you'll become much better at drawing!

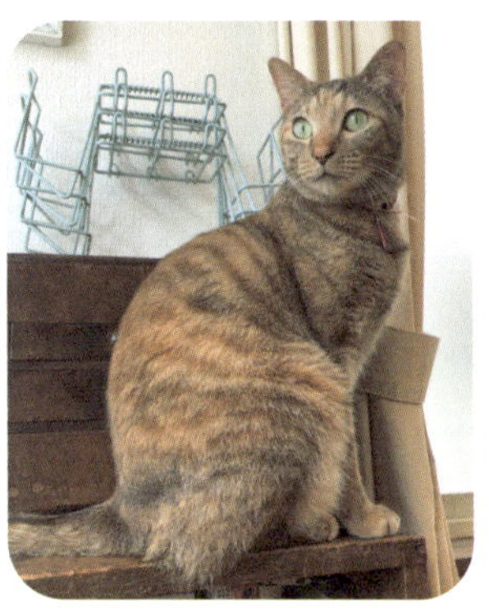

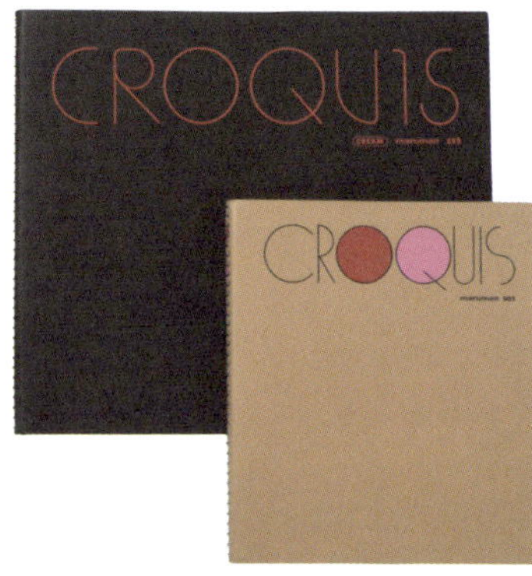

Croquis book

Each sheet is thin and lightly textured, making it easy to draw on and ideal for repeated practice. Don't aim to create a finished piece—just draw as much as you can for practice.

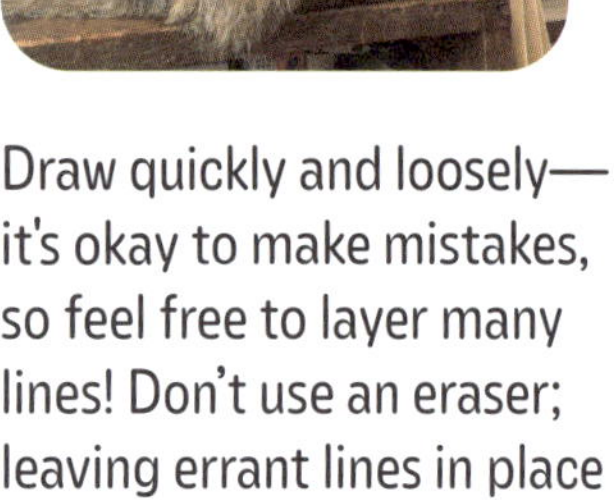

Draw quickly and loosely—it's okay to make mistakes, so feel free to layer many lines! Don't use an eraser; leaving errant lines in place is good practice.

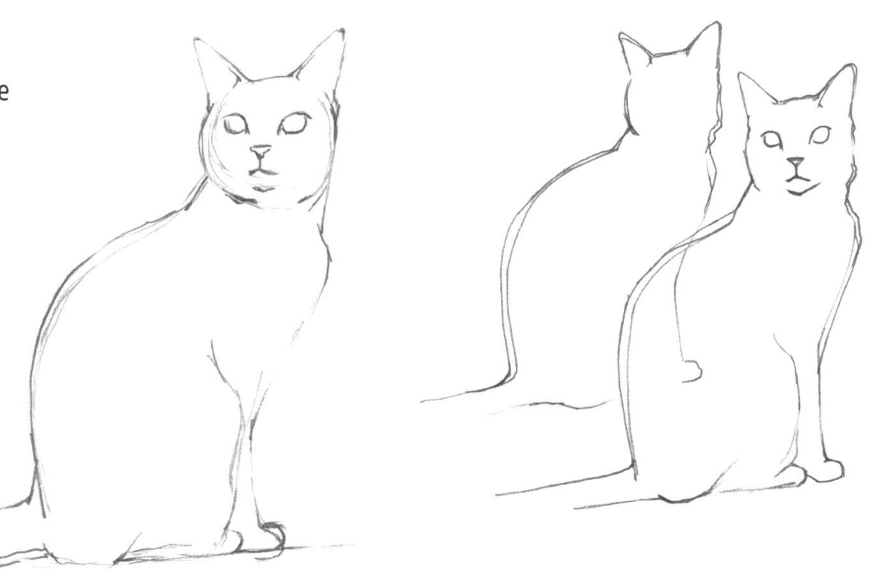

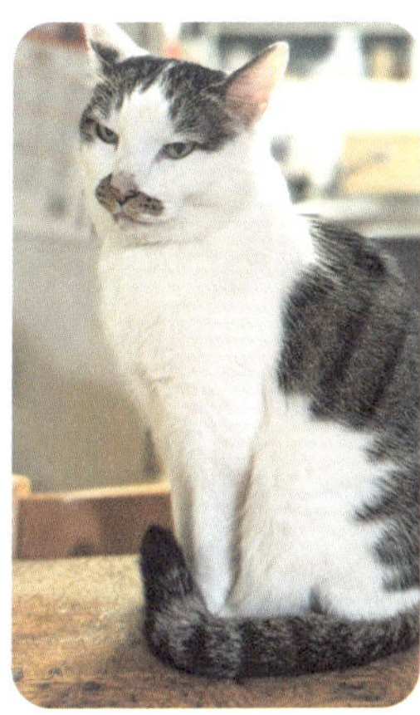

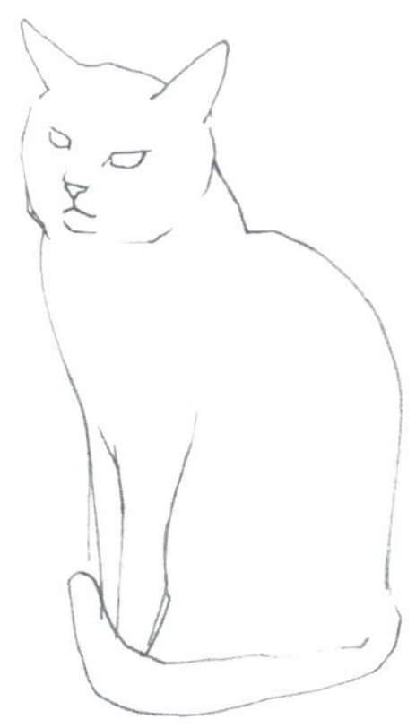

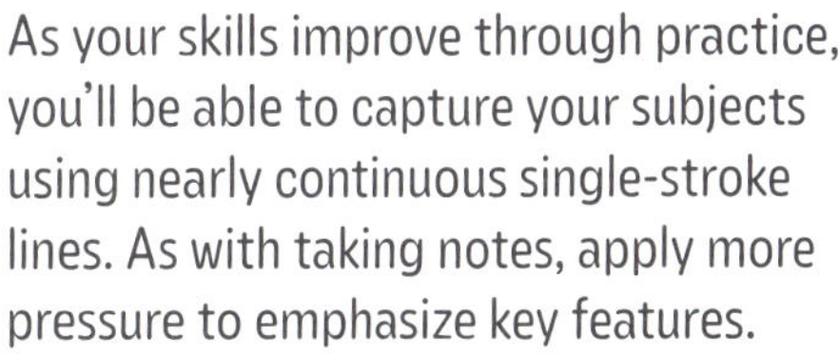

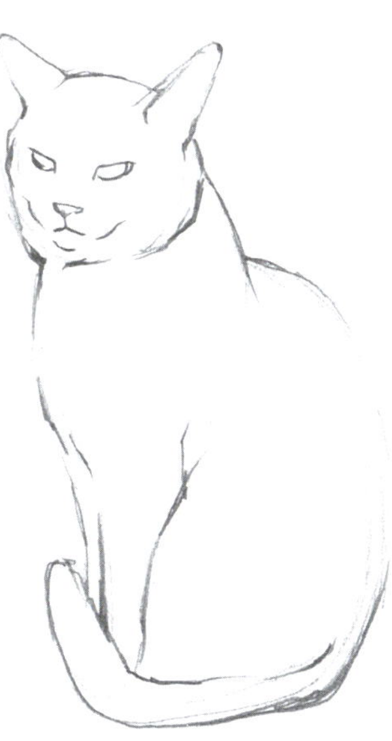

As your skills improve through practice, you'll be able to capture your subjects using nearly continuous single-stroke lines. As with taking notes, apply more pressure to emphasize key features.

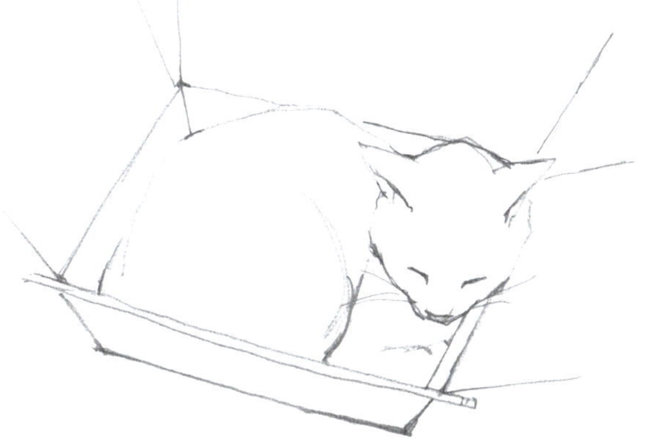

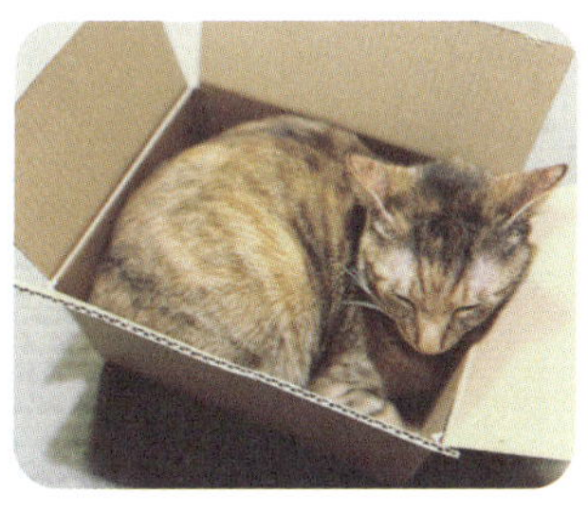

A sleeping cat doesn't move much, so it's the perfect subject to start with.

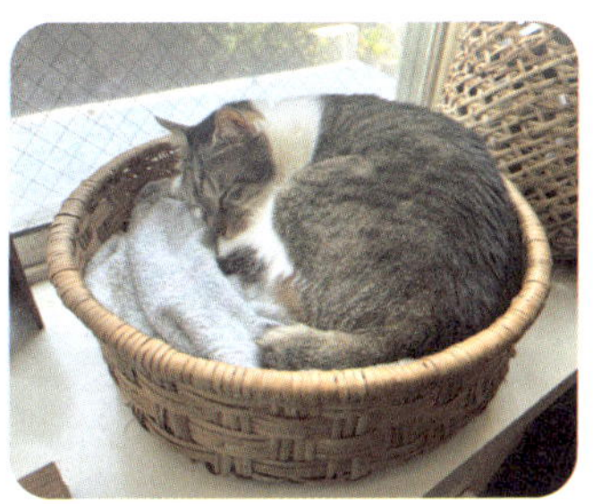

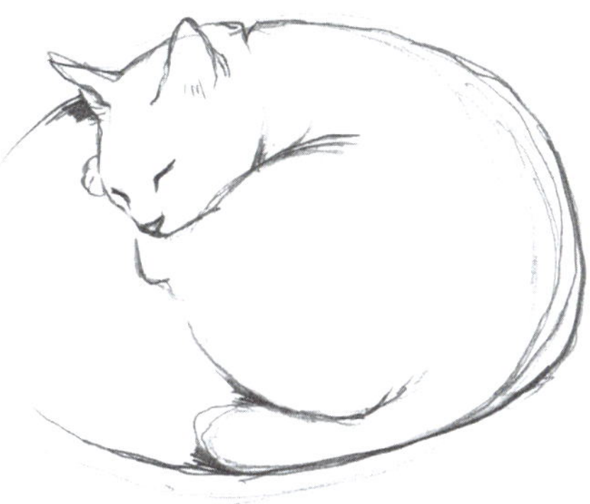

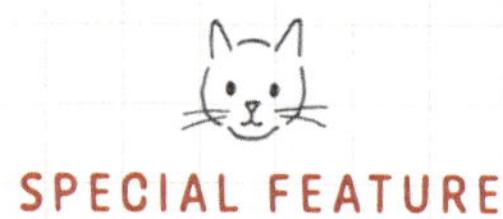

My favorite parts of a cat

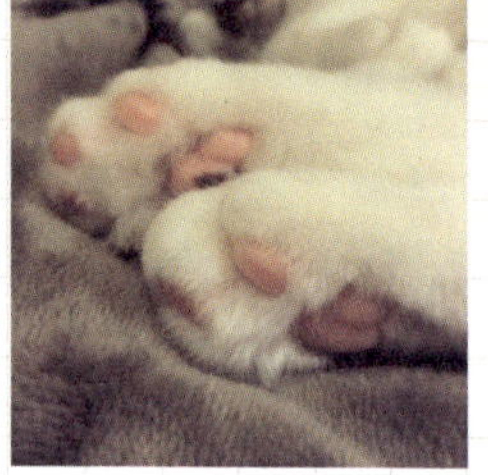

Let's take a little break.

What is your favorite part of a cat?

There are so many cute parts that are soothing just to look at,

but the part I particularly love is the "whisker pad!"

It's the area where the whiskers emerge from the fuzzy muzzle.

It's plump and puffed up, and I think it's the root of a cat's charm.

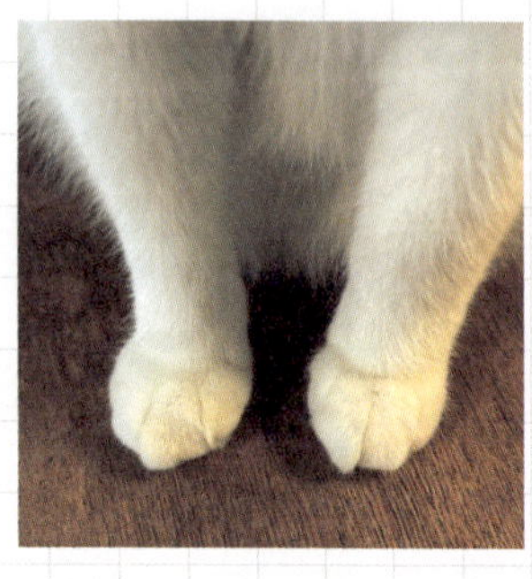

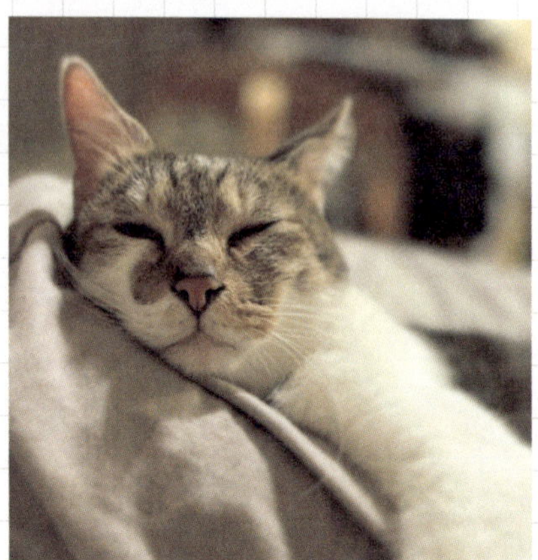

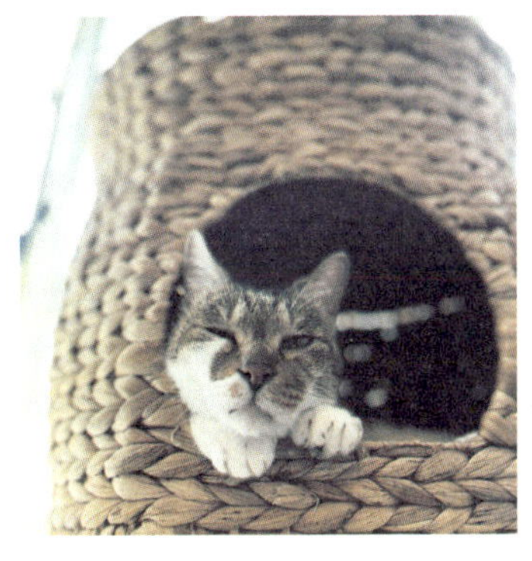 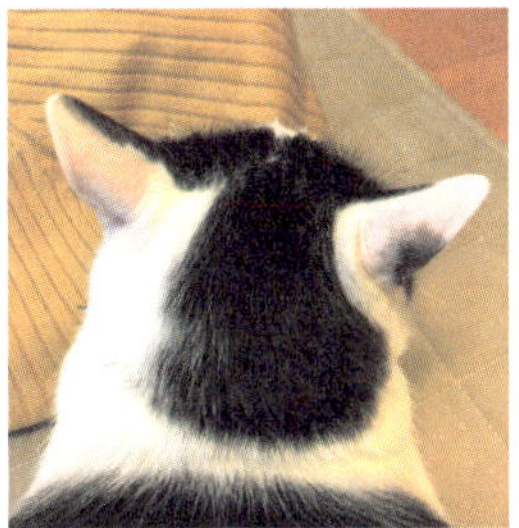

Squeezing this part between your thumb and index finger
and gently squashing it feels incredibly blissful.
Also, the soft fur behind their ears feels as fluffy
as cotton and is wonderfully soft.
Of course, I love their "toe beans" too!
But honestly, I really enjoy working my fingers into the gaps
between their paw pads—it's not overstating things to say
that this is a pastime of mine.

Sorry for suddenly bringing up such a niche and borderline-
fetishistic topic. But, when it comes to talking about cats,
I just can't stop myself from getting
excited and passionate!

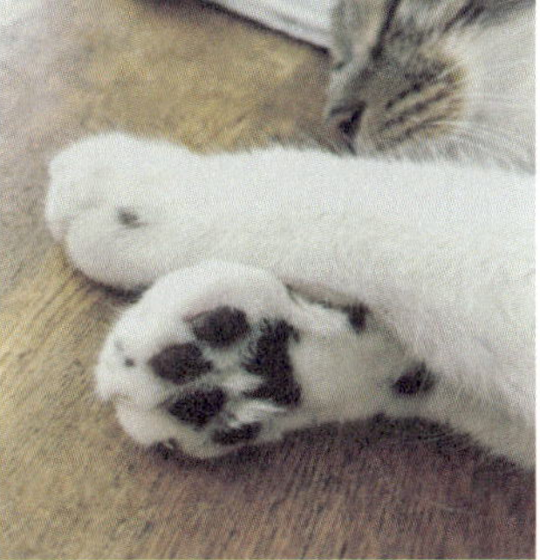

PART 2

Understanding Cat Shapes

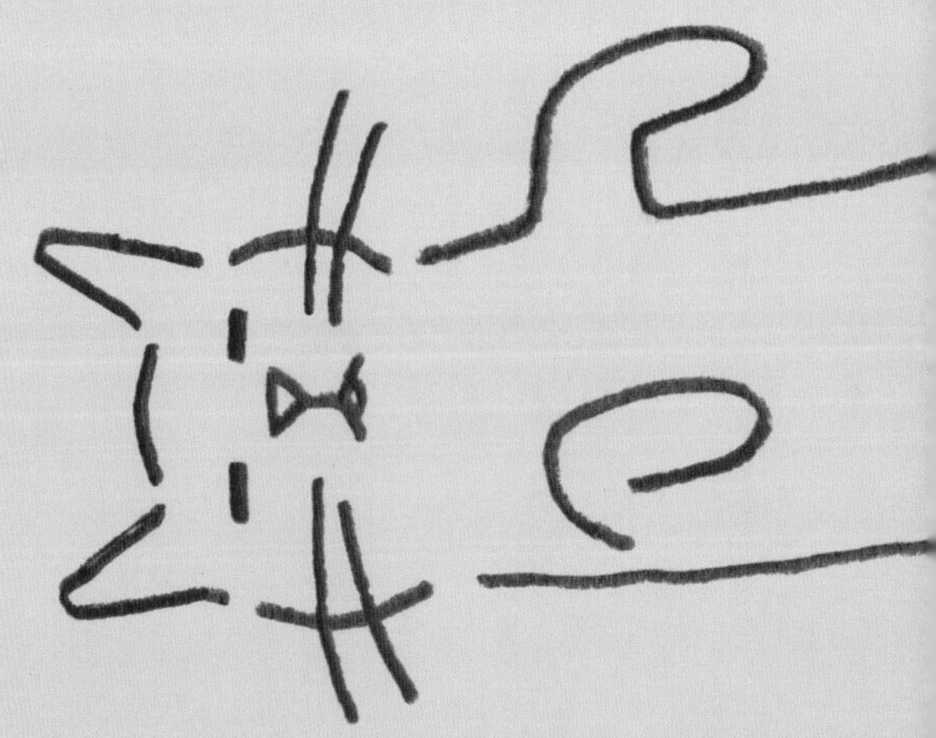

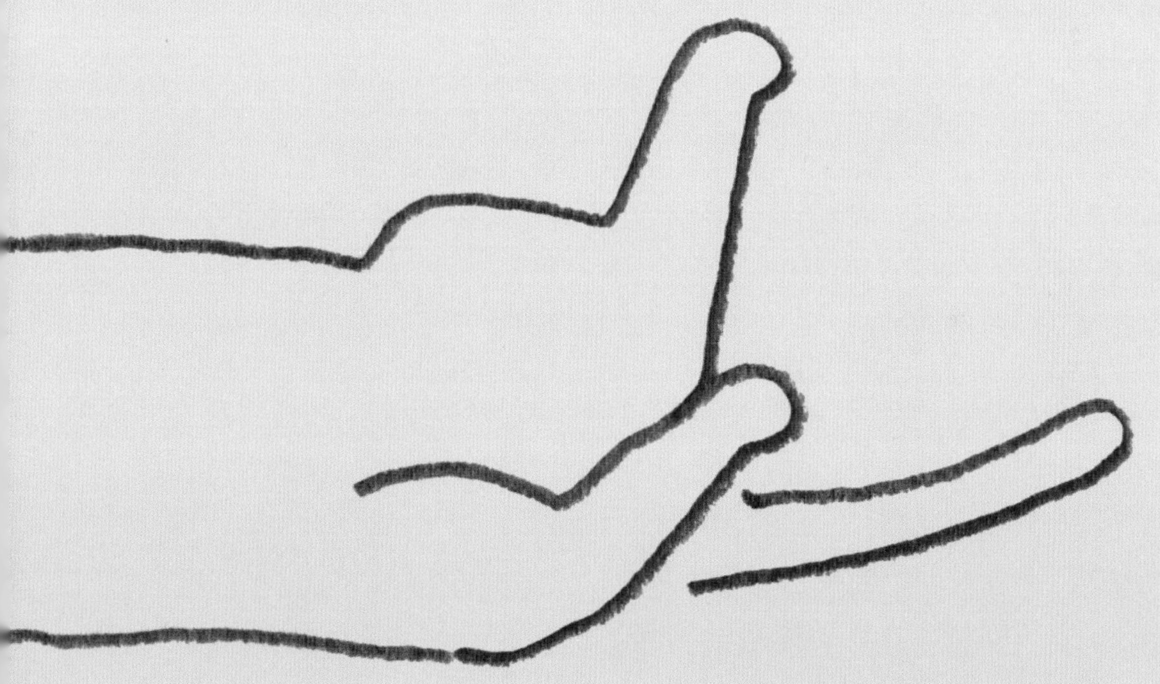

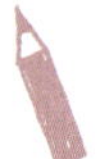# Understanding the cat's bone structure

When drawing a cat, being aware of its skeletal structure greatly improves the accuracy of your work. Cats are very flexible animals, but if you try to capture them as they are, the drawing can end up looking floppy. You don't need to understand the entire skeleton, but if you have a cat nearby, try feeling it to check its structure.

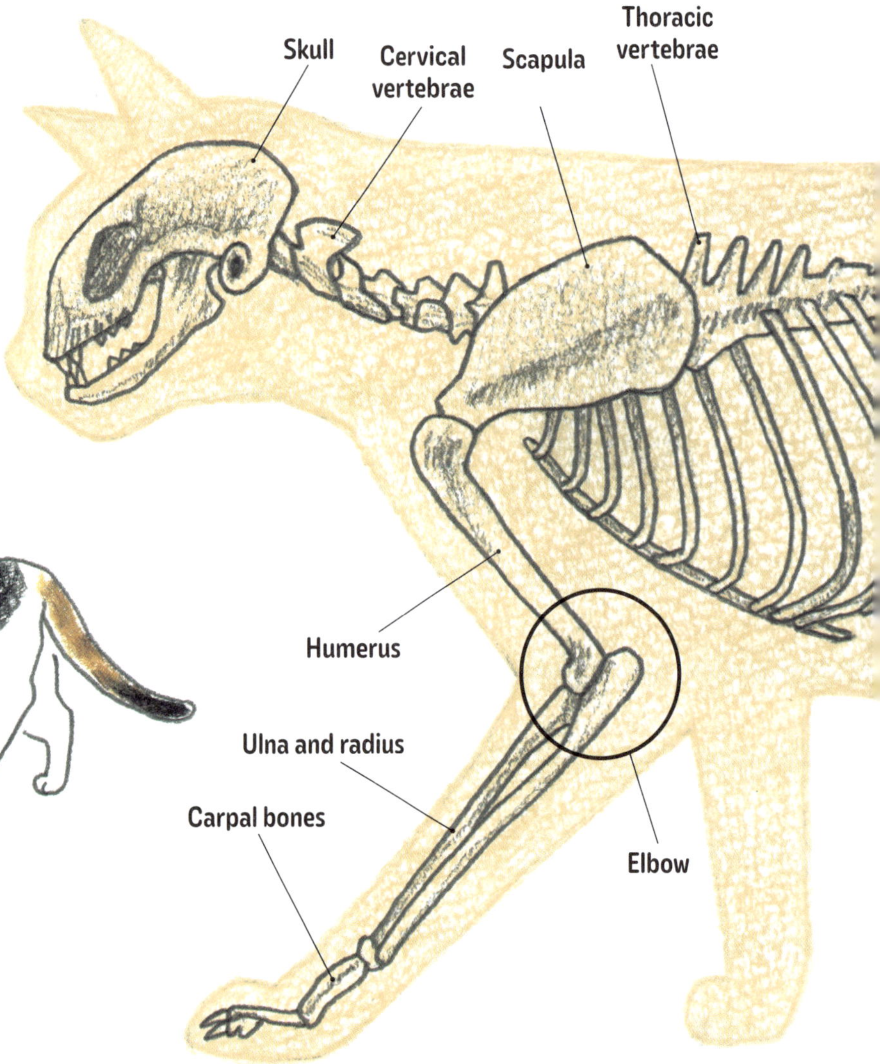

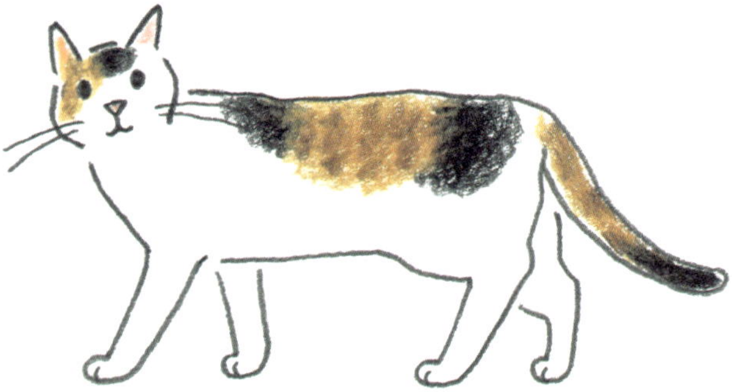

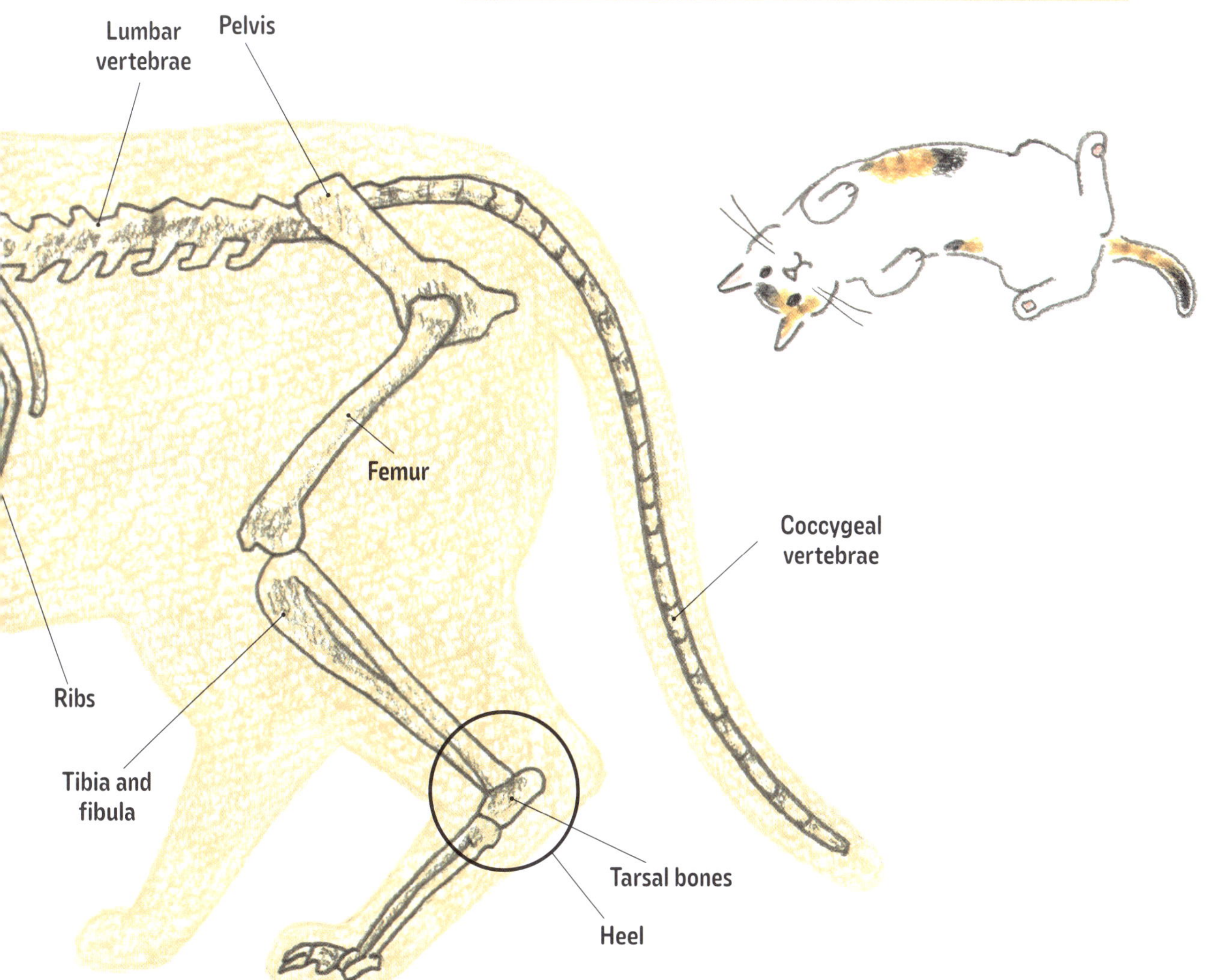

N O T E

Just being familiar with key bones like the shoulder blades, pelvis, elbows and heels makes it easier to capture a cat's form. It's also interesting to compare these with human anatomy. Observe and think about how the skeleton looks and moves in various cat poses. If it's your beloved cat, even its bones feel lovable....

Common cat poses with skeletal studies

Here are sketches paired with corresponding skeleton studies. Of course, you don't always need to create studies like these, but try drawing while visualizing what the skeleton looks like.

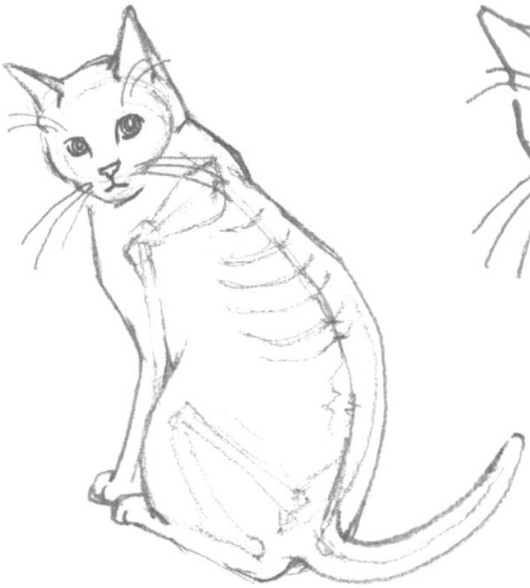

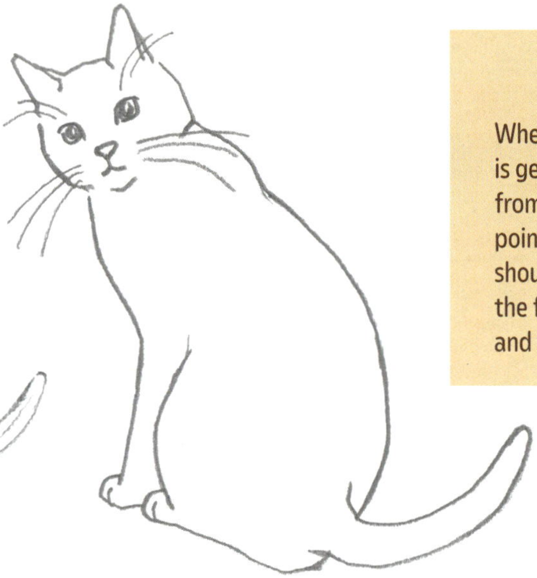

NOTE

When a cat is sitting, its spine is gently curved (as expected from a cat's hunched back!). Key points include the spread of the shoulder blades, the angles of the femur and lower leg bones and the position of the heels.

NOTE

Note the position of the reclining cat's upright neck, shoulder blades, elbows and pelvis. Also be aware of the soft, rounded belly (absent of bones) and the smooth slope of the back.

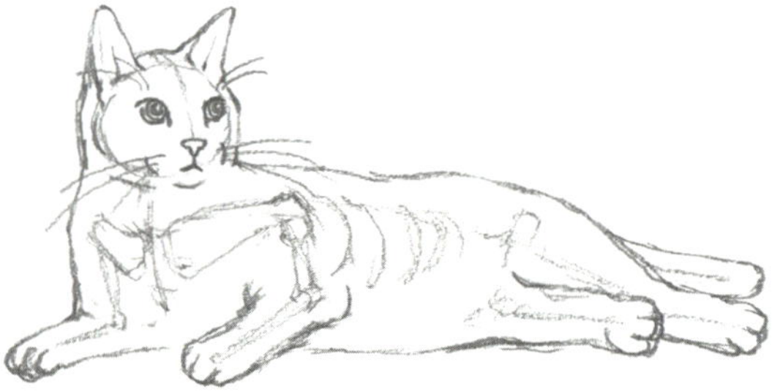

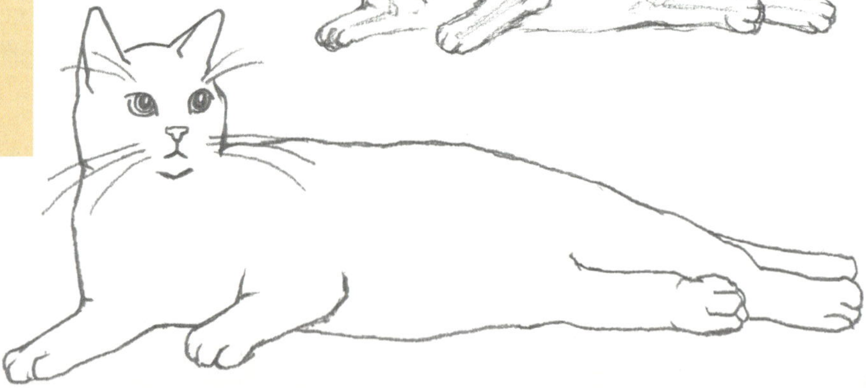

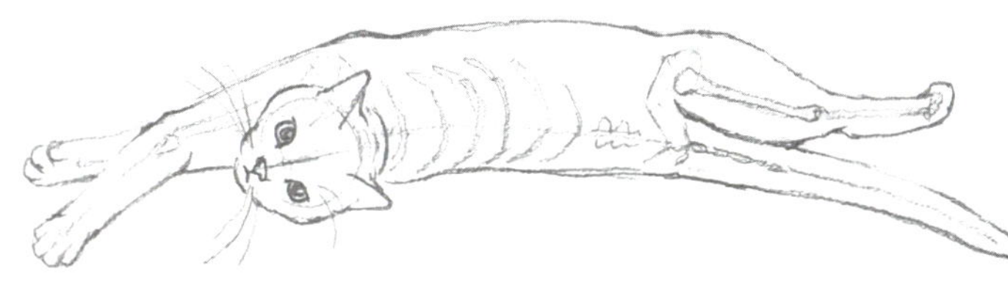

NOTE

When the cat is lying stretched out, observe how the head is positioned and the continuity from the spine to the tail bones. In flexible cat fashion, the front and back legs are fully extended.

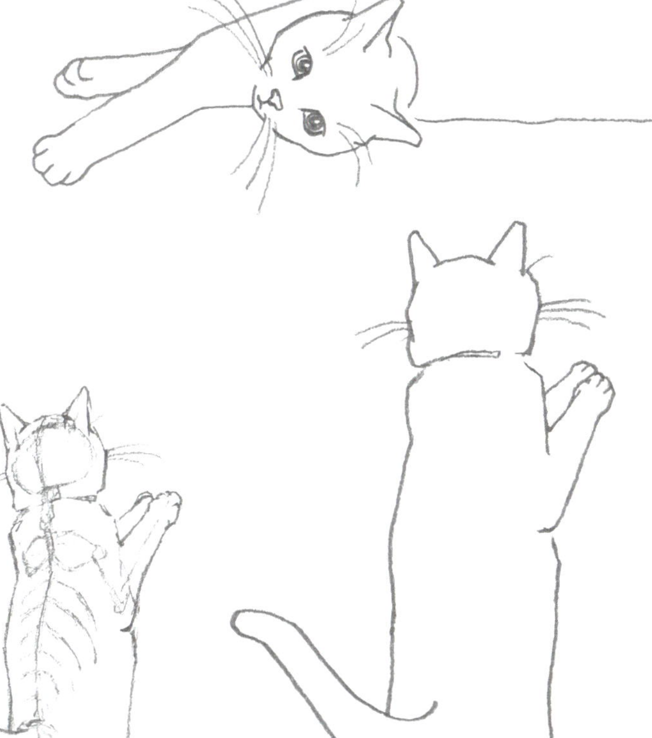

NOTE

A standing cat's posture forms a straight line from head to spine, its elbows are held close to the body, and the femurs, lower leg and tarsal bones are firmly extended to support its weight. The positions of the heels are also important.

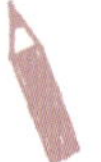 A collection of cat poses

Here are various cat poses, in all sorts of shapes and forms. I hope they'll serve as helpful references when drawing cats.

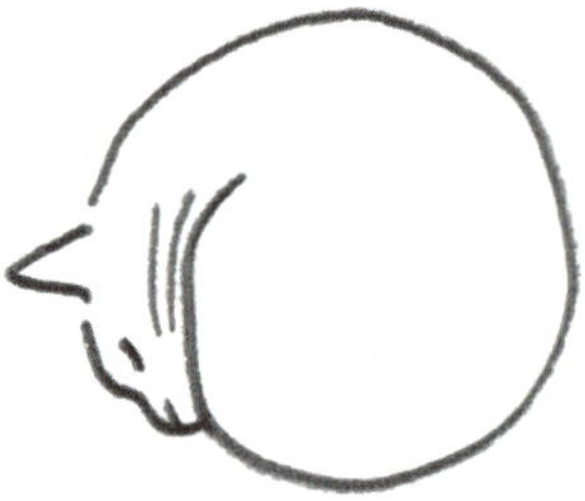

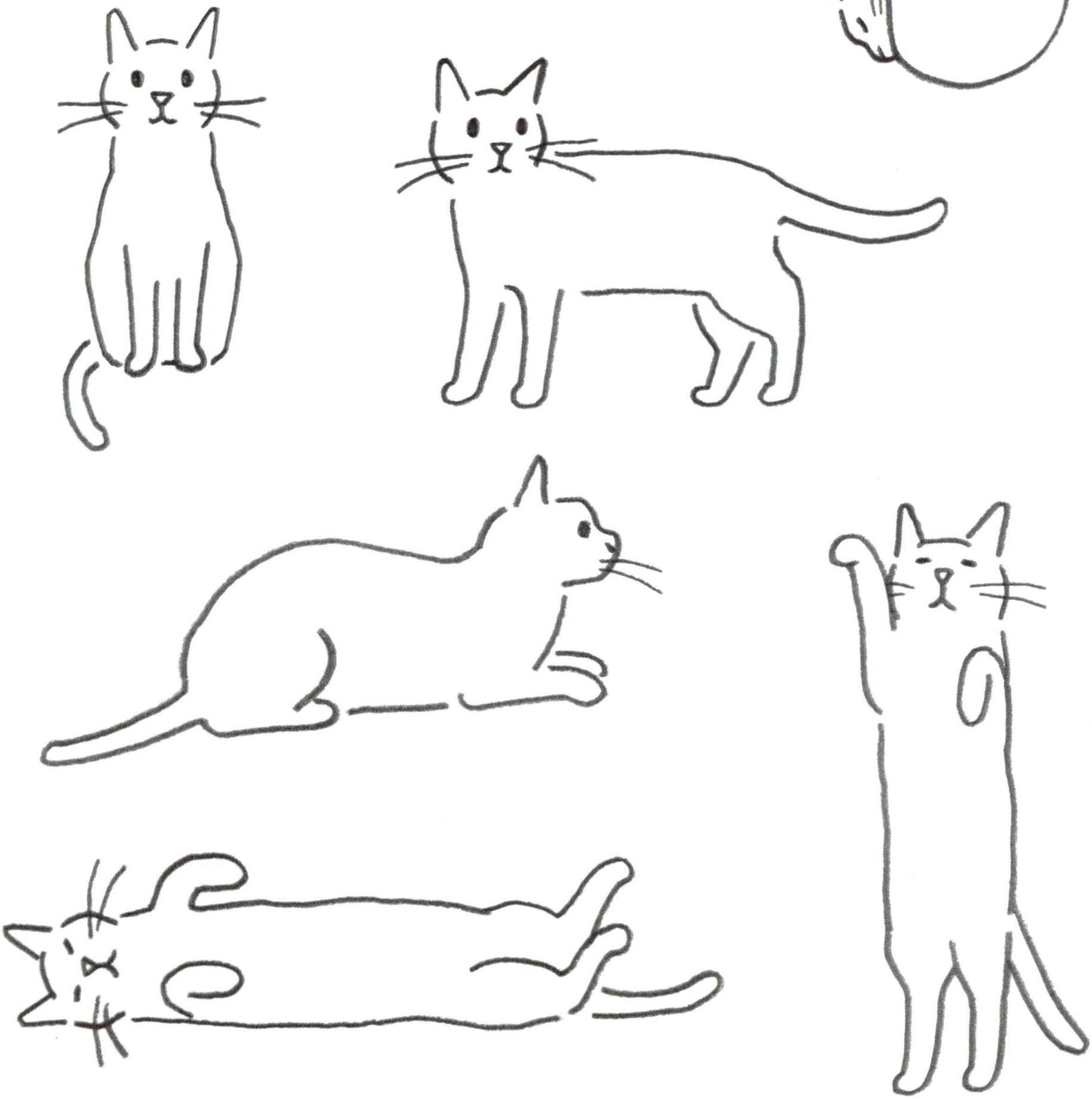

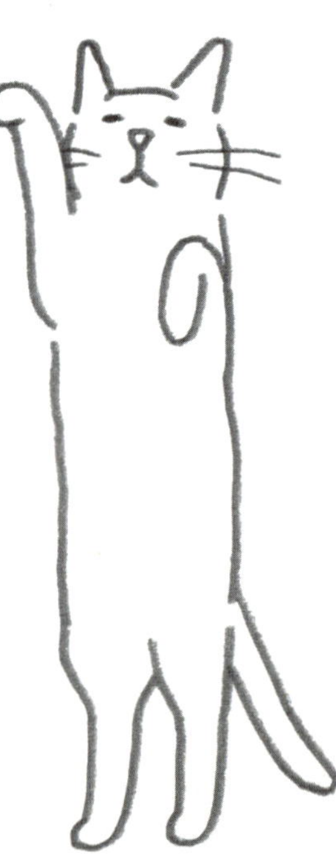

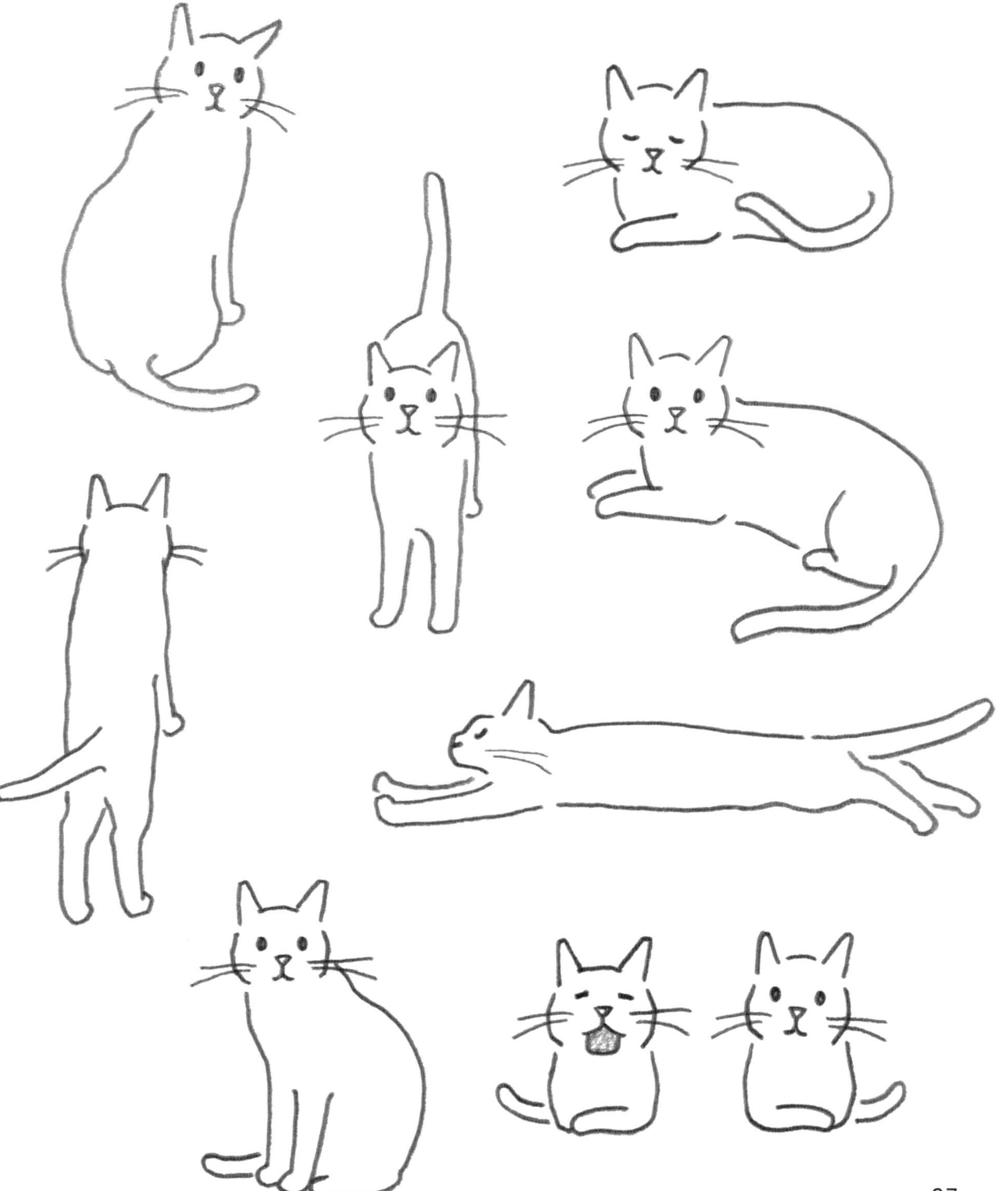

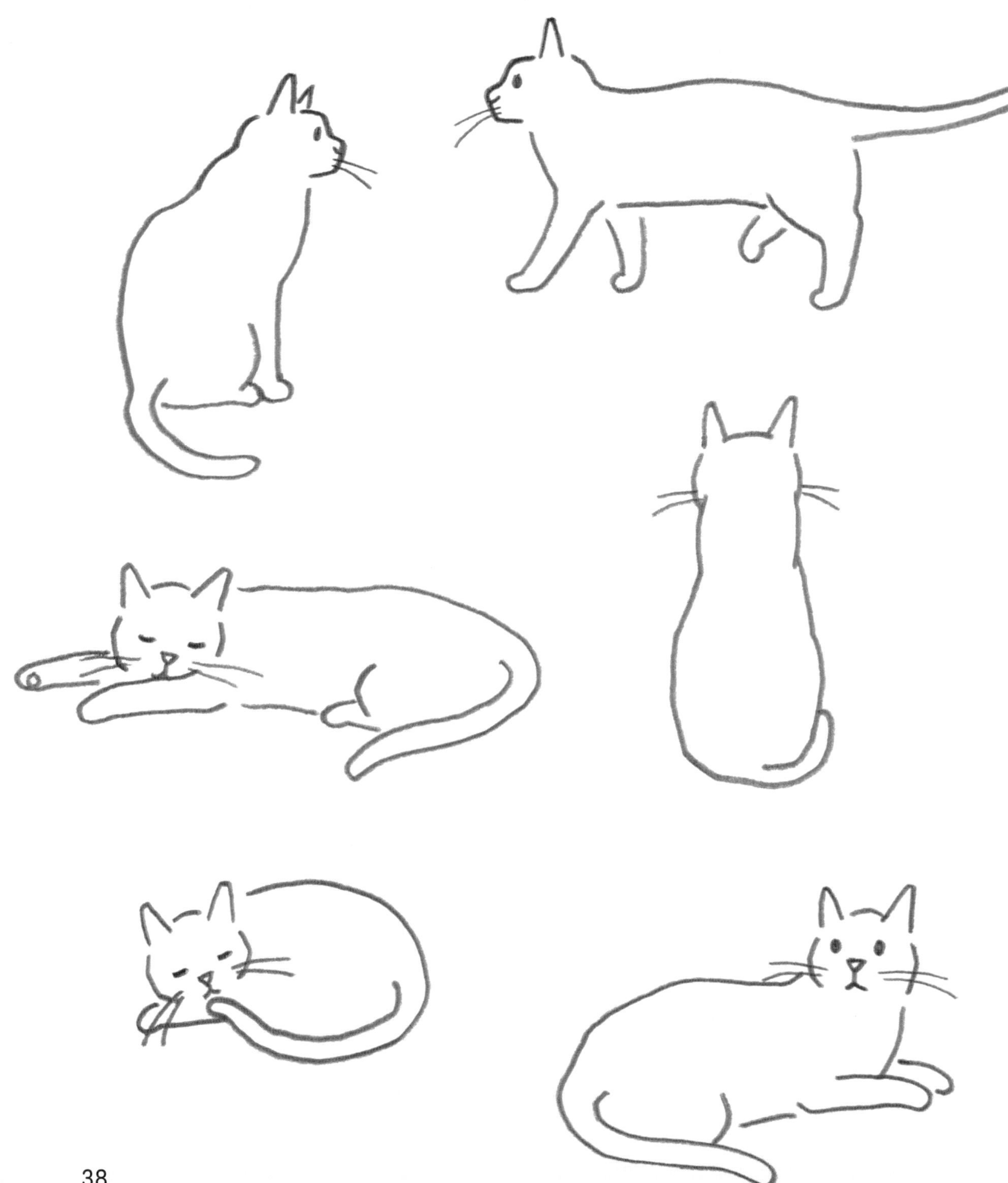

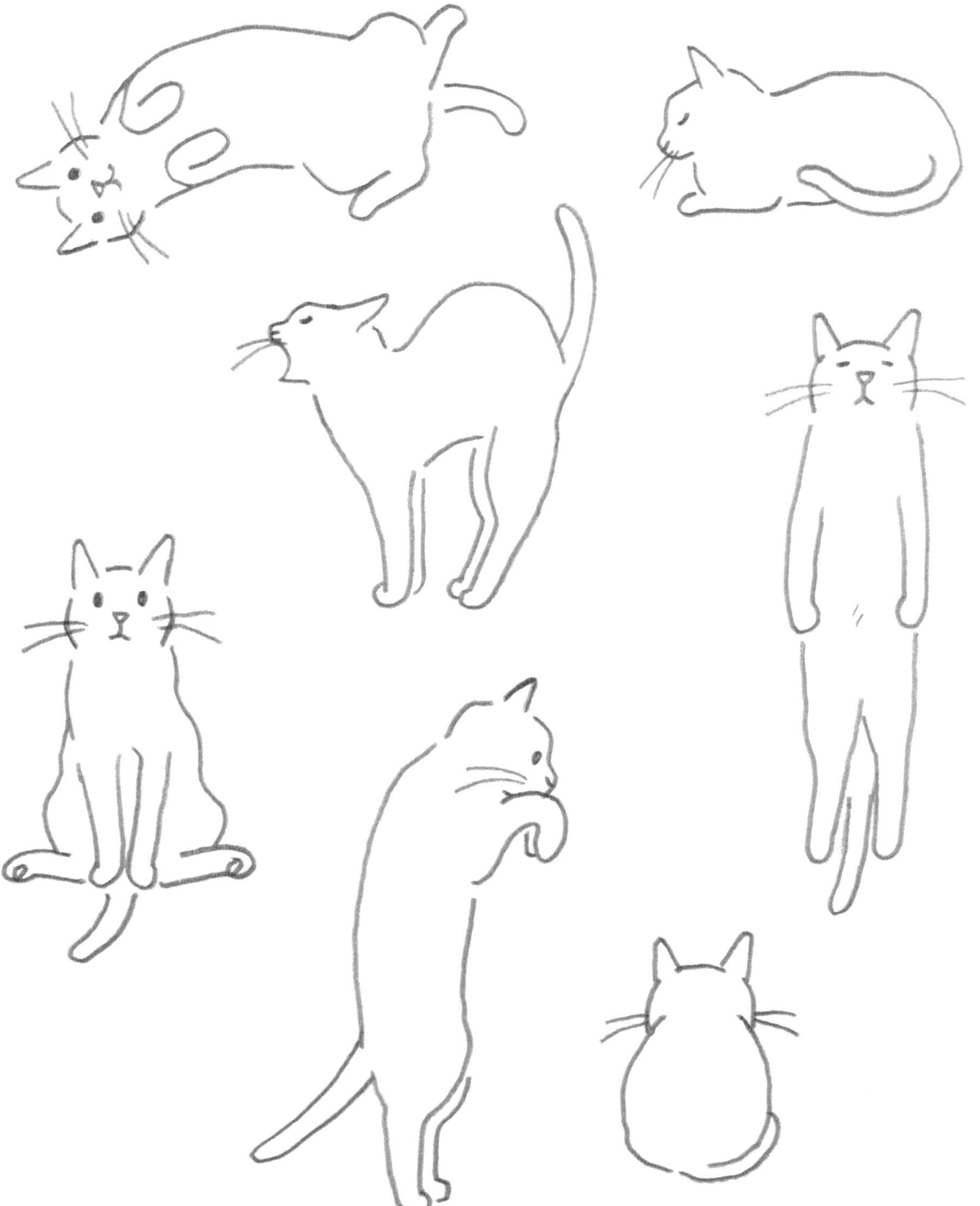

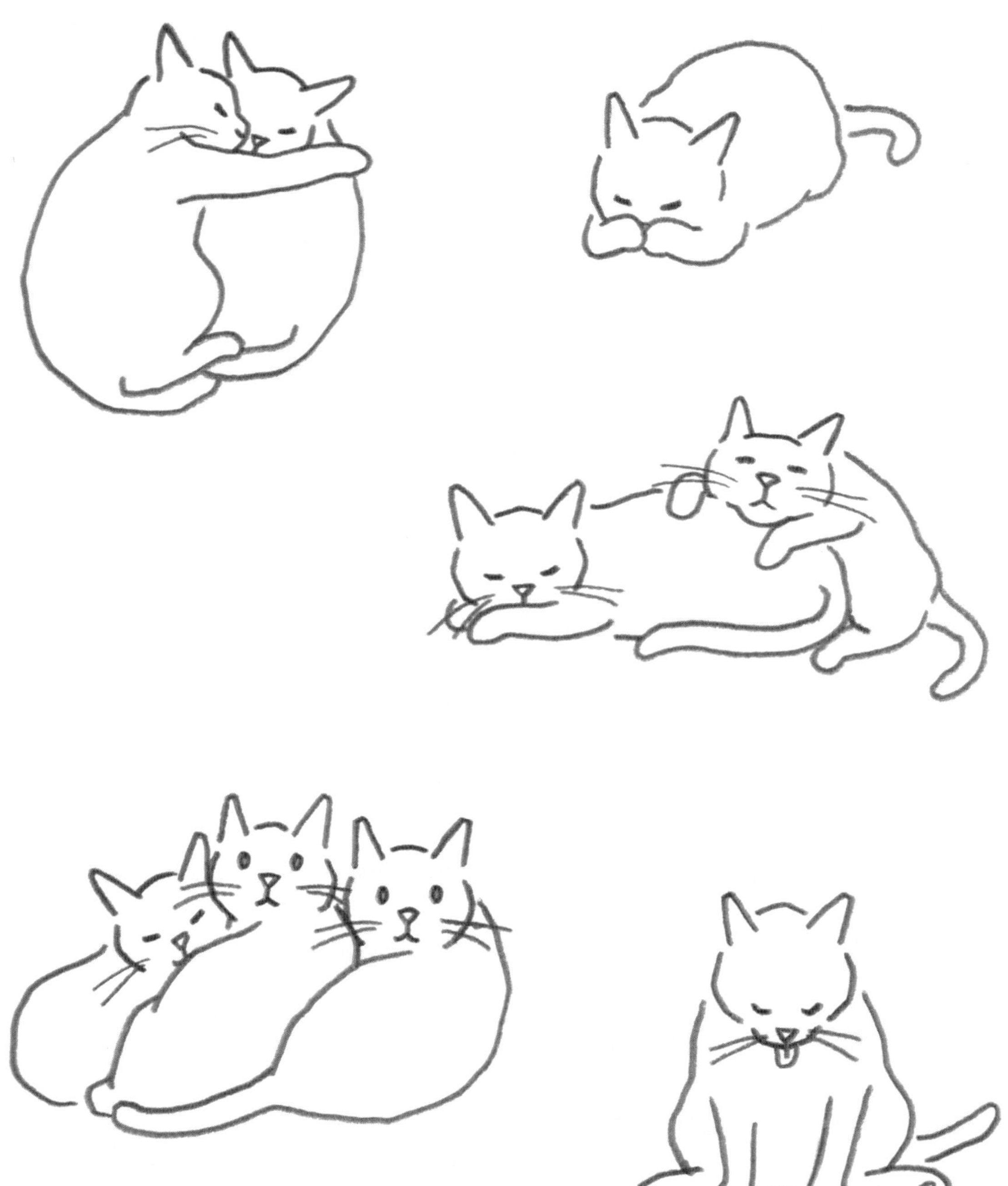

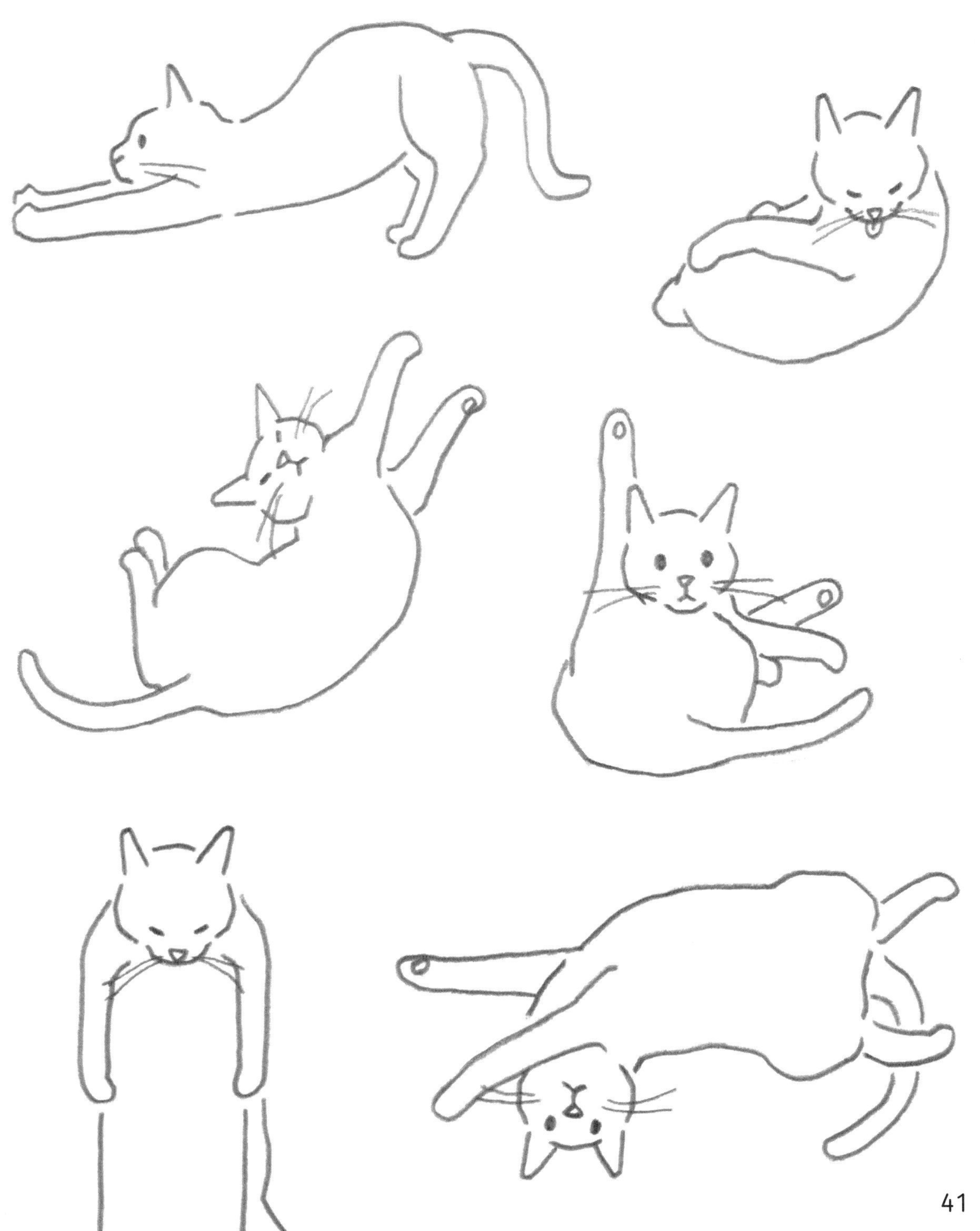

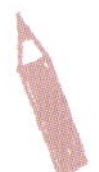

Drawing a cat's face

Next, let's try drawing a cat's face. This time, we'll look at a simple stylized (cartoon-style) version and a slightly more realistic cat face. Use these as a reference and absolutely give it a try!

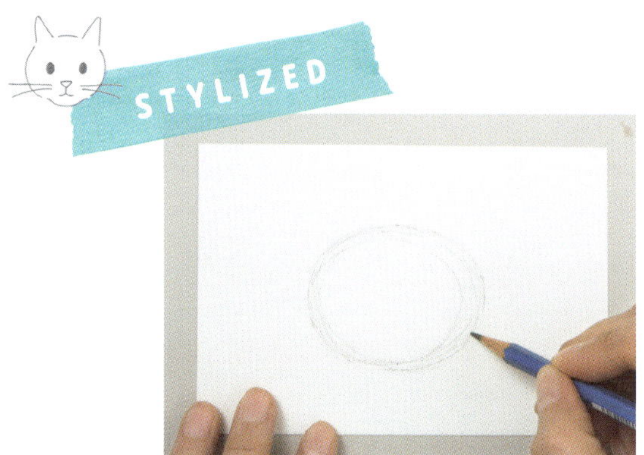

1 Start with a rough sketch of a slightly squat oval. Draw very lightly with a pencil.

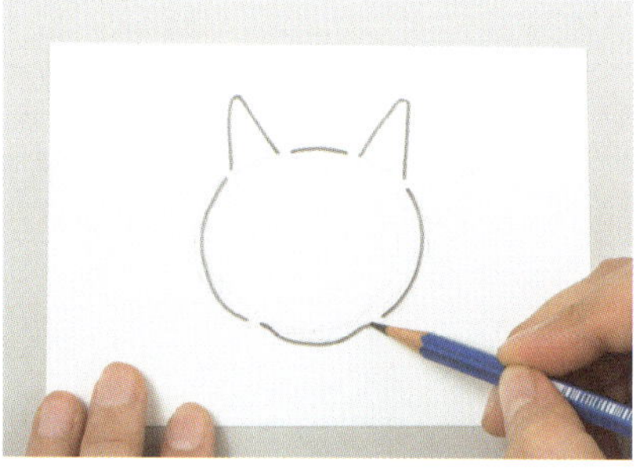

2 Add ears above the oval, and trace around the most well-formed curves of the oval to create the outline. Let the chin bulge slightly downward to give it a natural cat-like look.

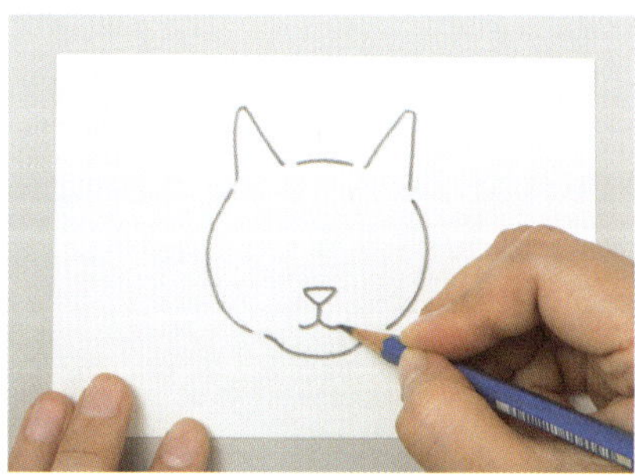

3 Gently erase any unnecessary lines from steps 1 and 2, leaving only the outline. Draw a rounded, upside-down-triangle nose slightly below the center, and add a mouth below it.

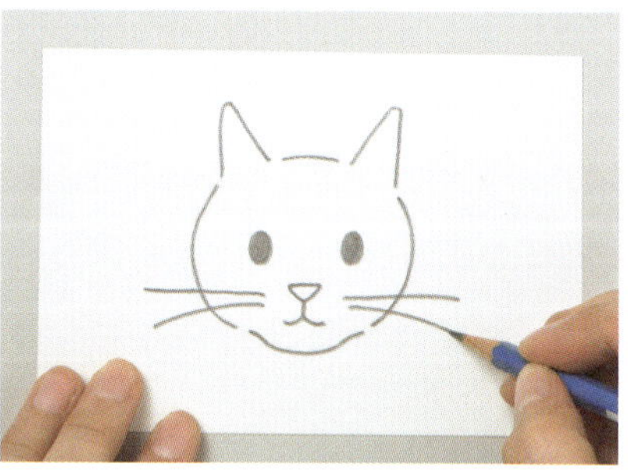

4 Draw the eyes as vertically oriented ovals for a cute impression. Add some whiskers, and you're done!

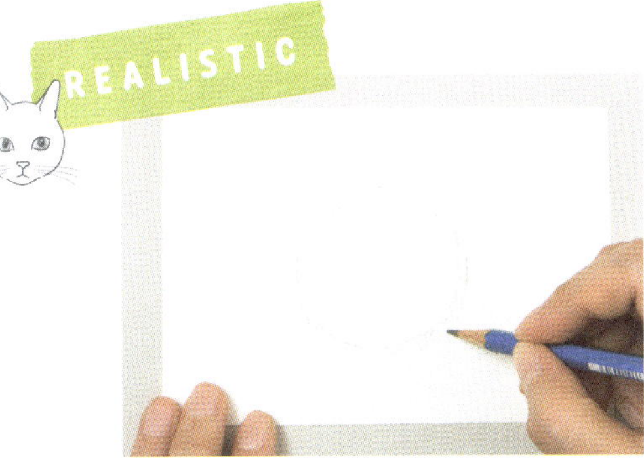

1 Start with a light sketch of an oval that's closer to a perfect circle than in the stylized version.

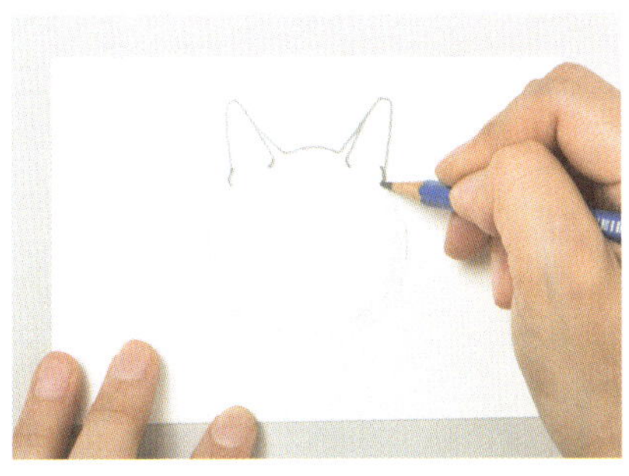

2 Draw the ears. Unlike in the stylized version, sketch in a way that captures more detail, like a croquis drawing.

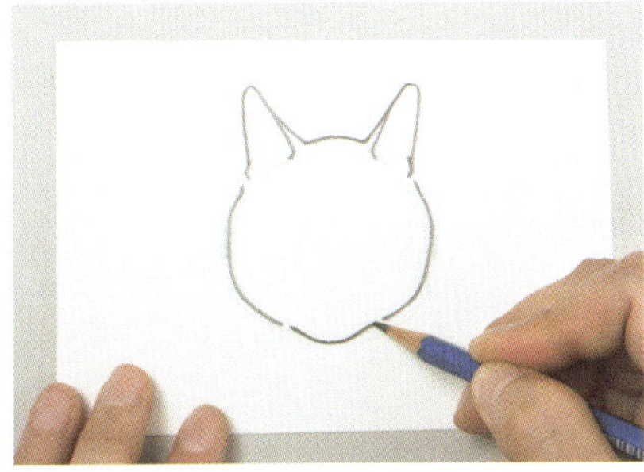

3 Draw the outline in the same way. Make the chin slightly more pointed than in the stylized version. Gently erase any extra sketch lines.

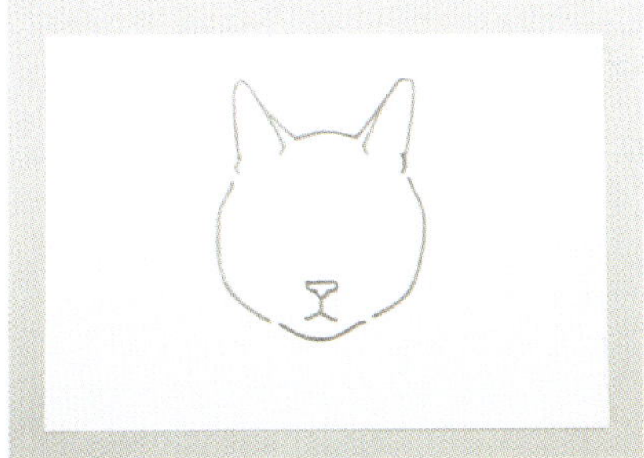

4 Draw an upside-down-triangle nose slightly below the center, and a mouth shaped like an inverted Y underneath it.

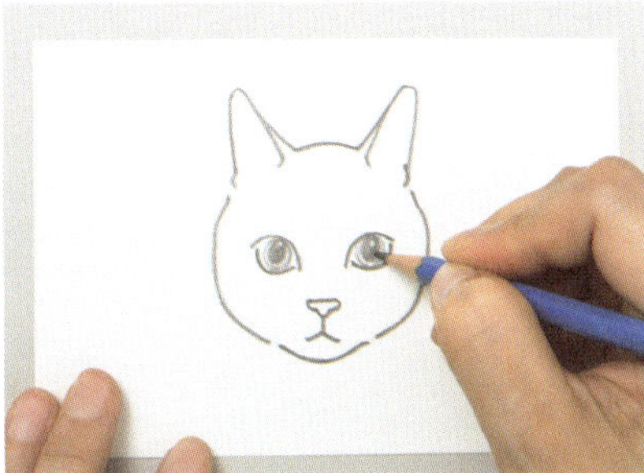

5 Draw the eyes with their inside corners starting above the left and right sides of the nose, slanting upward toward the outer corners. Round pupils give a soft look, while narrow pupils look sharper.

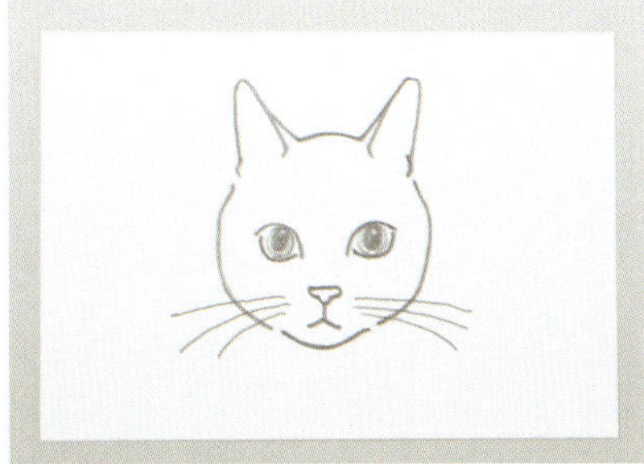

6 Draw a few more whiskers than in the stylized version, and it's complete!

Expressive cartoon-style faces 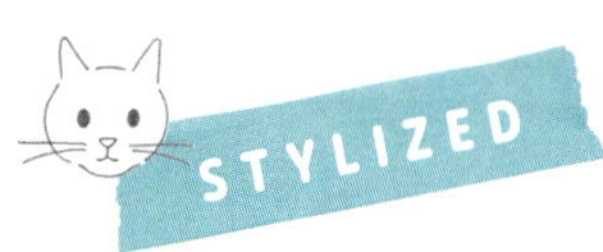

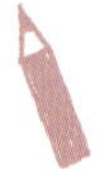

Using the cat face drawing techniques from the previous page, try drawing cats with various expressions. Just by shifting the positions of the eyes, nose and mouth or changing the shape of the eyes, you can create many variations.

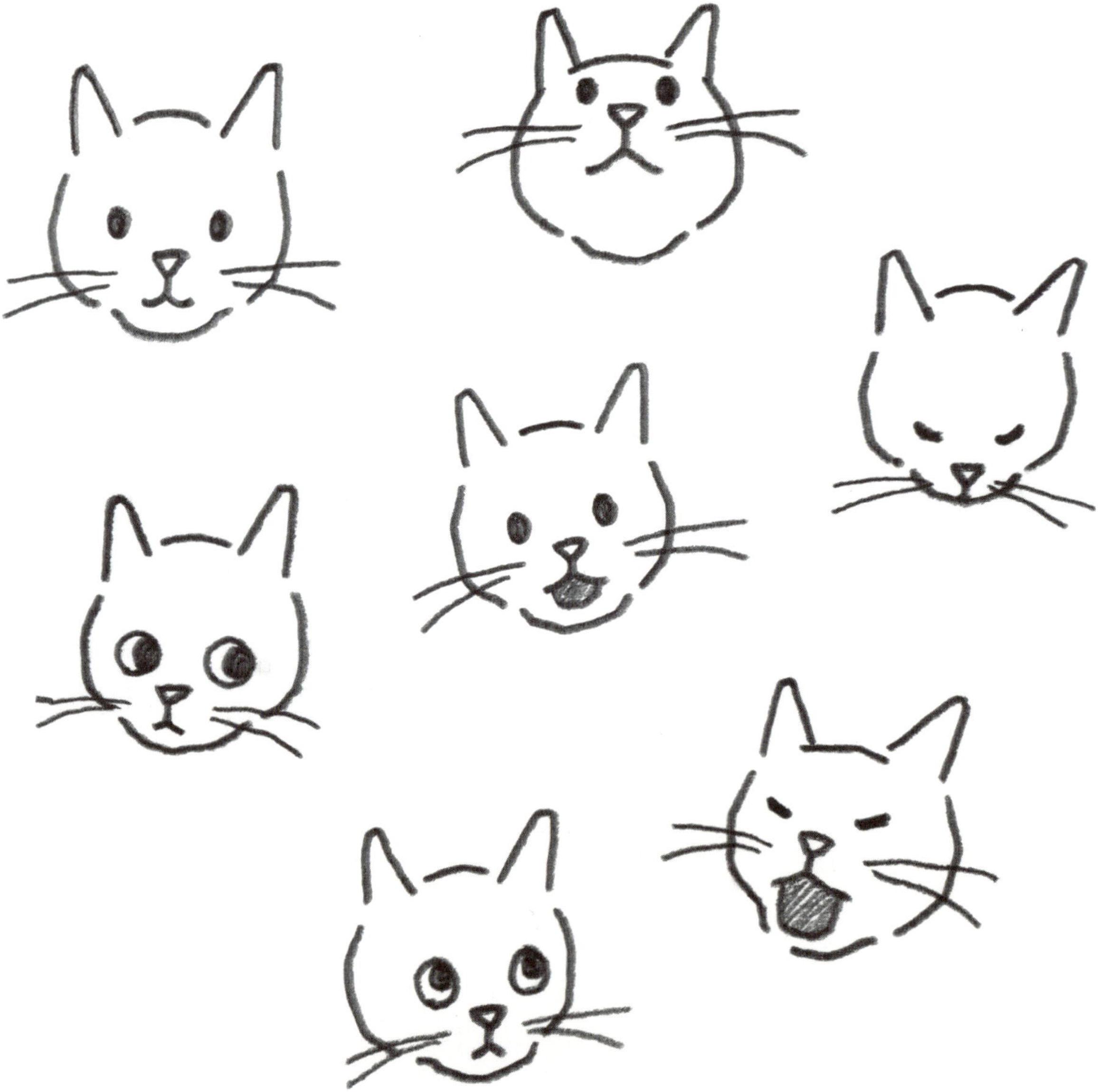

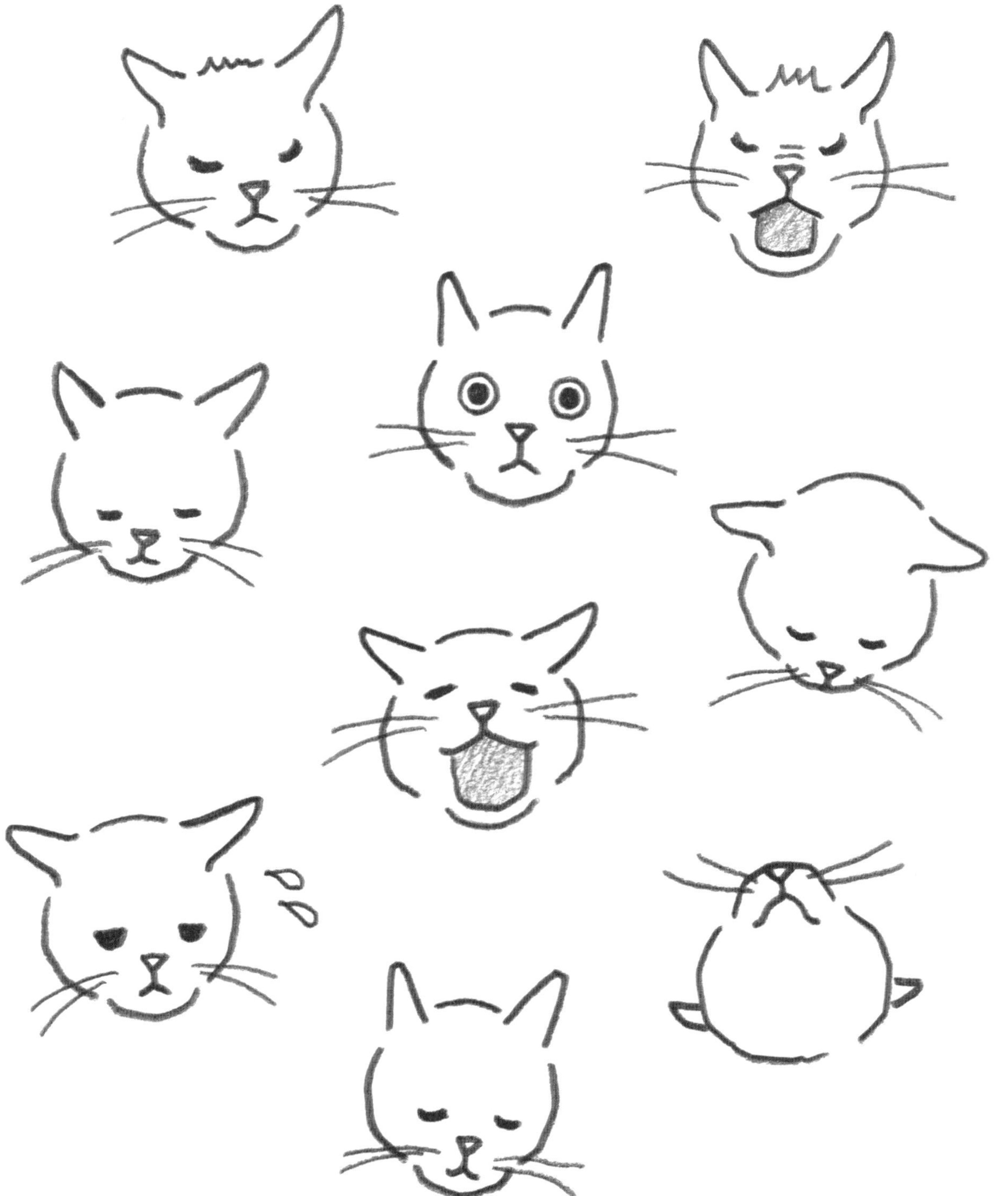

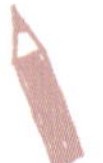

Expressive realistic faces

Here are various realistic cat expressions. In these, detailed noses have been drawn, along with whiskers above the eyes and fluffy hair inside the ears. These details create a more lifelike impression.

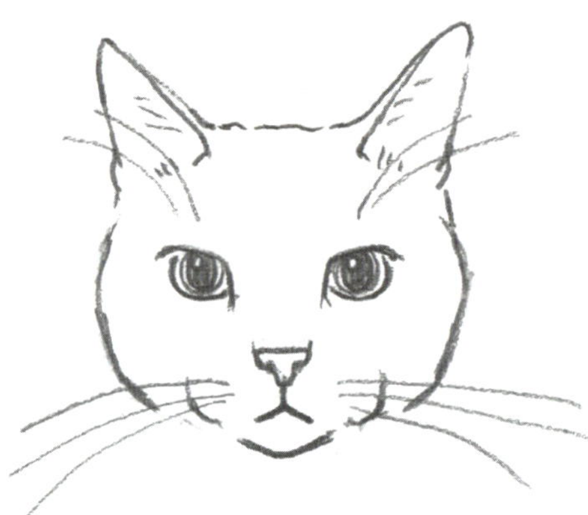

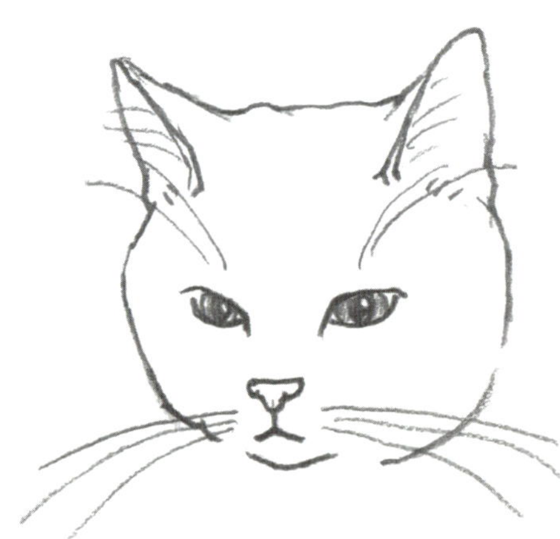

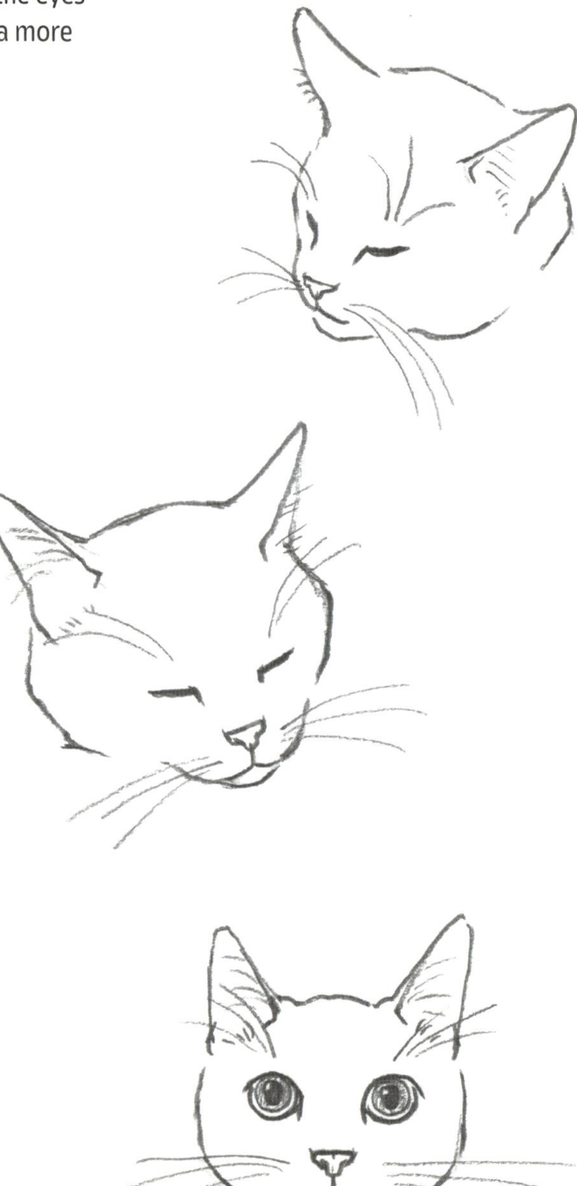

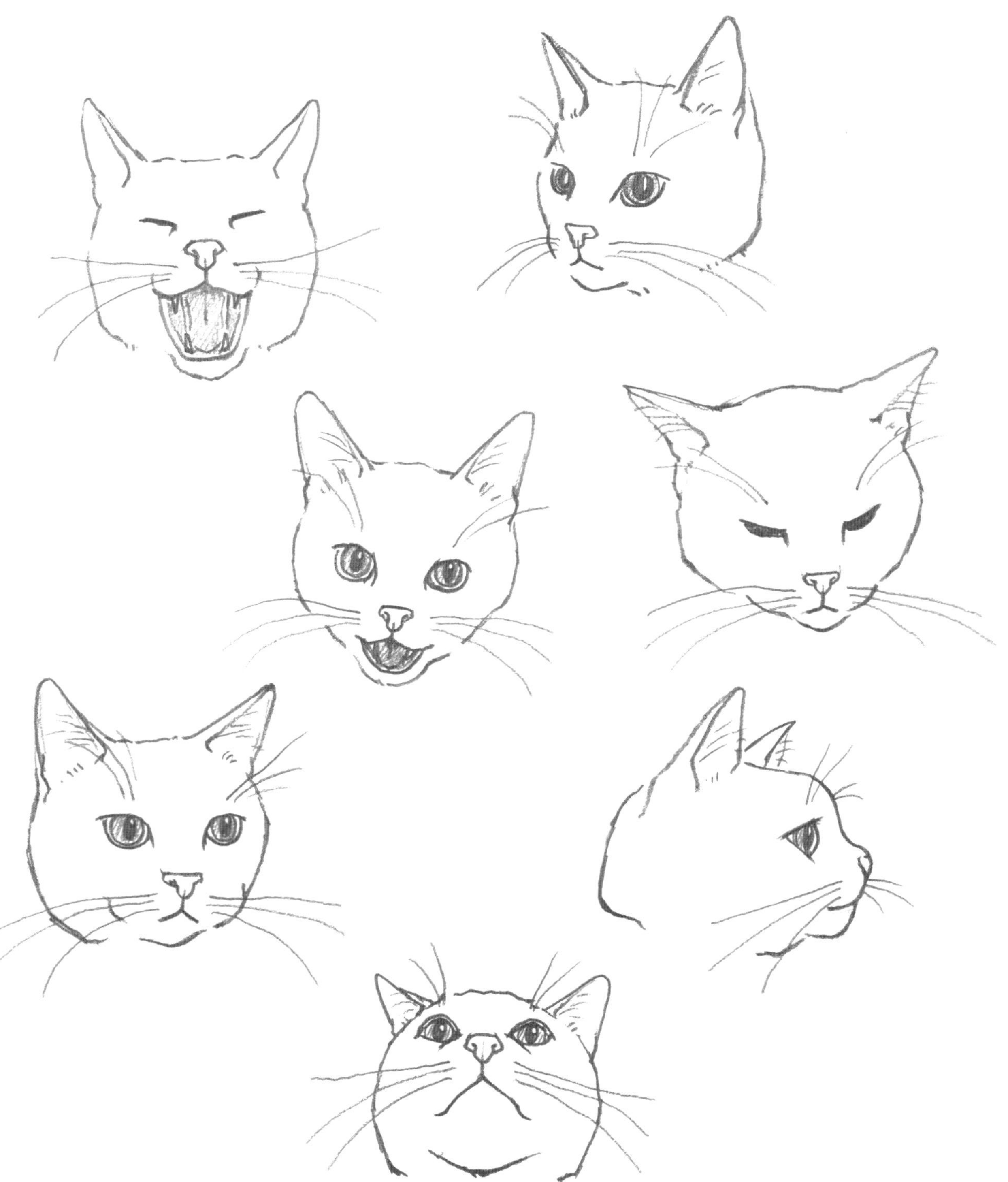

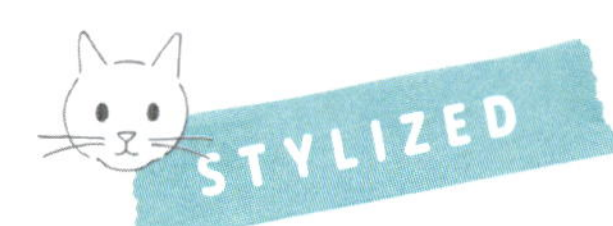

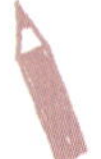 Different cats, different faces

All cats are cute, but each one is truly unique! Whether it's your house cat or a stray, each has a one-of-a-kind face. When you draw their charming features in a simple style, it looks like this. By just changing the shape or position of parts, you can express all kinds of personalities.

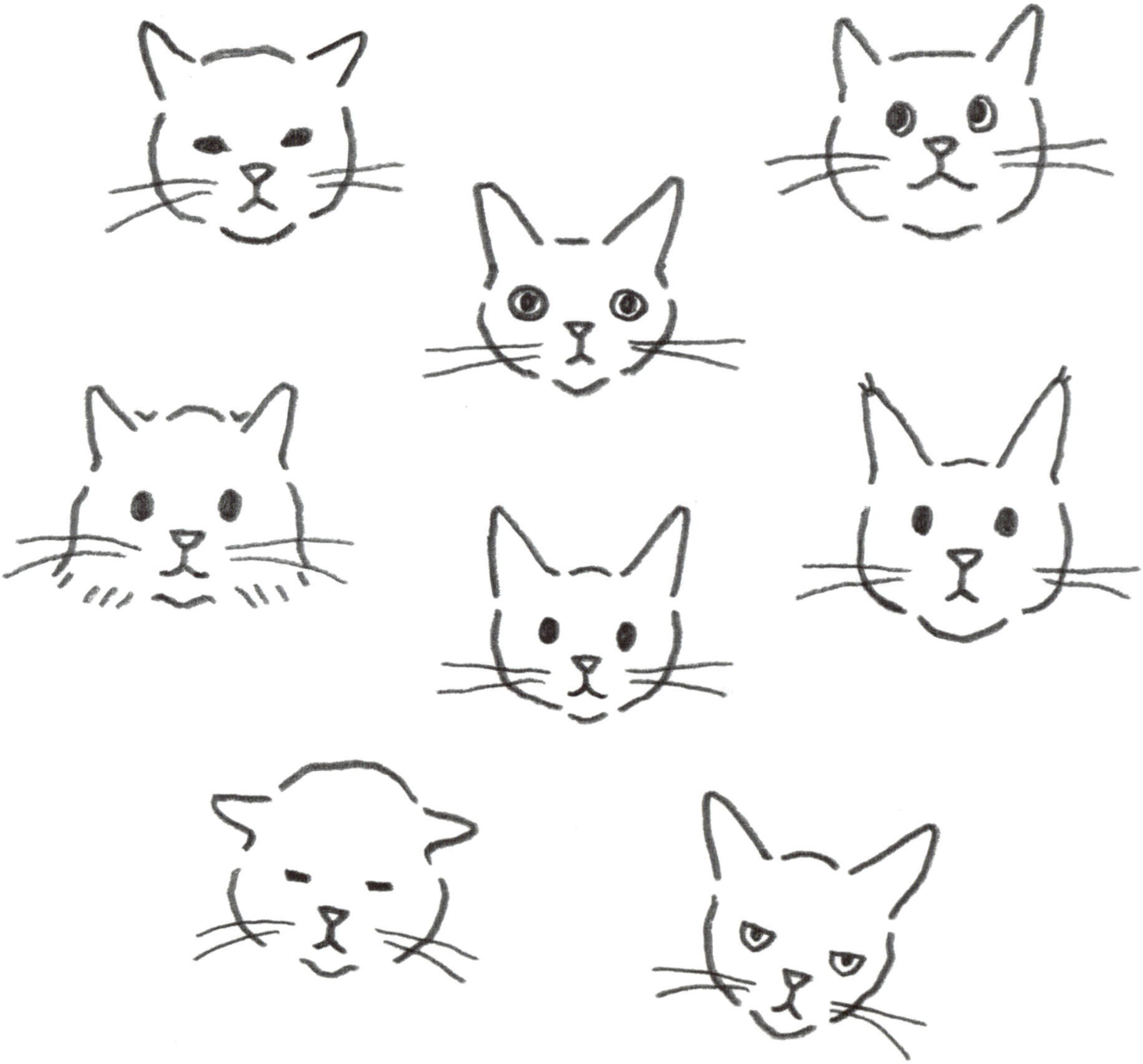

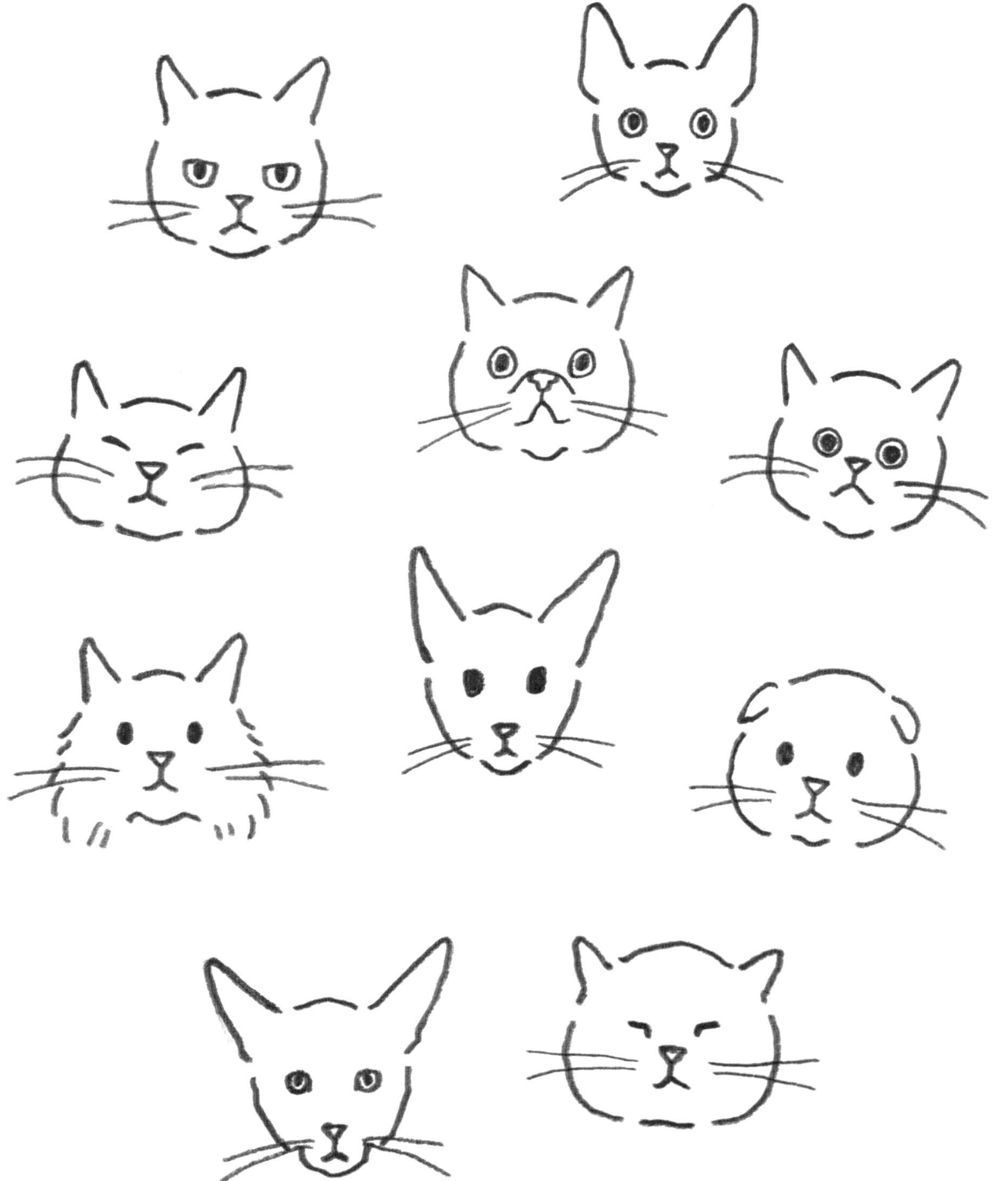

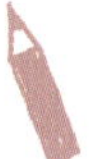

Different cats, different faces

When you depict cats' personalities in a realistic way, it looks like this. Each breed has its own traits—long-faced cats with narrow muzzles or cats with short, compact faces, Even faces with tightly arranged features are charming. Droopy eyes, gentle-looking faces, angular faces and more—look closely at their features. For long-haired cats, be particularly mindful of the underlying bone structure.

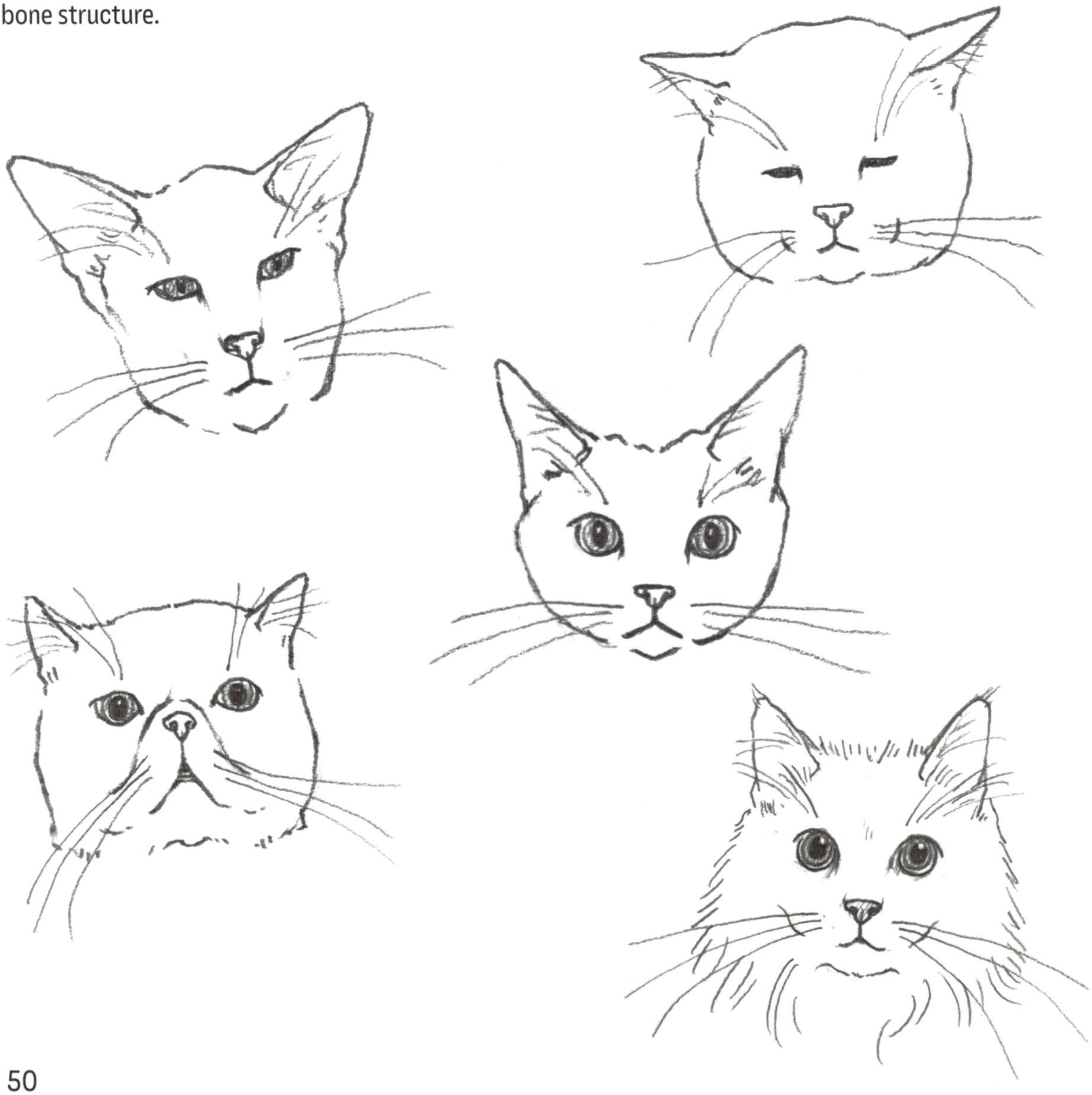

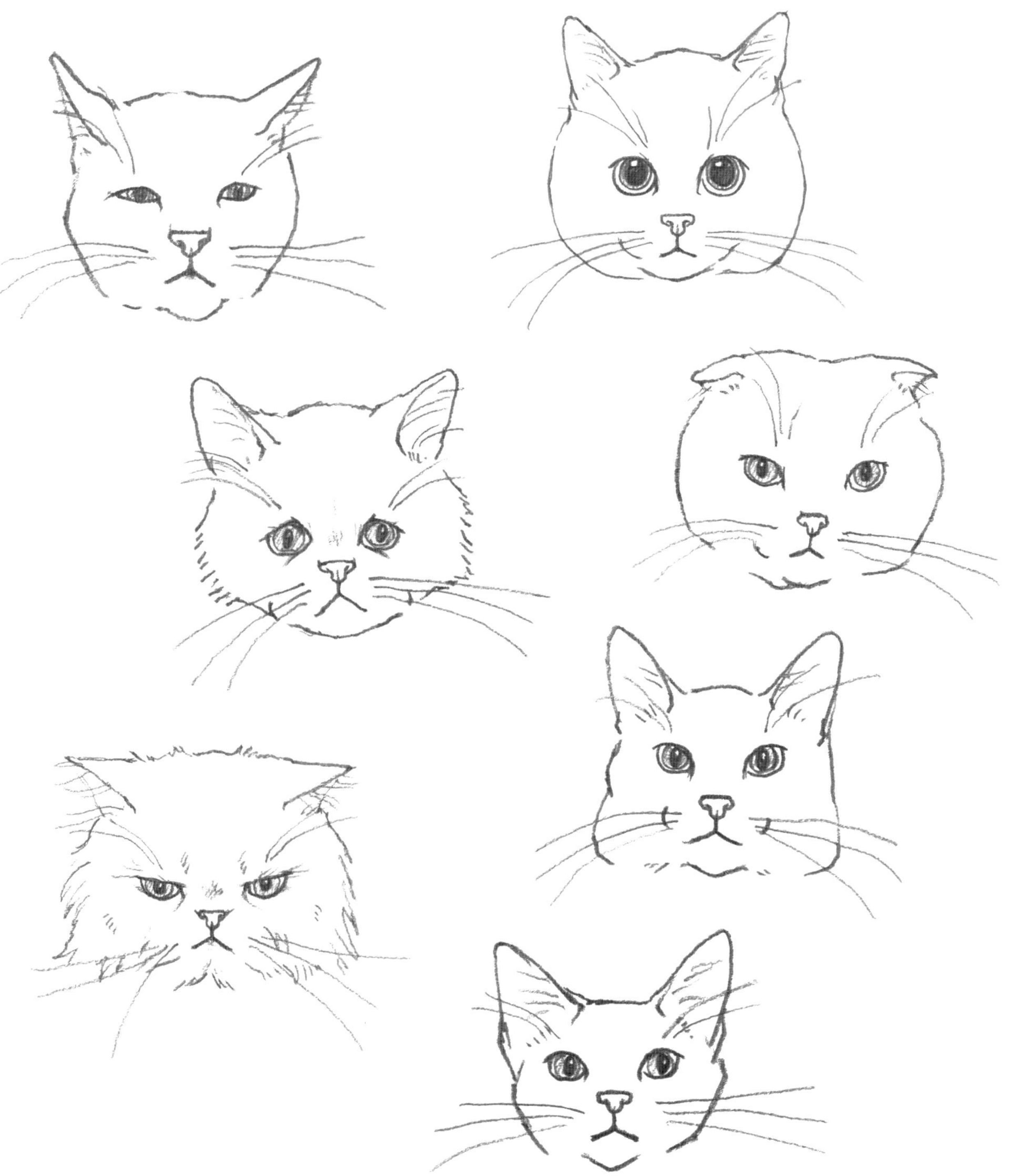

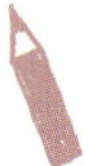

Drawing coat patterns in monochrome

Cat fur patterns are often mottled and fascinating. Here, each coat is intentionally rendered in monochrome.

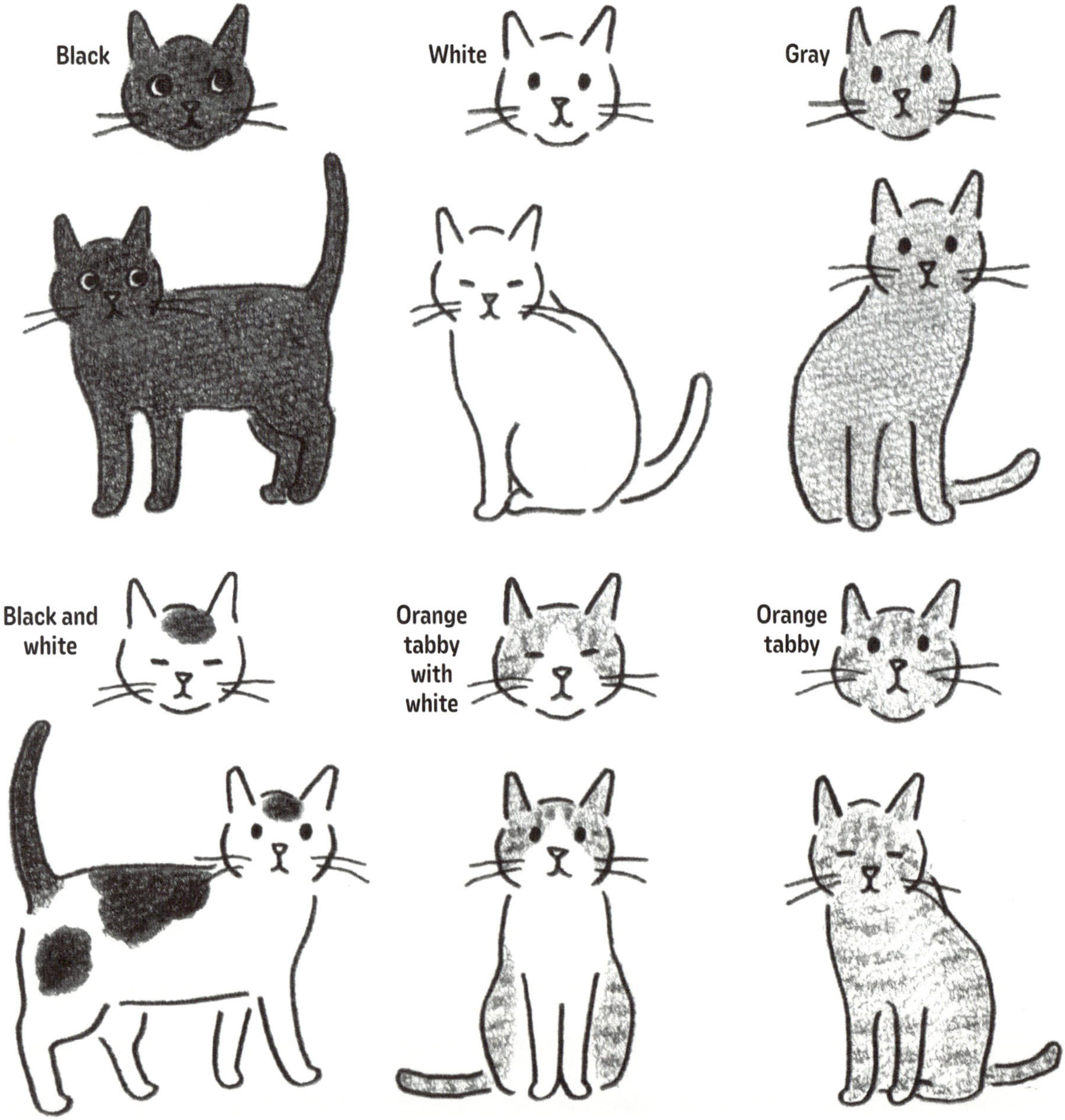

Black

White

Gray

Black and white

Orange tabby with white

Orange tabby

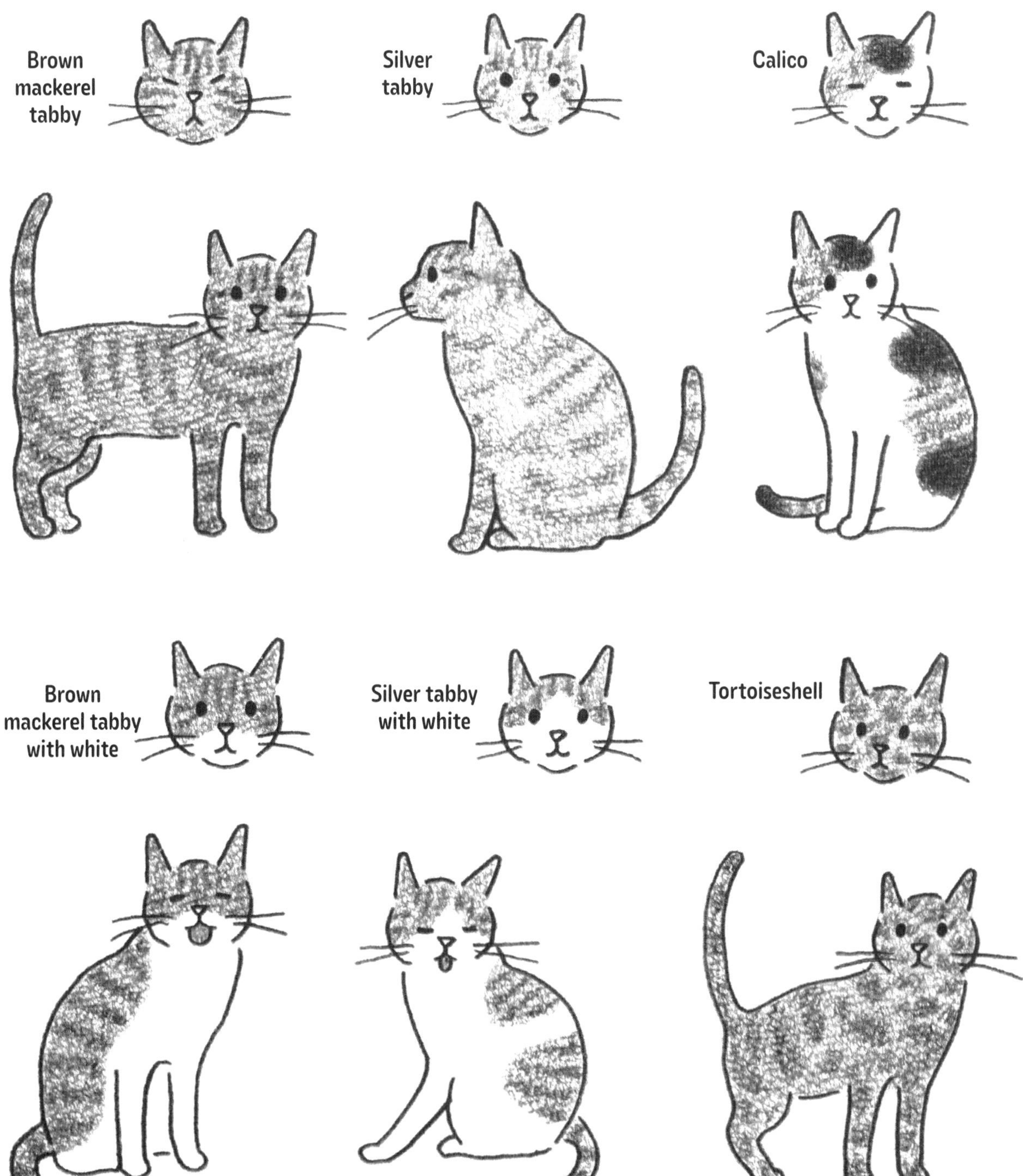

Brown mackerel tabby
Silver tabby
Calico
Brown mackerel tabby with white
Silver tabby with white
Tortoiseshell

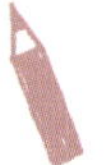

Drawing coat patterns in color

Adding color makes cats' coats even more varied. Colors used include black, white, gray, brown, ocher, beige and orange.

Black

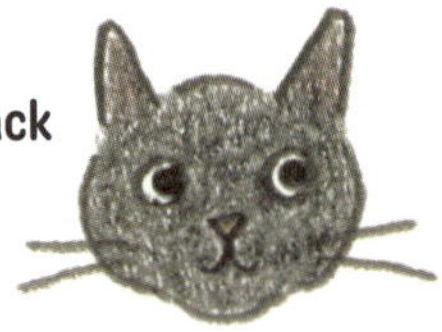

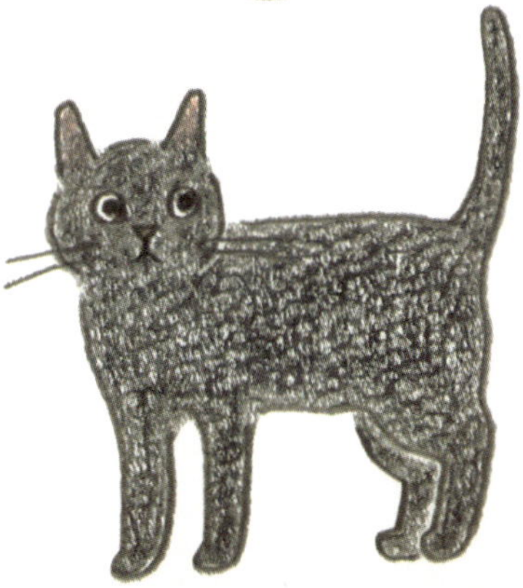

White

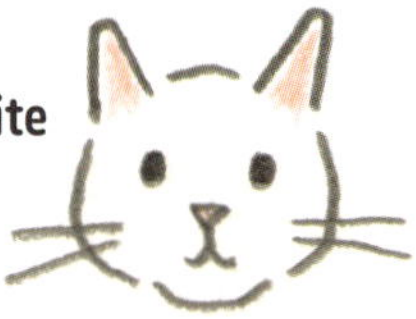

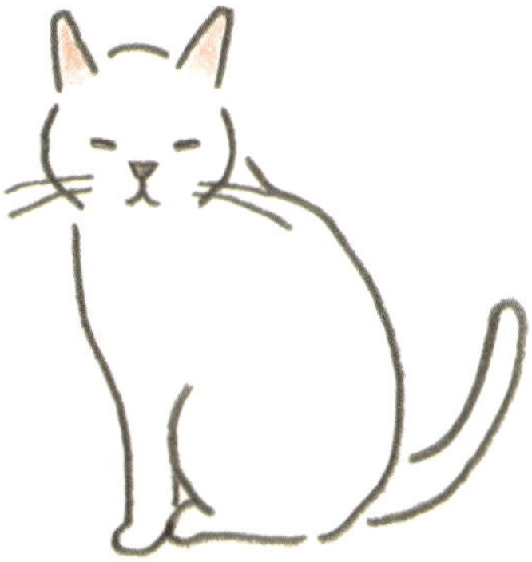

Gray

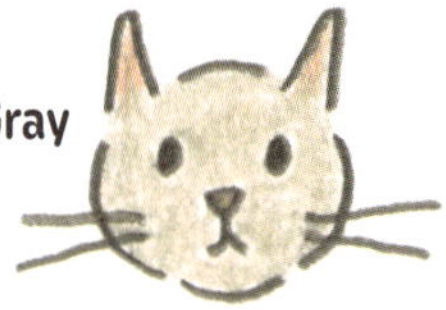

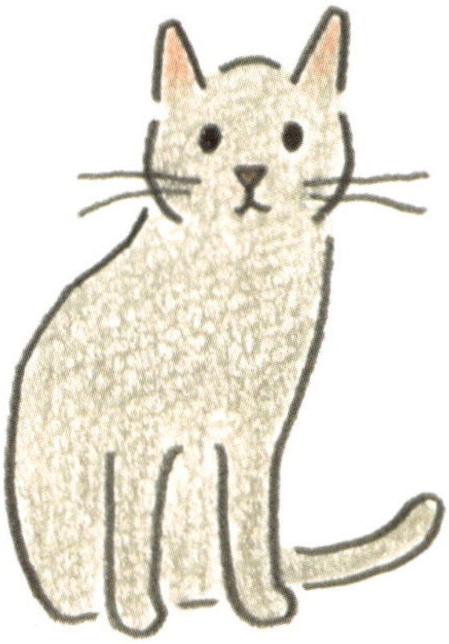

Black and white

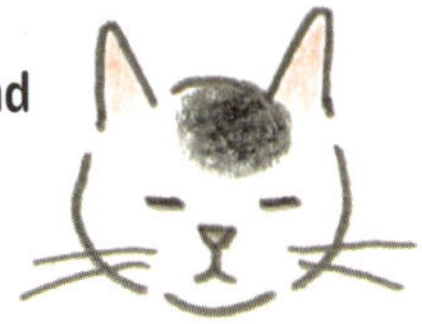

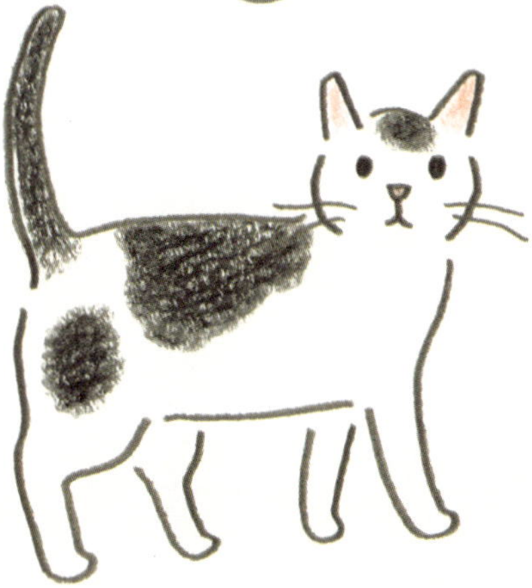

Orange tabby with white

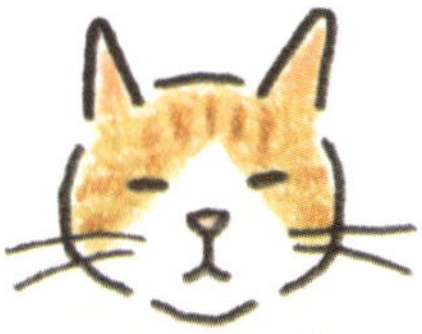

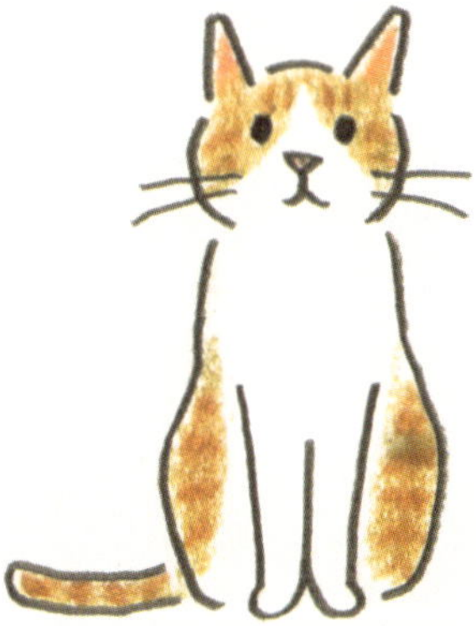

Orange tabby

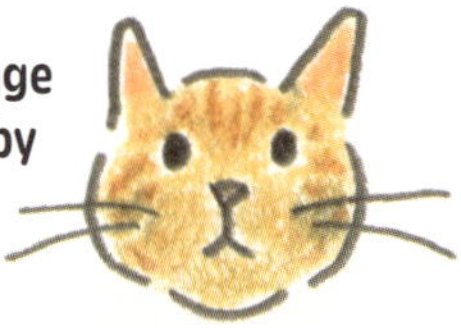

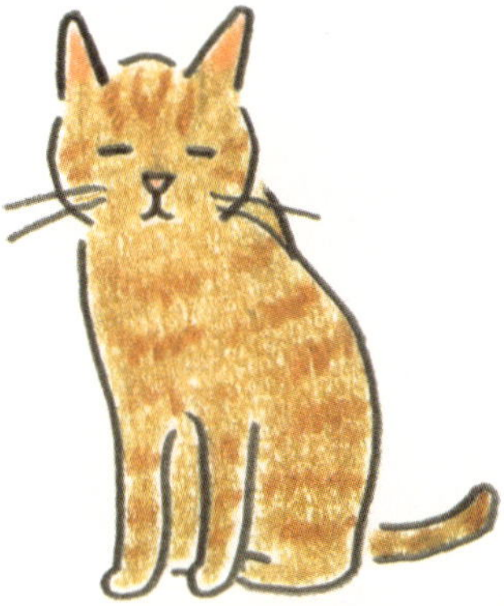

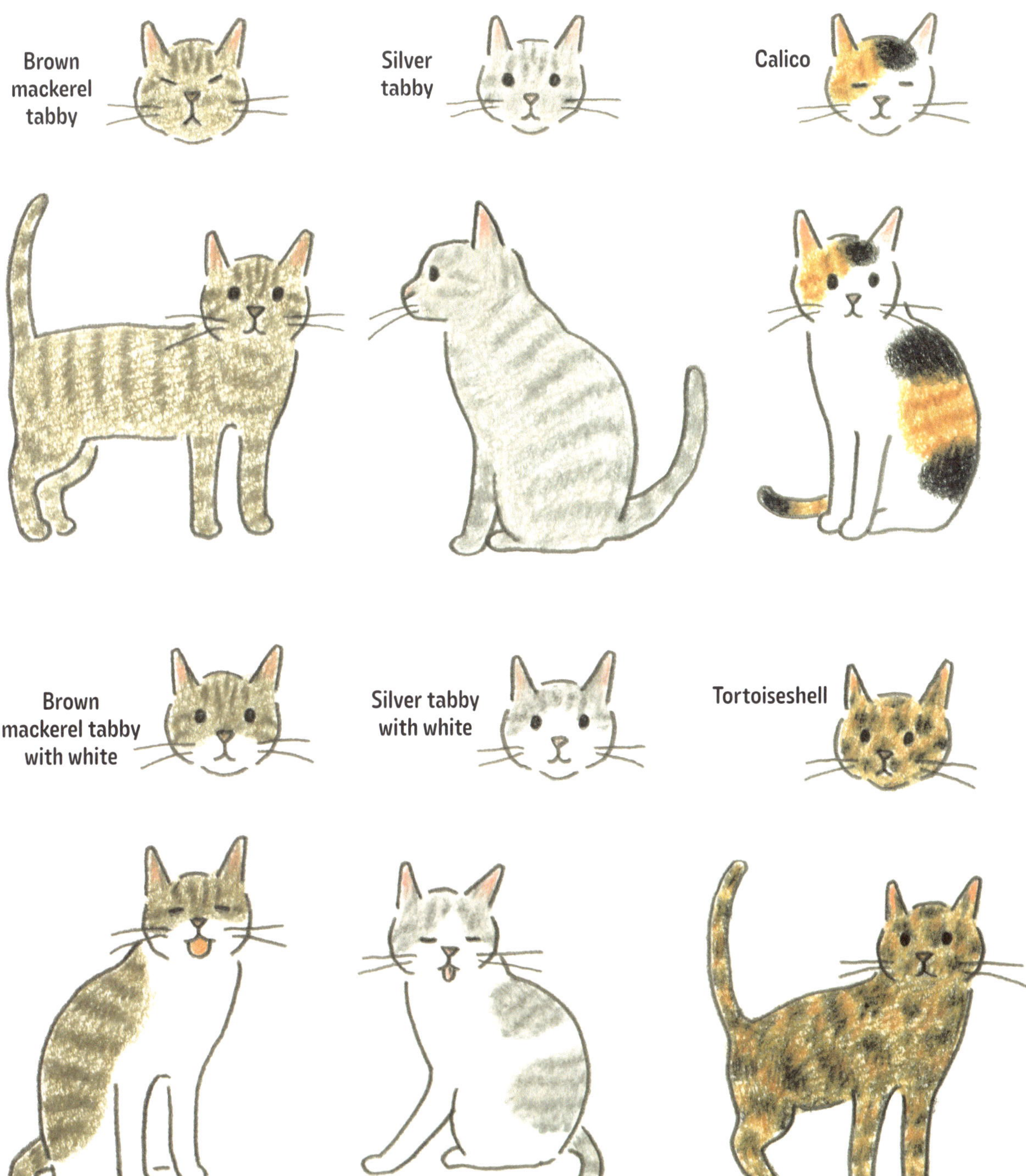

Brown
mackerel
tabby
Silver
tabby
Calico
Brown
mackerel tabby
with white
Silver tabby
with white
Tortoiseshell

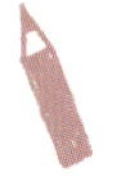# Bringing it all together: forms, poses, expressions and patterns!

By combining the forms, poses, expressions and patterns you've practiced so far, you can draw an endless variety of adorable cats. Enjoy drawing your very own feline motifs—expressions unique to your drawing style.

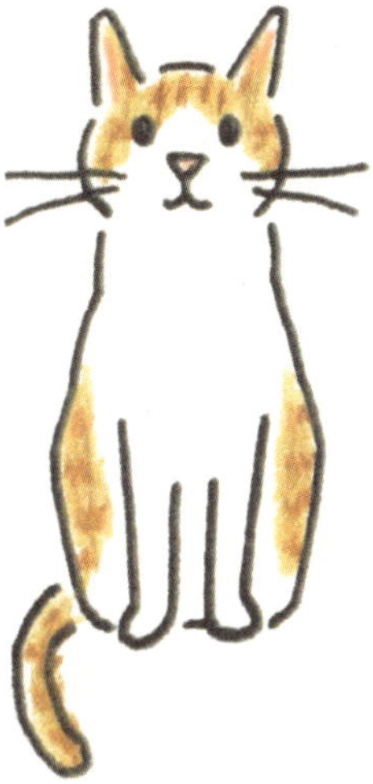

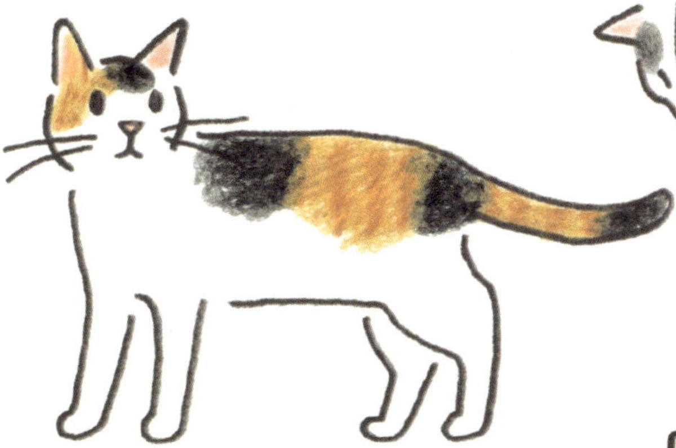

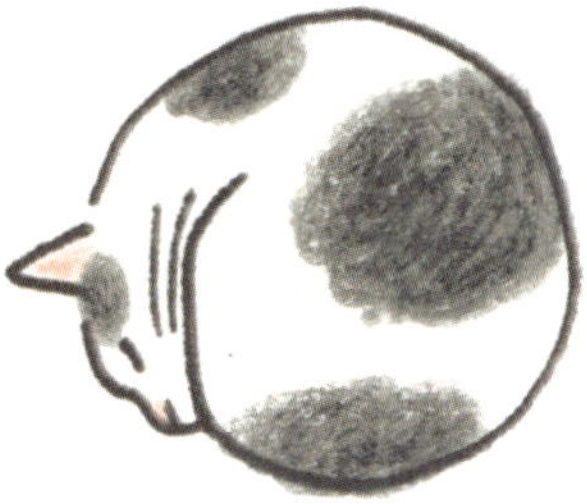

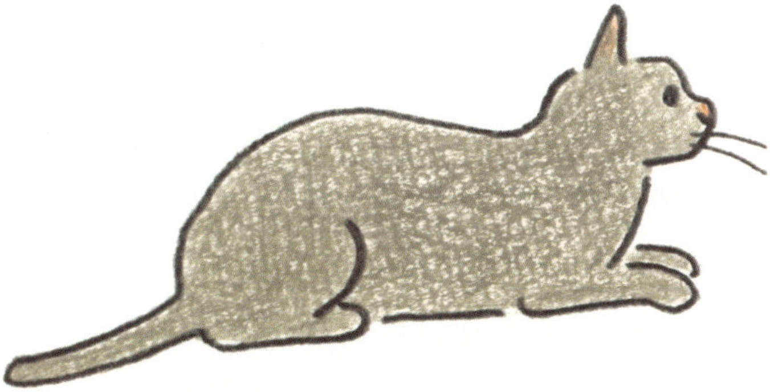

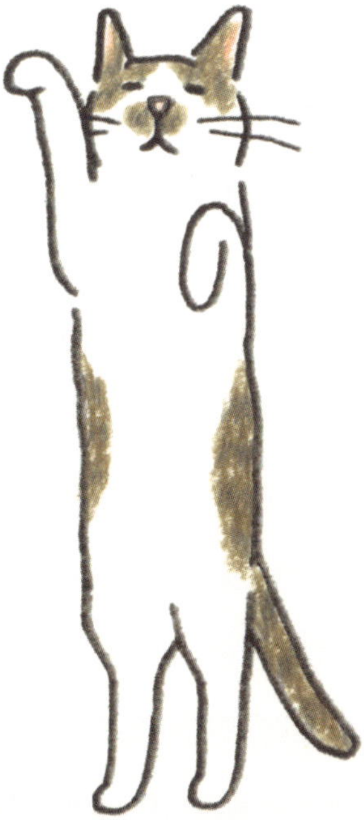

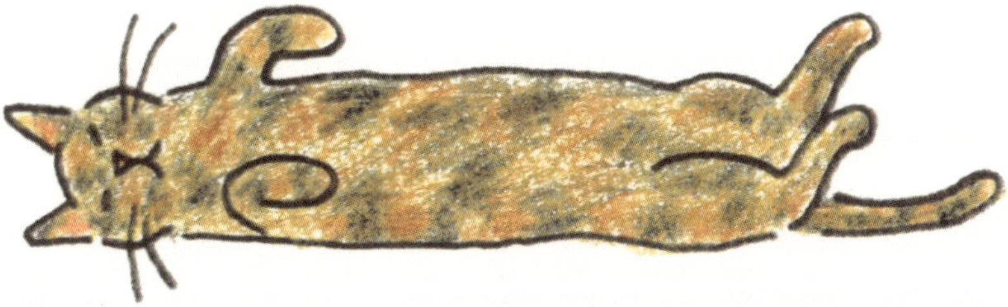

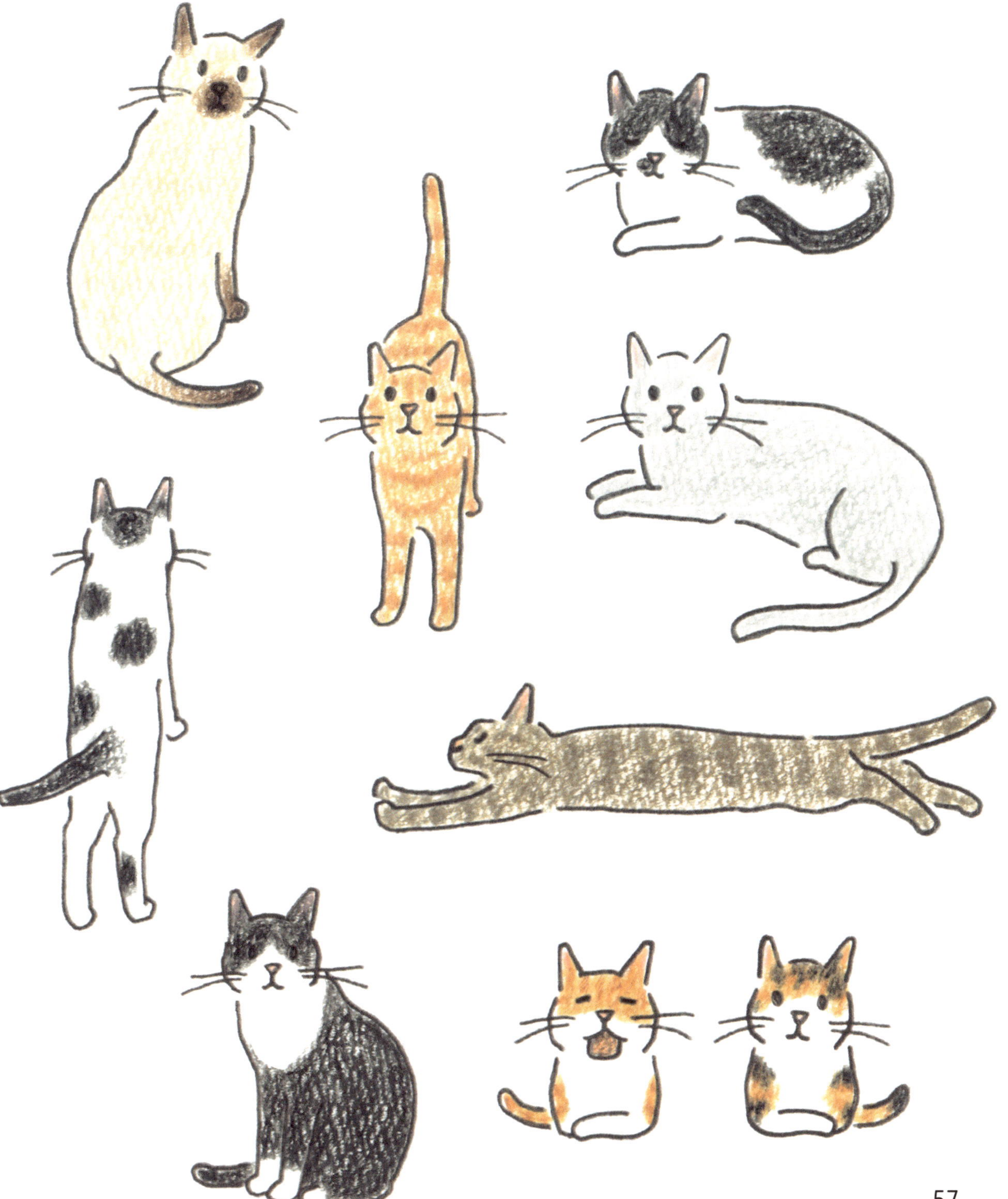

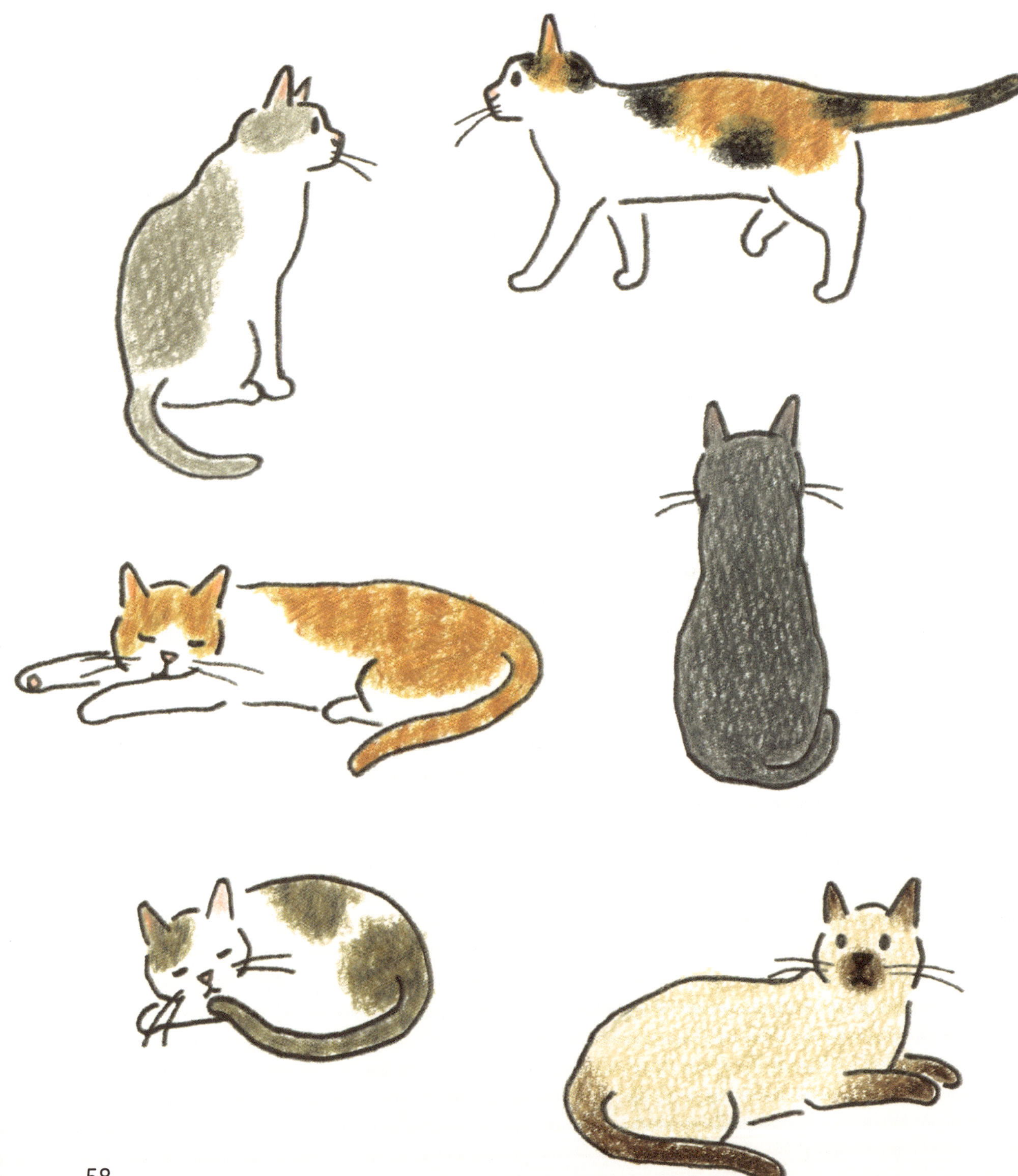

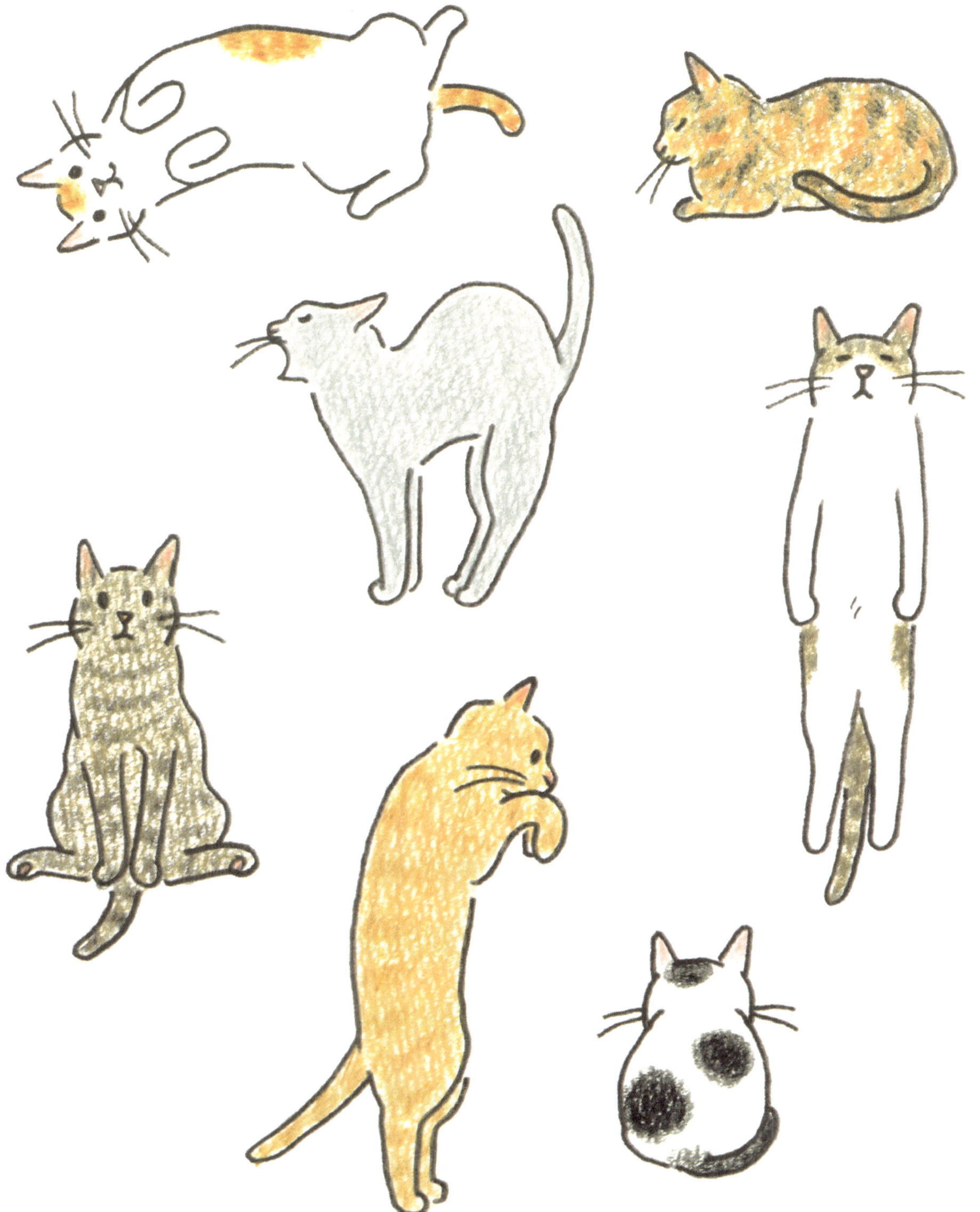

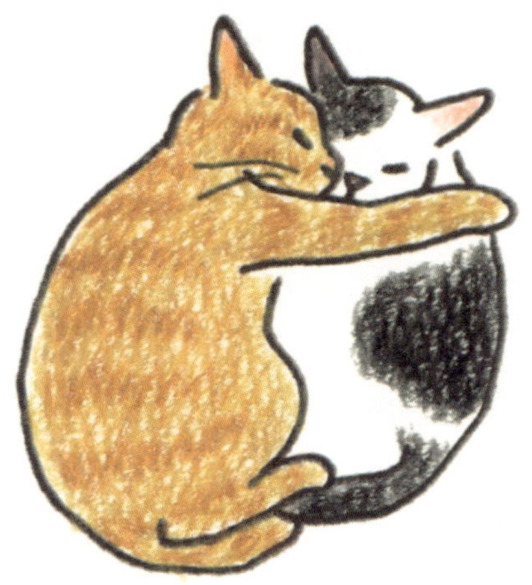

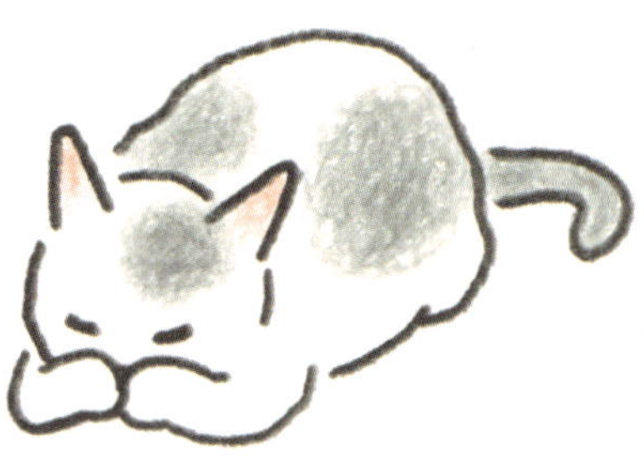

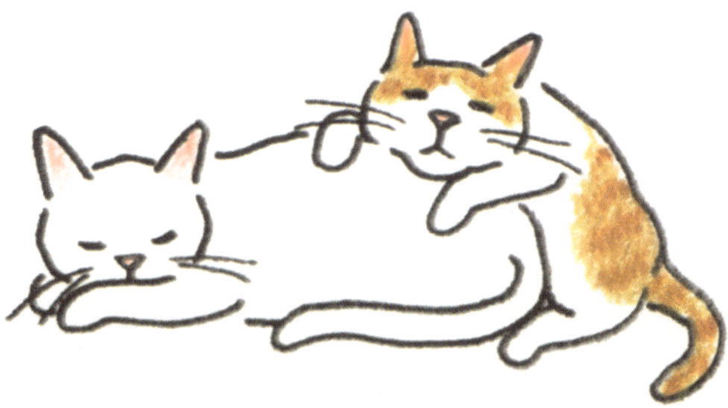

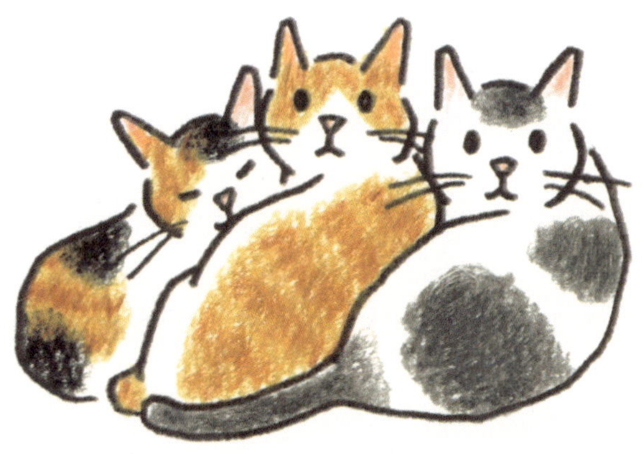

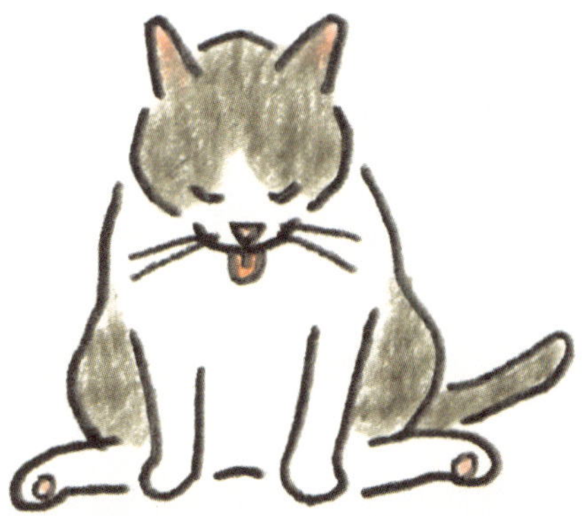

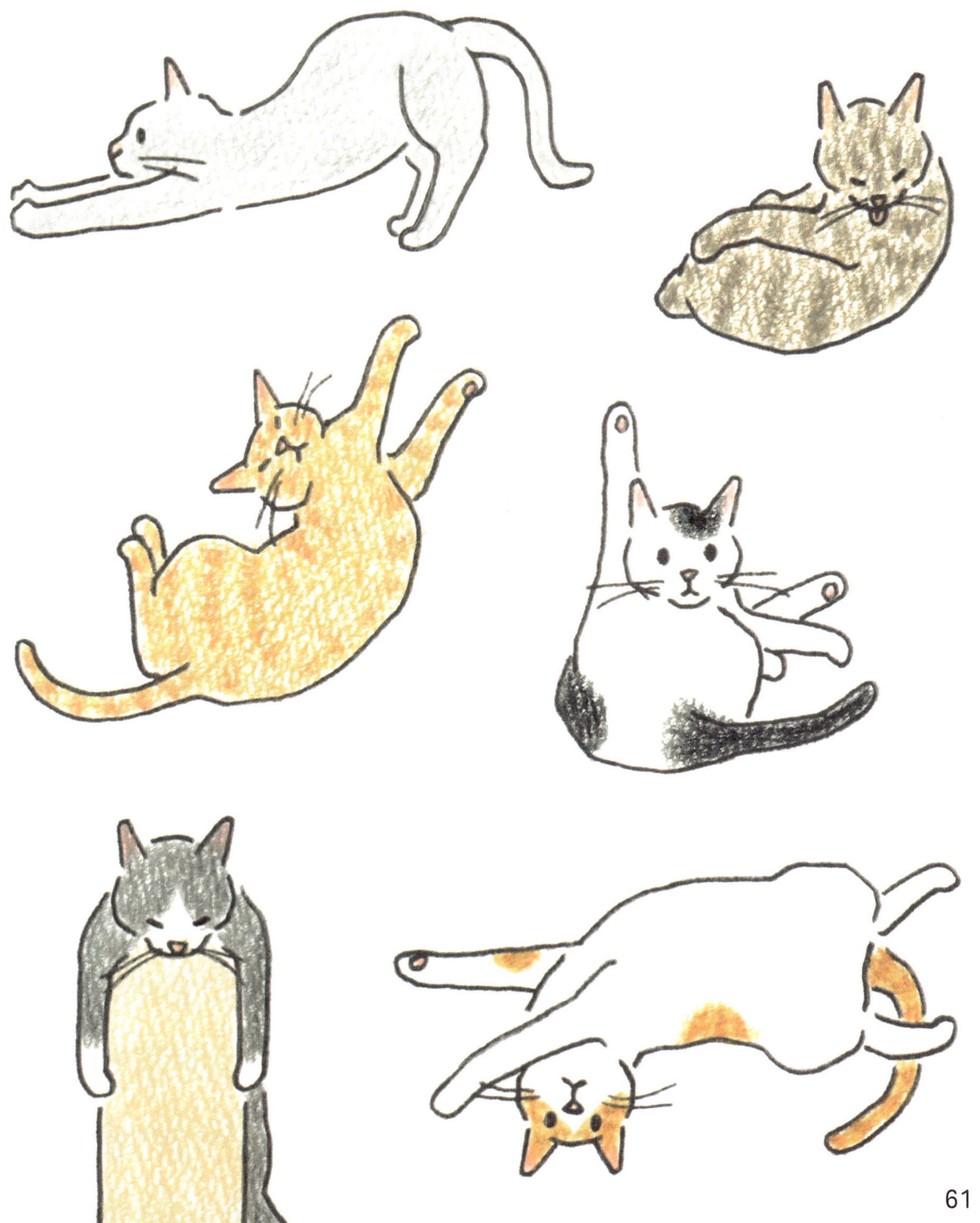

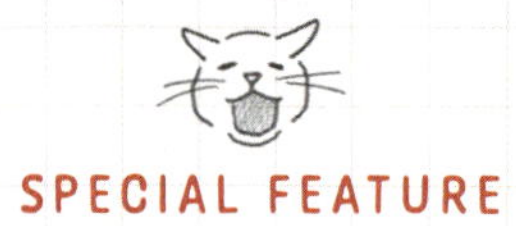

Our precious cats

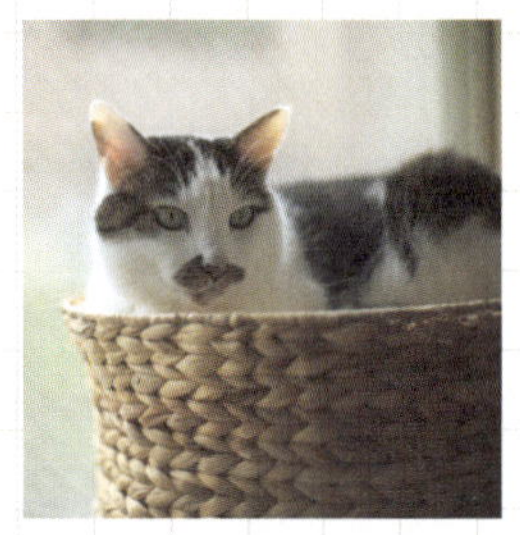

Kanjirō

Currently, three cats live in our home. Kanjirō (male) has a large frame, bandit-like markings on his face and intense eyes—he's an imposing presence. But contrary to that intimidating face, he's a kind older brother who easily shares his sleeping spot or allows others to take it. We thought he was a mischievous biter, but ever since the younger two cats arrived, he seems to have learned how to show affection to humans—a clumsy, sweet boy.

Seto (female), with her graceful body and long, straight tail that she proudly sways, is the very image of a cat—lively and athletic.

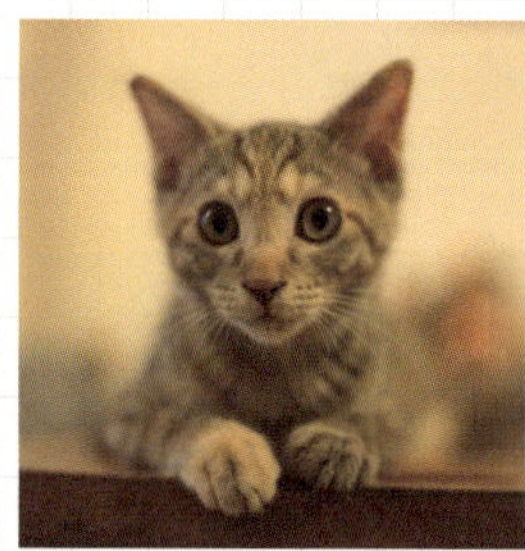

Seto

Siblings with crossed paws

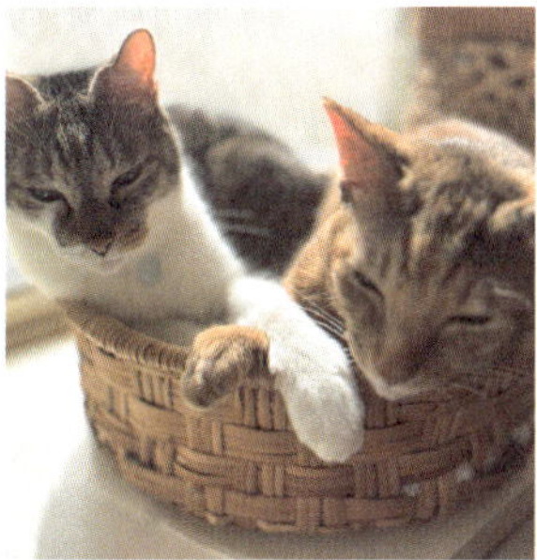

She's the only girl, but sometimes sleeps in very unladylike poses, gets groomed by the others, or doesn't bother to cover her poop!

And the youngest, Otojirō (male), is Seto's brother—we adopted the two of them together. He's the opposite of Seto—calm and relaxed. Because of his easygoing nature, everyone likes to watch him. He's like a little idol. His charming features include his downturned mouth and short, wiggly, curved tail. He's quite neat and even diligently covers up Seto's litter-box faux pas.

These three have a perfect balance of personalities and get along very well. Just having them around brings happiness—I can't even imagine life without them!

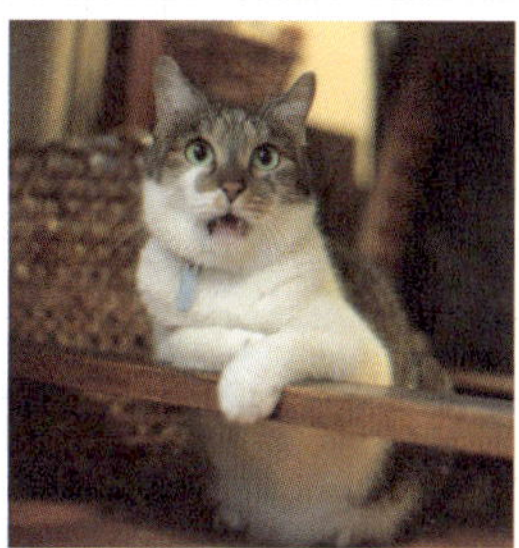

Otojirō

Drawing Techniques by Medium

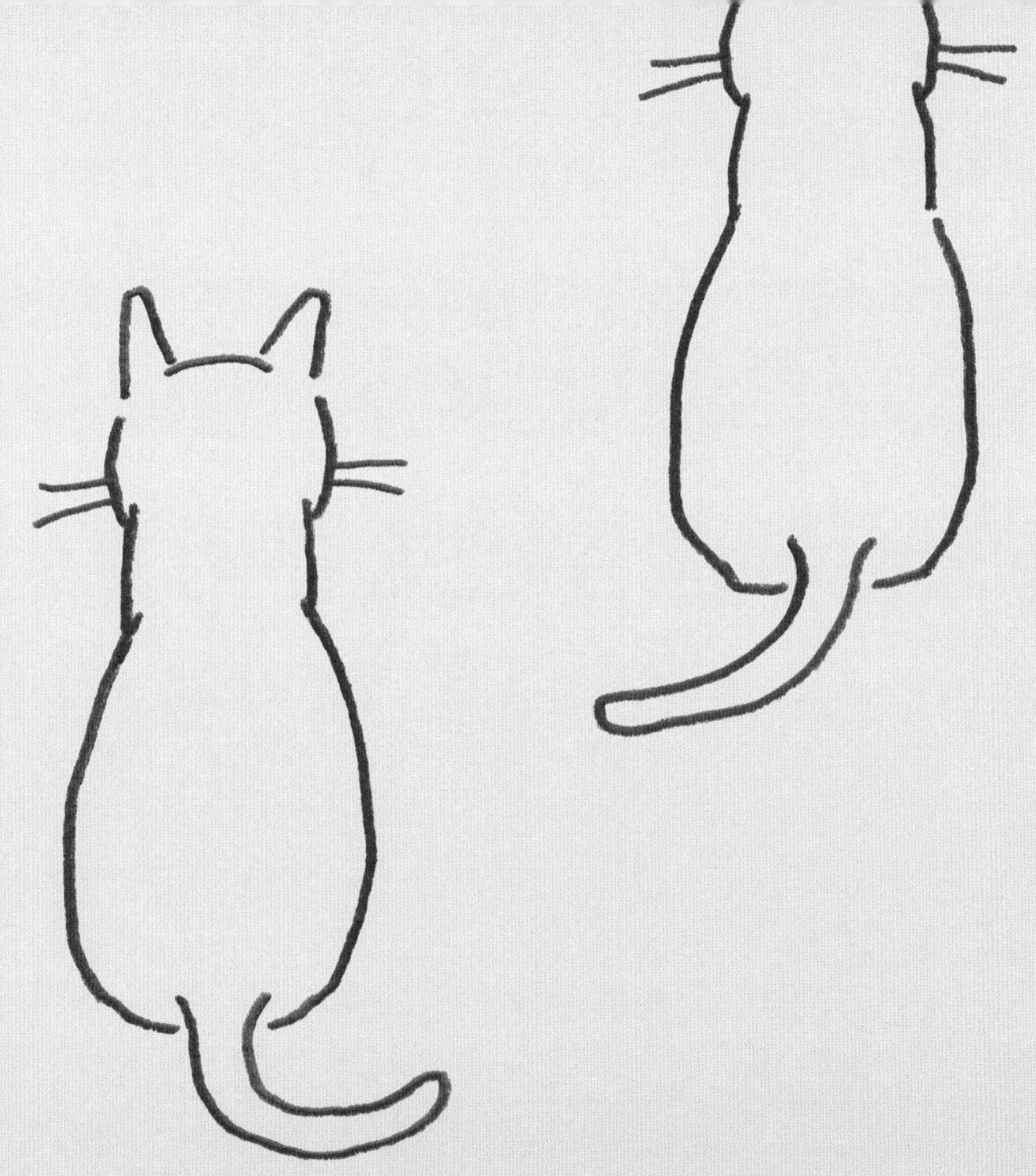

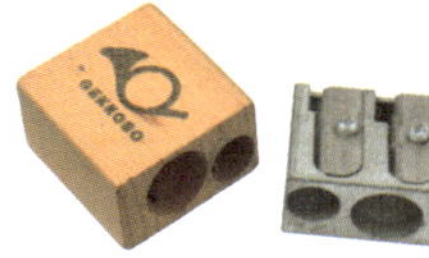 Drawing with a pencil

From here, I'll explain drawing techniques for various tools. The look of your drawing will vary depending on the materials used. Let's start by practicing drawing with a pencil.

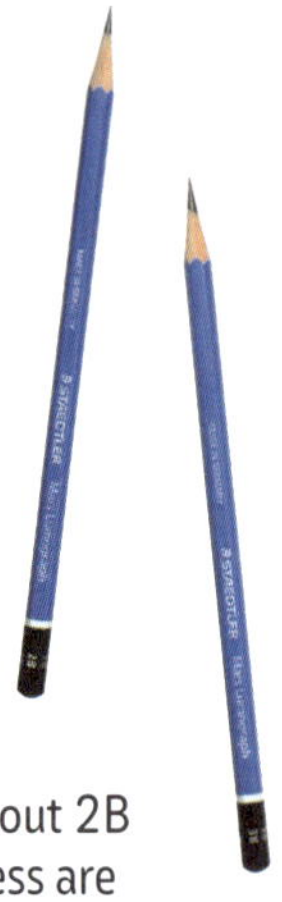

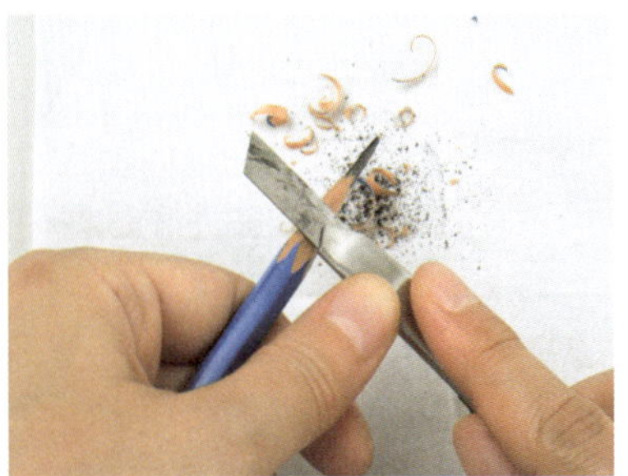

If possible, begin by sharpening the pencil yourself with a utility knife. Hold the pencil in your left hand, with your thumb on top, and grip it firmly. Use your thumb to push the back of the knife blade away from you and shave away material. The lead should extend about 3/16–7/16 in (5–10 mm).

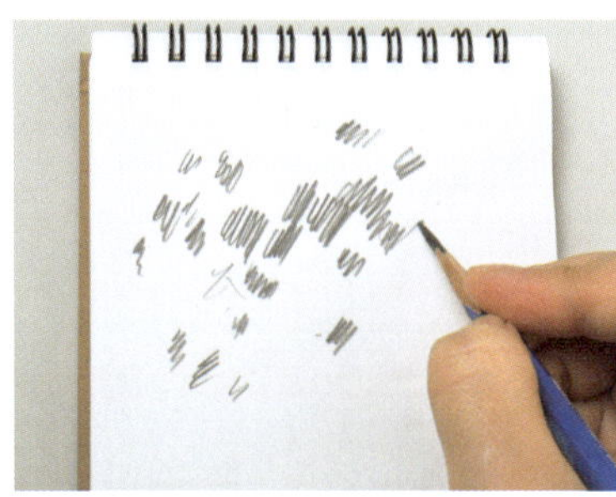

If the tip is too sharp, it will move smoothly, so gently blunt it on a scrap piece of paper. Rotate the pencil as you move it against the paper to round the tip evenly.

Pencils of about 2B to 3B hardness are easier to work with.

If you're not comfortable sharpening your pencil with a knife, feel free to use a pencil sharpener! Just don't forget to slightly blunt the lead afterward.

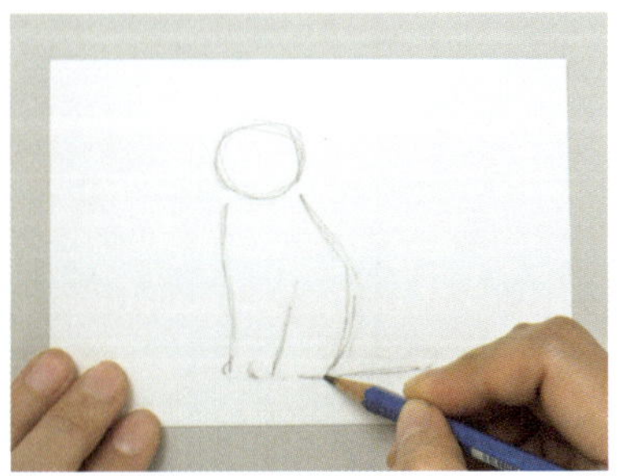

1 Imagine the shape of the cat you want to draw and make a light, rough sketch of it as a guideline.

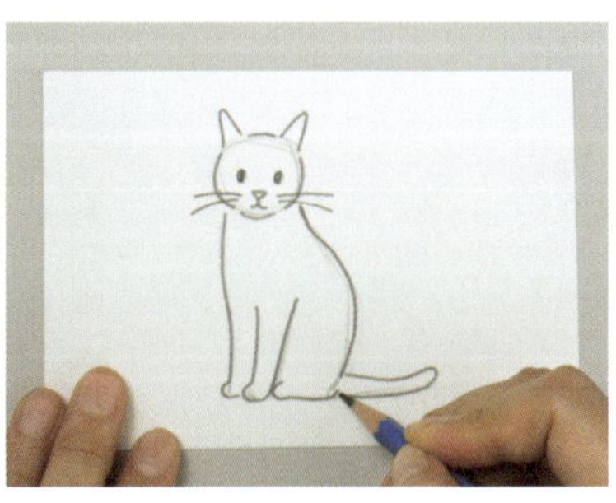

2 Trace over the lines you like from the sketch to define them more clearly.

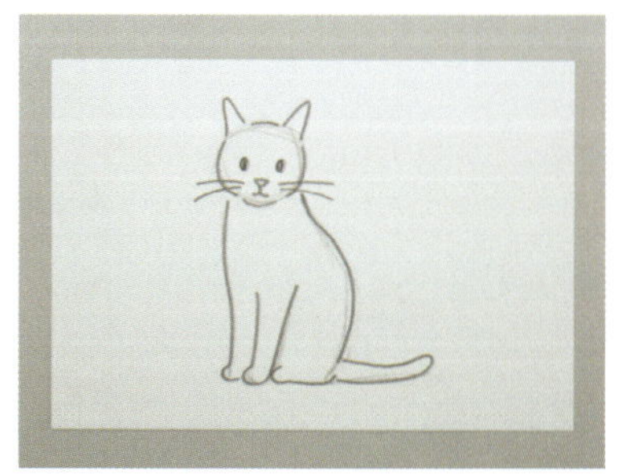

3 Finished.

Drawing with a water-based pen

Next, let's try drawing with water-based pens. There are many thicknesses available, so choose one that suits your style. For a delicate image, a fine pen is best; for a casual look, a thicker pen is recommended.

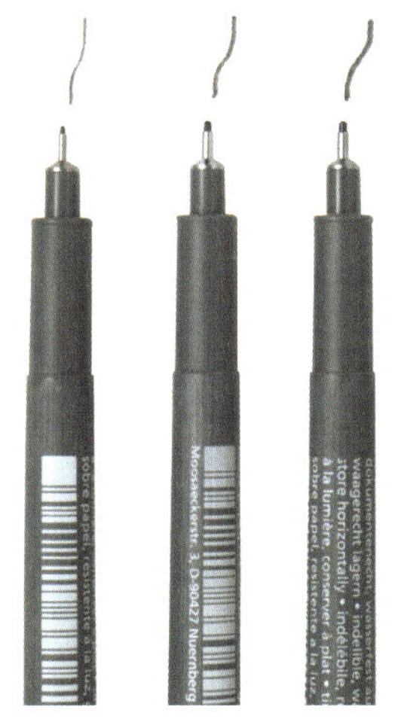

Staedtler Pigment Liners—from left: 0.3, 0.5 and 0.8 mm.

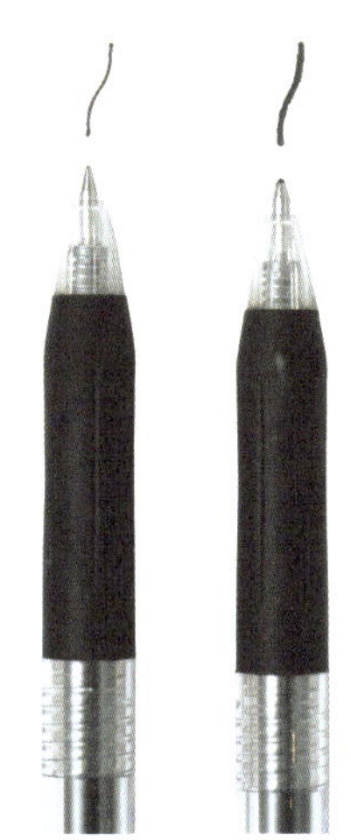

Zebra Sarasa Clips—from left: 0.5 and 1.0 mm.

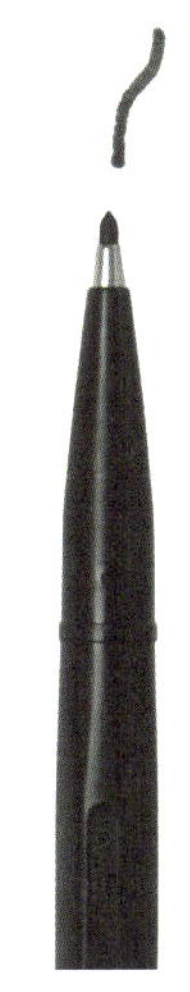

Pentel Sign Pen

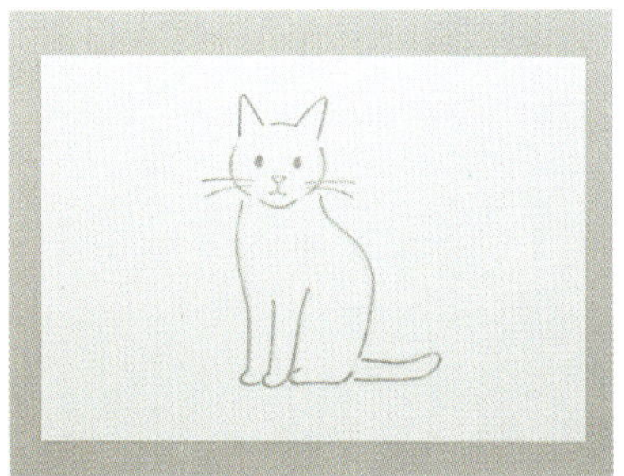

1 Prepare the cat drawing. See page 66, "Drawing with a pencil."

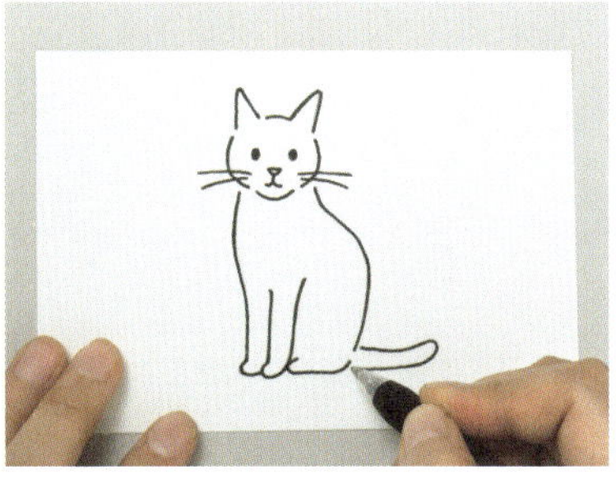

2 Trace over it with your preferred pen. Once the ink has dried, erase the pencil lines.

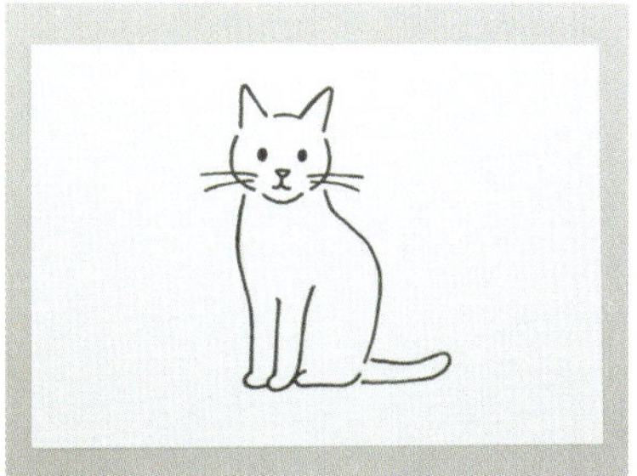

3 Finished.

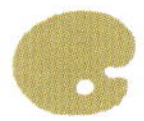 # Drawing with colored pencils

Once you can draw cats with pencil or water-based pen, try adding some color. Colored pencils are easy to use for coloring, so give them a try. Avoid being too precise—keeping it loose gives a cute finish.

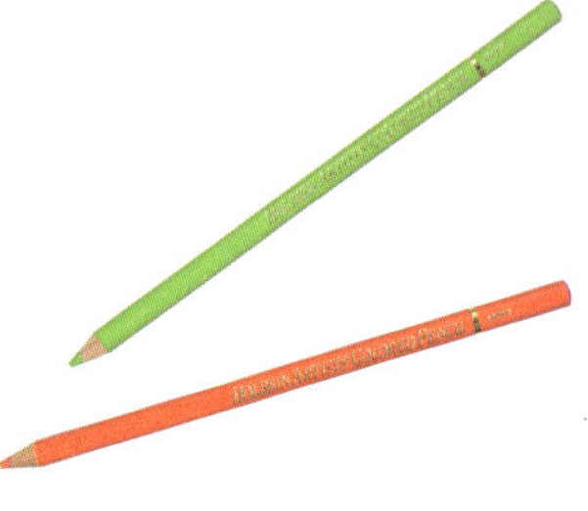

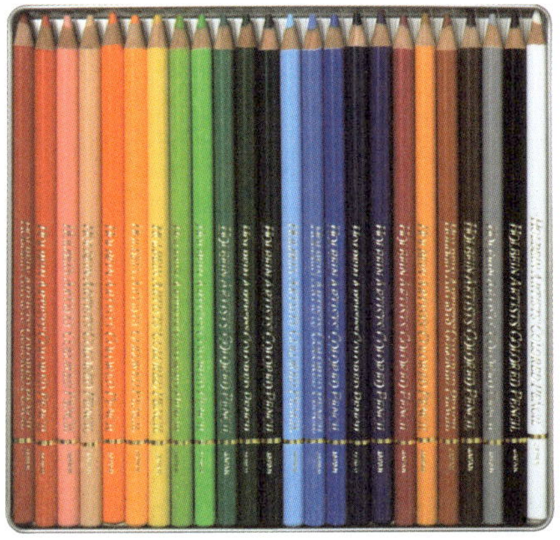

Holbein Artist Colored Pencils are smooth and easy to handle, so I recommend them.

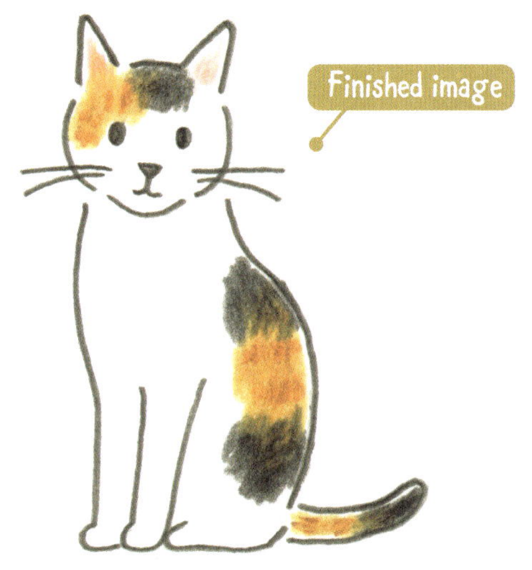

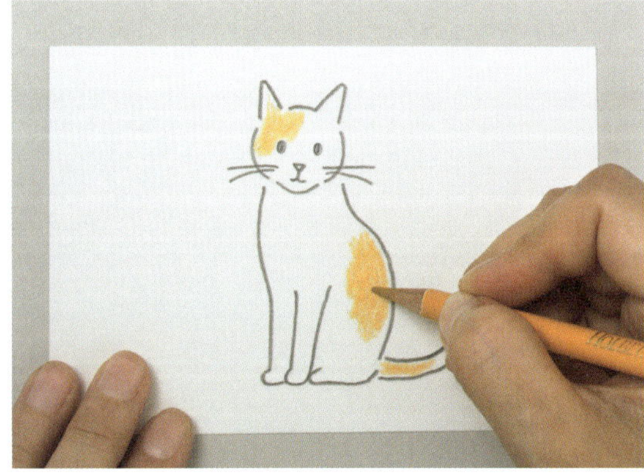

1 Using the cat illustration you completed on pages 66–67, start coloring roughly with the lightest color needed for your drawing.

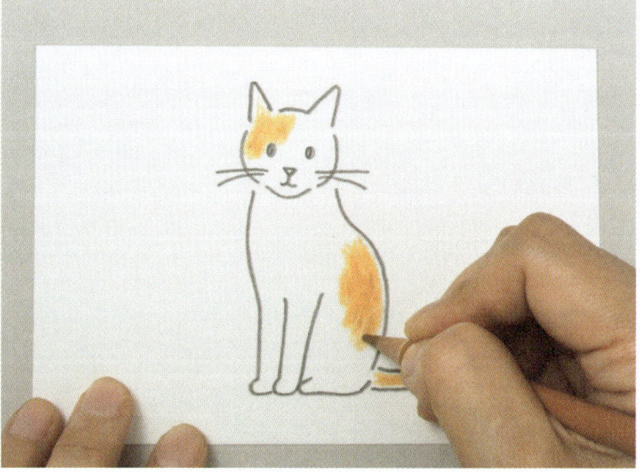

2 Layer a slightly darker color over the step-1 shading. Color it lightly, just like in step 1.

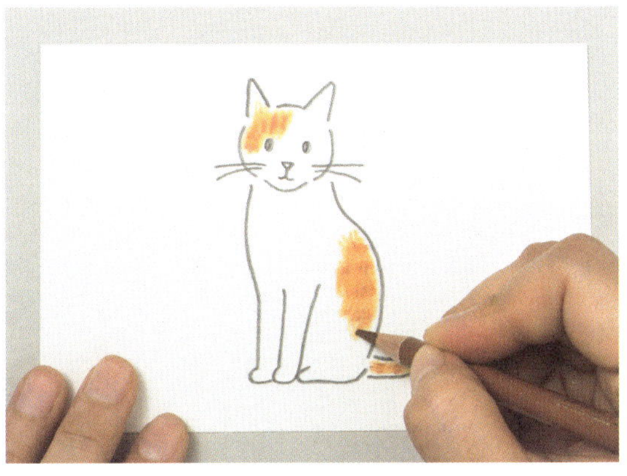

3 Draw the darkest stripes of the coat with an even darker tone.

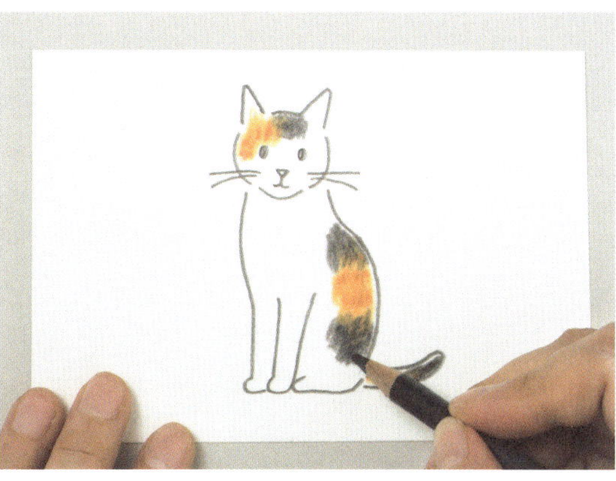

4 Color the black parts of the calico pattern. Overlap the brownish striped area from step 3 slightly for a smooth transition.

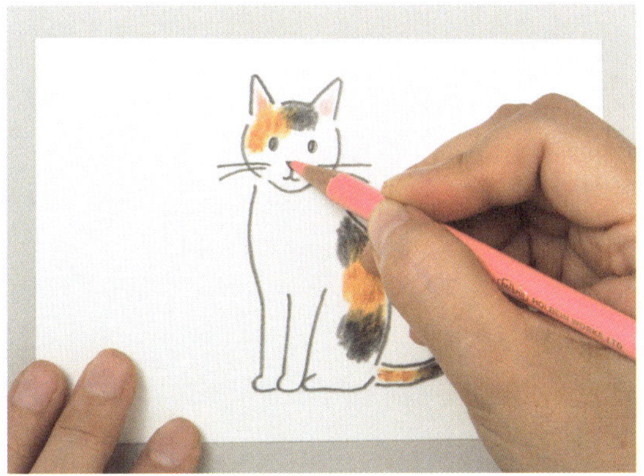

5 Color the ears and nose with pink. Use a lighter touch for the ears and a more saturated tone for the nose.

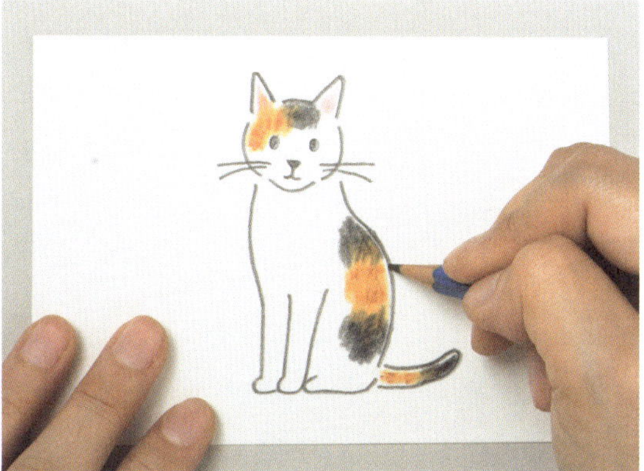

6 Go over any pencil (or pen) outlines that have been obscured by colored pencil to make them crisply defined again—then it's done!

N O T E

Don't press too hard—color gently. Rough, slightly-outside-the-lines coloring yields a charming result.

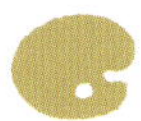 # Painting with watercolors

Next, let's try coloring with watercolor paints. Because you'll need to use additional tools, it's a bit more of a challenge, but it gives a different impression compared to colored pencils—and the rewards are worth the extra effort.

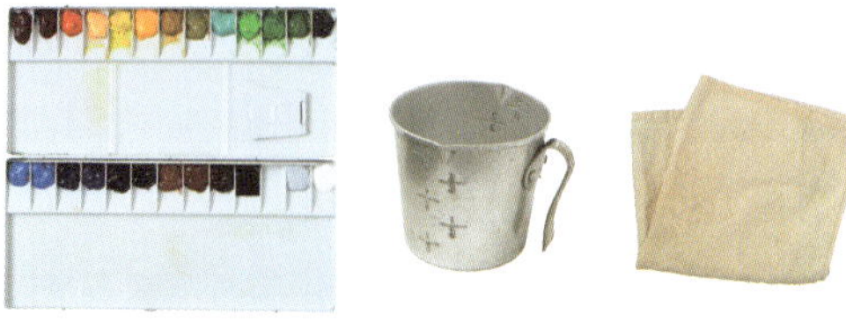

You'll need a palette, brush-cleaning cup (any small, watertight container is fine) and an unused cloth.

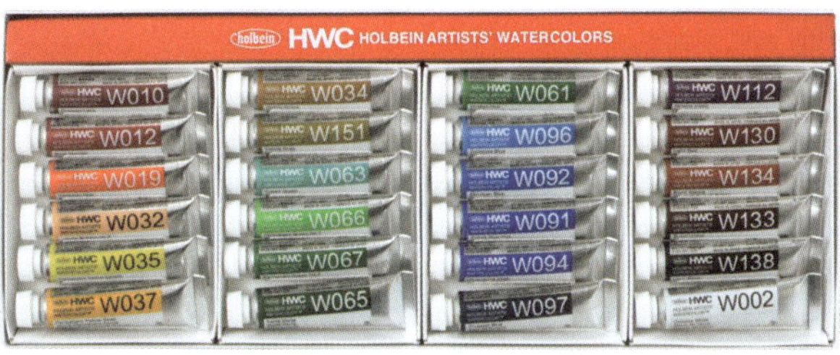

Holbein Transparent Watercolors
Transparent types are recommended because they layer more beautifully than opaque ones.

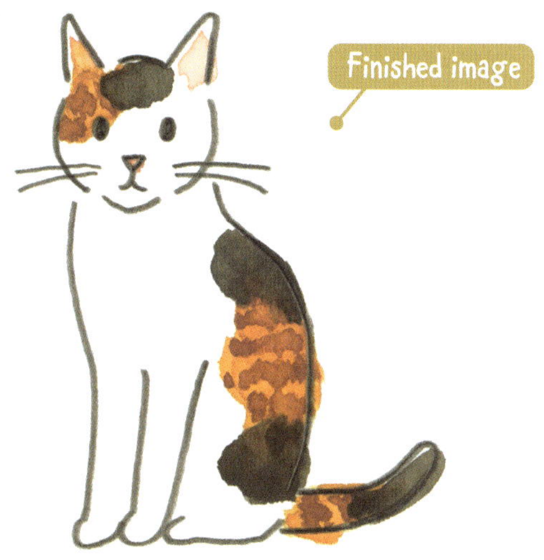

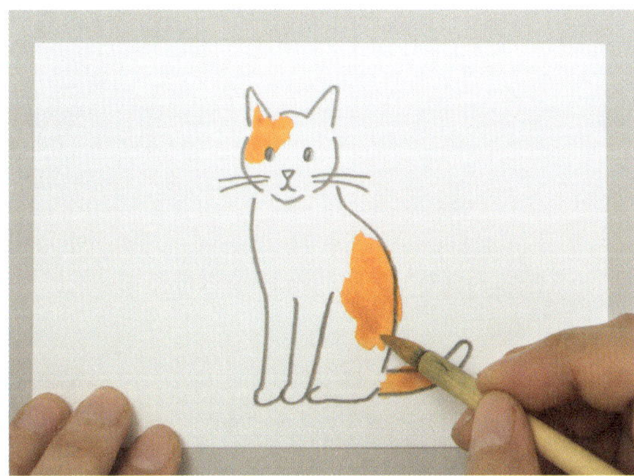

1 Prepare a cat illustration you've drawn with pencil. Mix paint in the palette and apply the lightest brown. Because you'll layer it, thin with a lot of water to keep it very light.

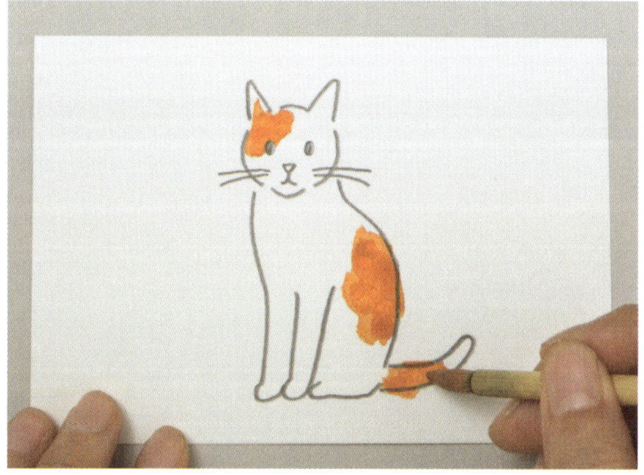

2 Once the step-1 paint is dry, add a slightly darker brown, also very diluted. Just gently touch the areas to be colored with the tip of the brush.

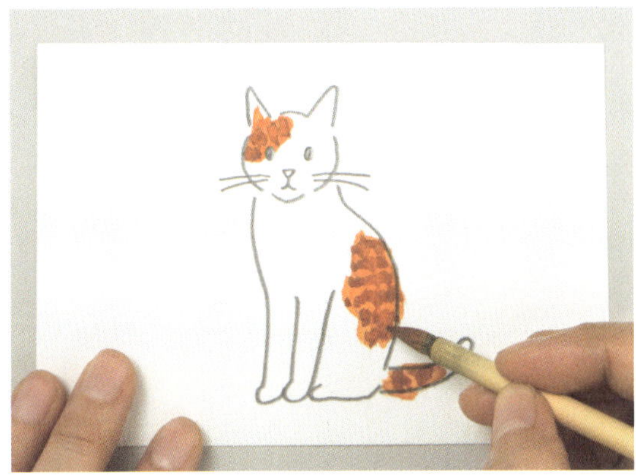

3 After the step-2 paint has dried, layer in the stripes of the brown tabby. Indicate the pattern by lightly dabbing the paint with the tip of the brush.

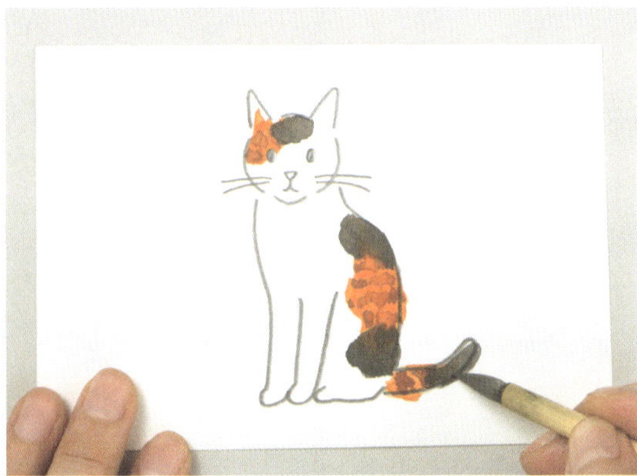

4 With the step-3 paint not yet fully dry, layer black over it. Don't use pure black—make it grayish. Let it slightly overlap the brown from step 3 and gently bleed into the still damp paint.

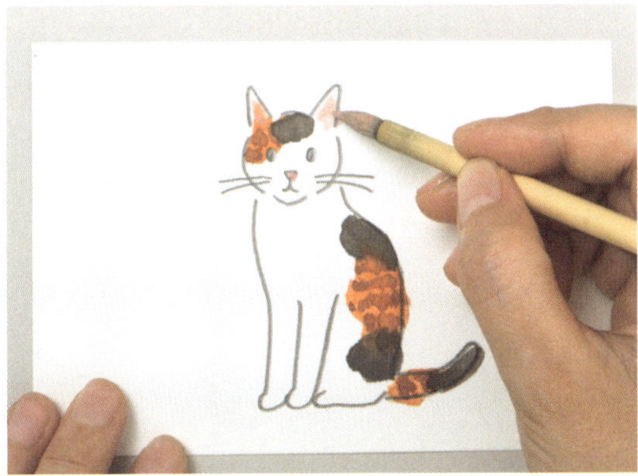

5 Paint the ears and nose with pink. Use a diluted mix with more water for the ears and just lightly dab with the brush. Make the pink on the nose a bit stronger.

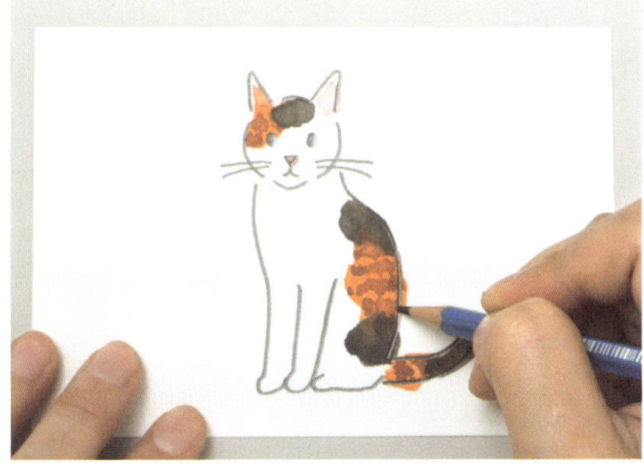

6 Trace over the pencil lines that have been obscured by the layering to make them crisply defined again, and you're done!

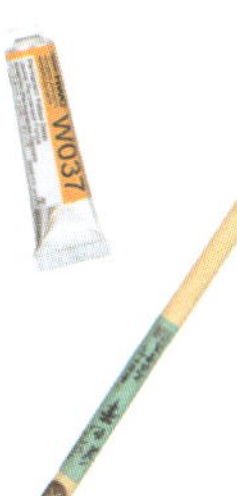

N O T E

Timing is important when it comes to taking advantage of the qualities of wet or dry paint! If you want to blend layers, do so before the previous layer is completely dry. The amount of water changes the color intensity, so make sure to adjust the moisture loaded onto your brush with an unused cloth before painting.

Watercolor painting tips

Here are a few tips for painting with watercolors. Once you get the hang of it, your range of expression will expand, and painting will become even more fun. Give them a try!

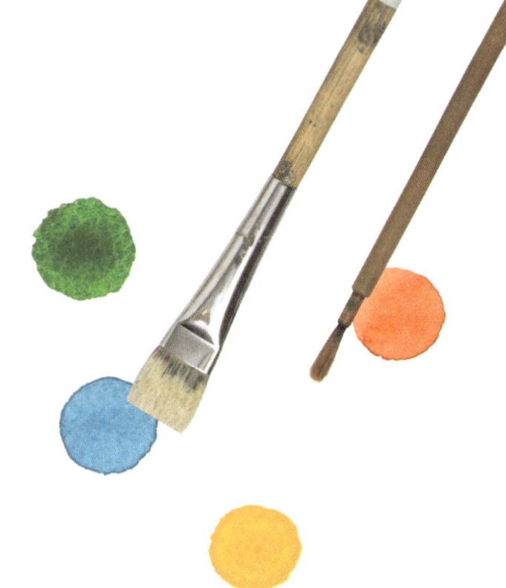

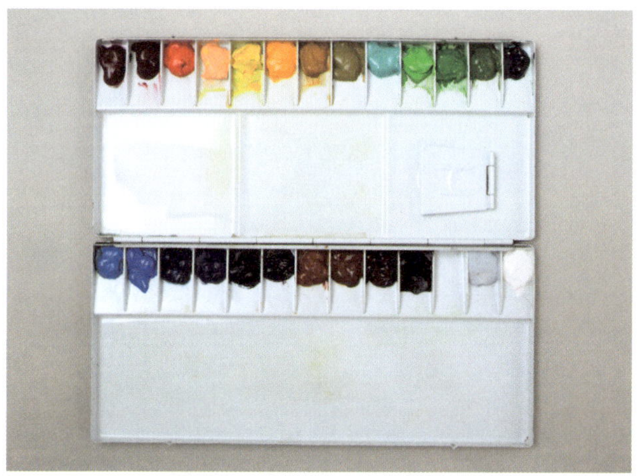

Dispense all colors onto your palette

Watercolor paints can be reconstituted with water even after they dry and harden, so you can squeeze out all the colors you plan to use onto the palette compartments in the same order as they appear in the set. Because they can be stored as-is, they're always ready to use at any time.

The amount of water used affects the strength of the color

The ratio of paint to water changes the intensity of the color, so adjust the amount according to the requirements of your artwork or your personal preference. Use scrap cloth or tissue paper to control the amount of paint or water loaded onto the brush.

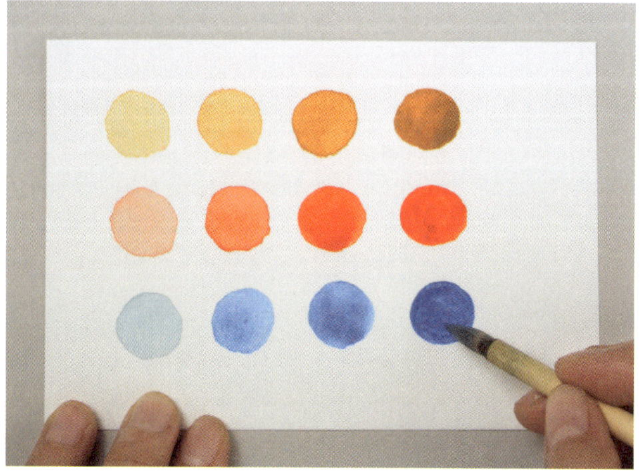

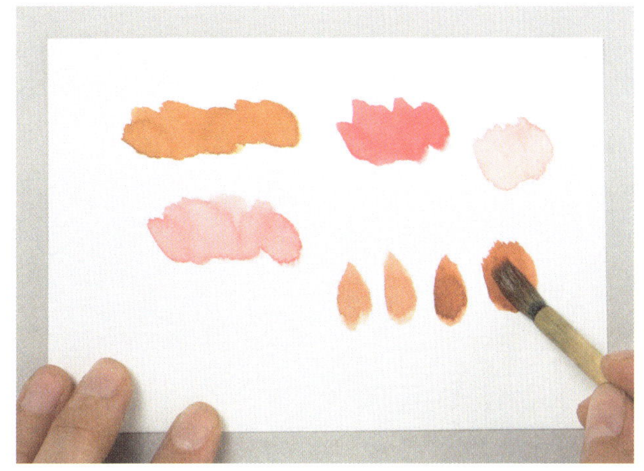

Use a separate sheet to check color and shading

Always mix your colors on the palette before applying them to your artwork. Avoid mixing directly on the drawing as doing so will cause the colors to become muddy. Use a separate sheet of paper to test the color you are about to apply.

When layering, use diluted paint

When layering colors, keep both the base and overlapping layers of color very light and dilute. If you want a subtle blending effect, apply the successive layer before the previous one dries completely.

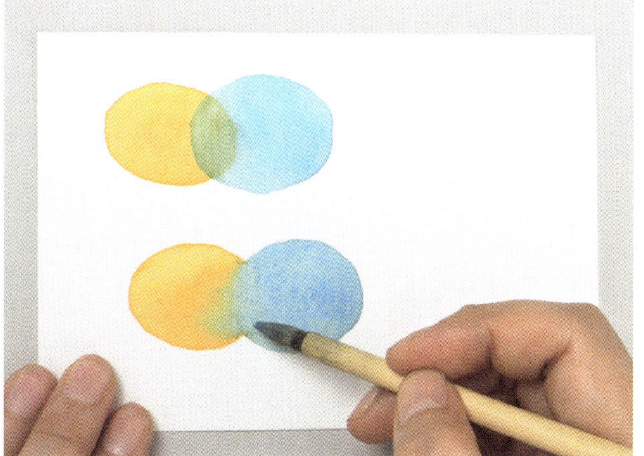

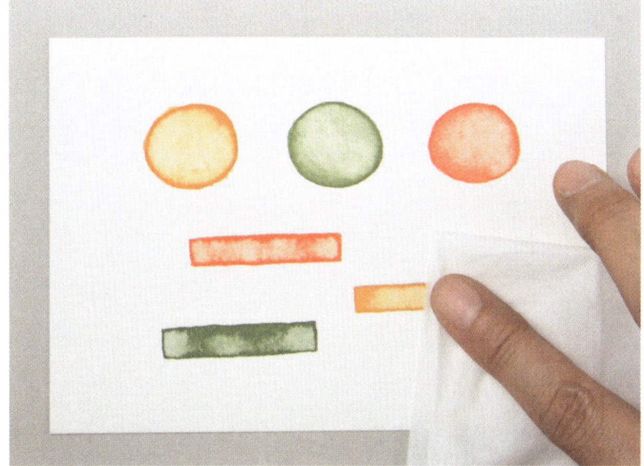

Dab paint with a tissue before it dries completely

Pressing a tissue firmly over the painted area before it dries creates a pleasing intentional unevenness, giving it a texture similar to that of a woodblock print.

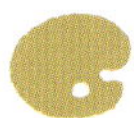 # Painting with acrylics

Acrylic paint is also thinned with water, but it gives a different result than transparent watercolor. It becomes matte and bold in color, giving a more informal impression.

Paper palette
Because acrylics don't dissolve once dried, use a disposable paper palette.

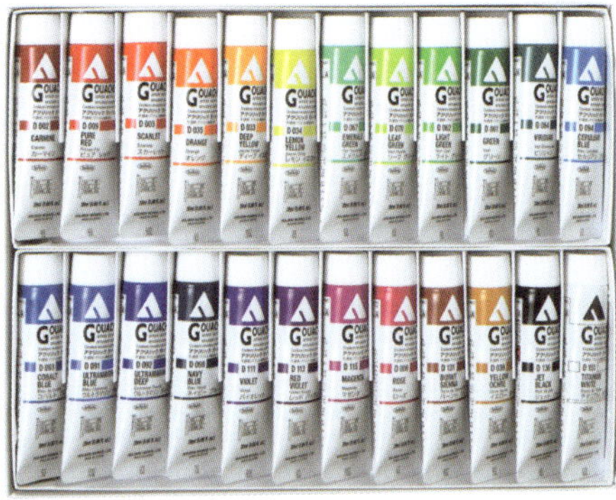

Holbein Acrylic Gouache
This opaque paint has a smooth, spreadable texture and is easy to handle.

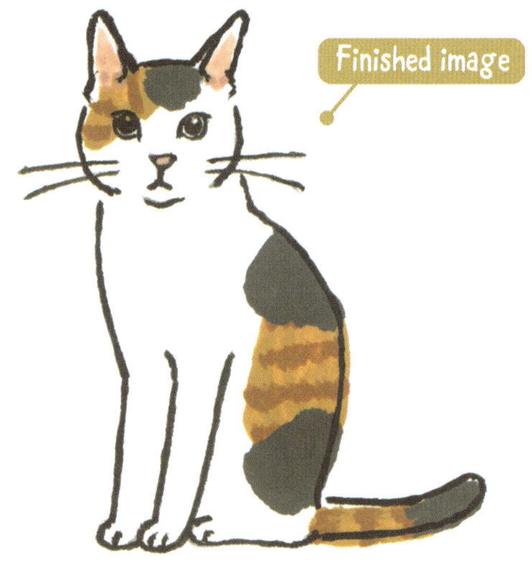

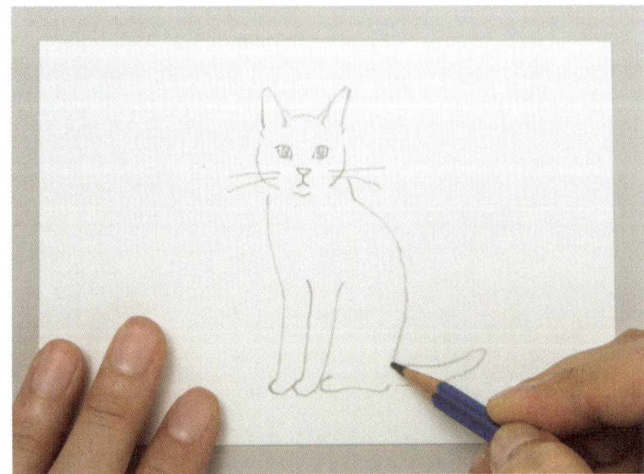

1 Prepare a lightly sketched cat drawing in pencil. Because you'll trace over the lines with paint later, a faint outline is fine.

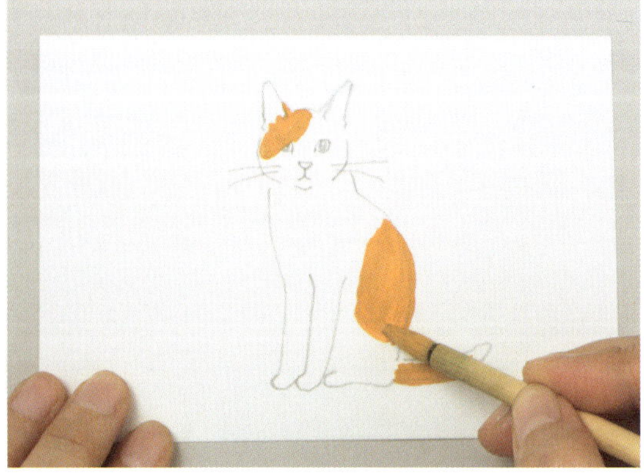

2 As with the transparent watercolor technique, start with a light brown, but use less water— just enough for the brush to move smoothly.

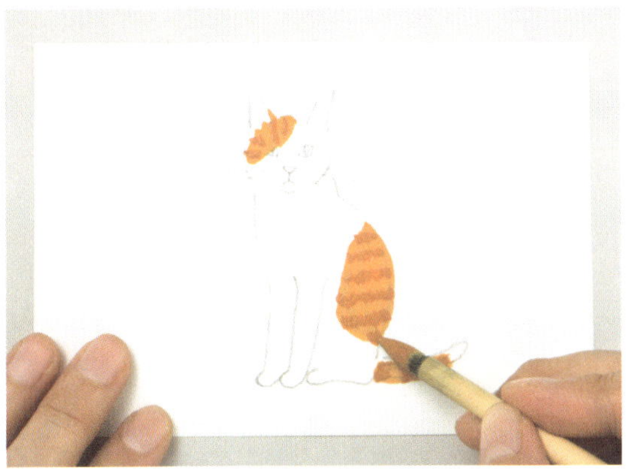

3 Unlike watercolors, acrylics don't bleed, so wait until the base layer is fully dry, then use a darker brown to paint the stripes.

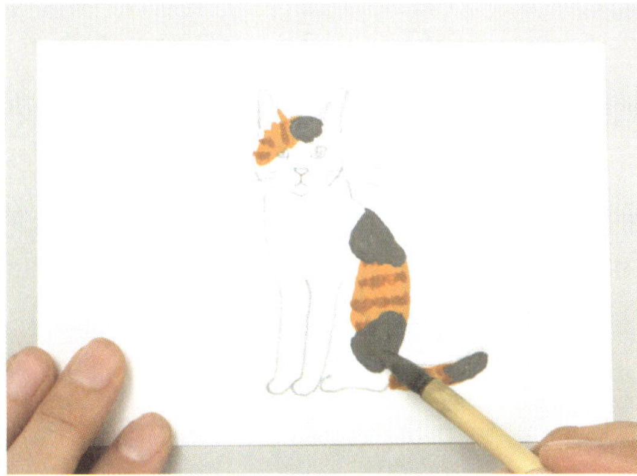

4 Once the step-3 paint is dry, apply a dark gray. Rather than the loose strokes used with watercolor paint, work more carefully here.

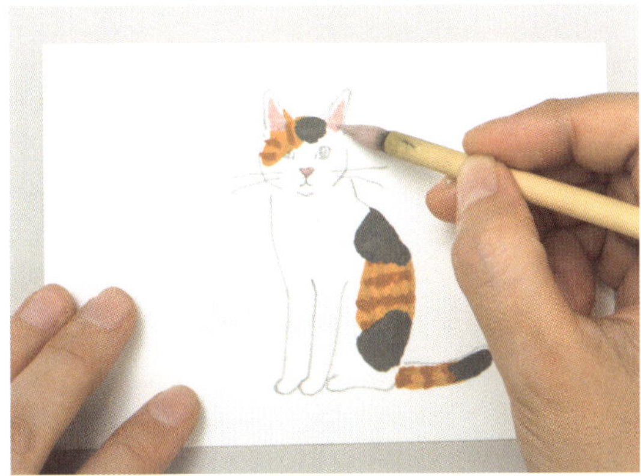

5 Add pink to the ears and nose. Use the same color strength for the nose as for the fur pattern, but dilute the color for the ears and apply just a touch.

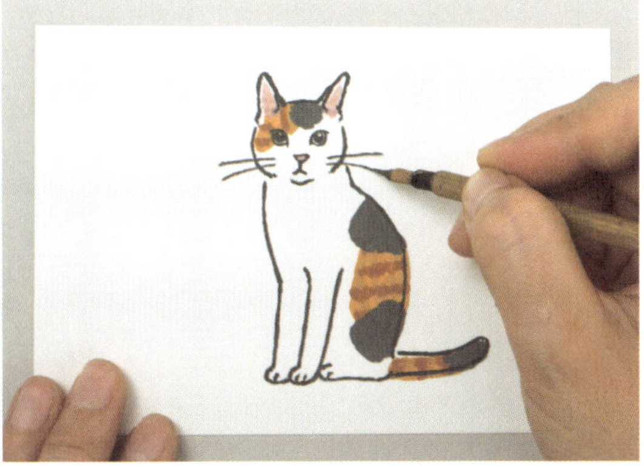

6 Once the color pattern colors are dry, trace the pencil lines with a dark gray. Apply the paint carefully and deliberately, but don't worry about achieving perfection—a slight wobble in the brushstrokes adds character.

NOTE

Rather than using the paint colors straight from the tube, try mixing several colors together on a paper palette. Adding a little white creates a softer, toned-down color.

Acrylic painting tips

Even though acrylic paints are water-based like watercolors, there are some different tricks to using them. Unlike the delicate layering of transparent watercolor, acrylics are better applied boldly, with distinct areas of color for a more modern finish.

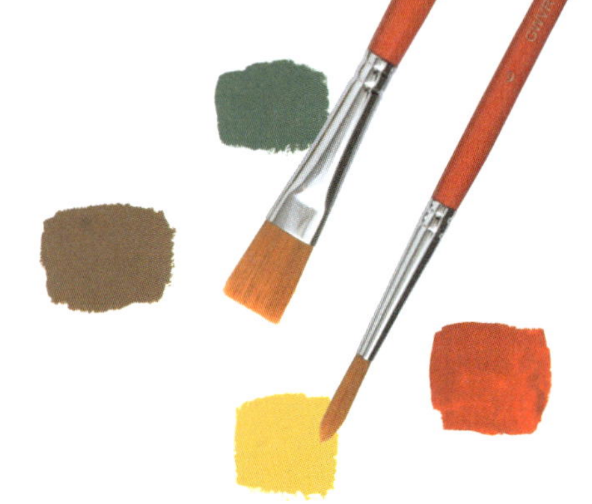

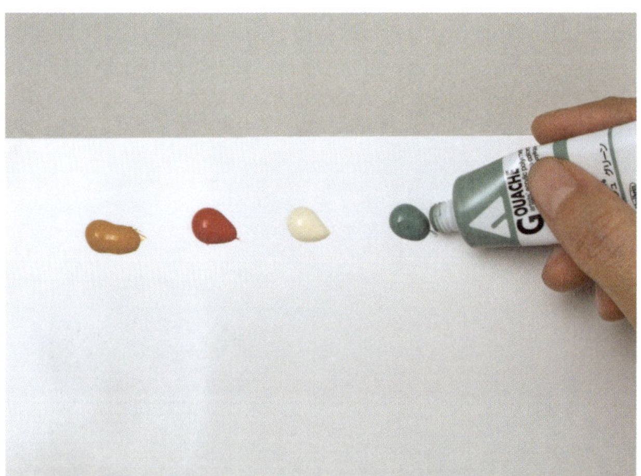

TIP 1 — Use a disposable paper palette

Unlike watercolors, acrylics dry and harden quickly. So, dispense only the colors you need, a little at a time, onto a paper palette. You can use thick coated paper, cardboard or aluminum foil as a substitute for a paper palette if needed.

TIP 2 — Limit the amount of water you add

Too much water can cause uneven coverage. Just mix in enough water for your brush to move smoothly. You can also use almost no water at all and apply the paint thickly, as with oil paints, which makes for a fun, layered effect.

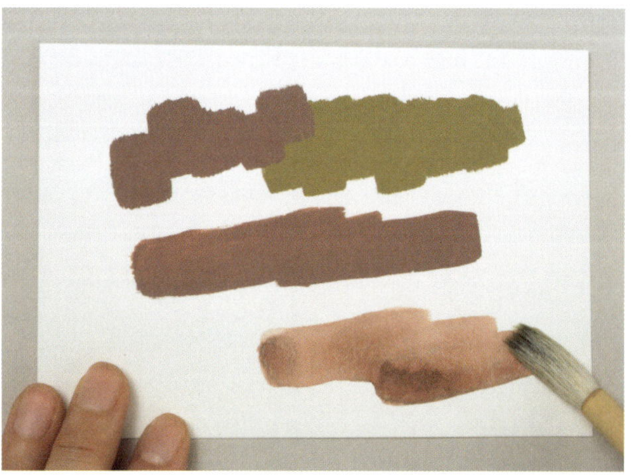

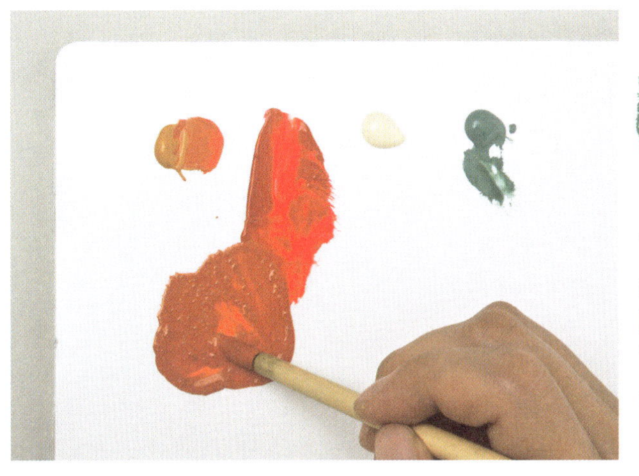

Mix and thin your colors on a paper palette to dial in the tone, intensity and viscosity

Thoroughly mix your colors on a paper palette, adjusting the amount of water added as needed before beginning to apply paint to your artwork. Test the colors on a separate sheet of paper to confirm that you've achieved the desired result.

Deliberately uneven lines can be interesting

When painting outlines or detail lines with a fine brush, hold the brush upright and apply the paint slowly and carefully. Creating slightly uneven lines on purpose can add character and make the artwork more dynamic and engaging.

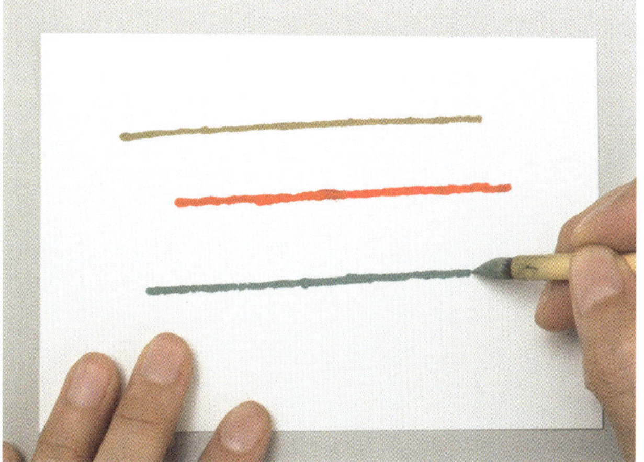

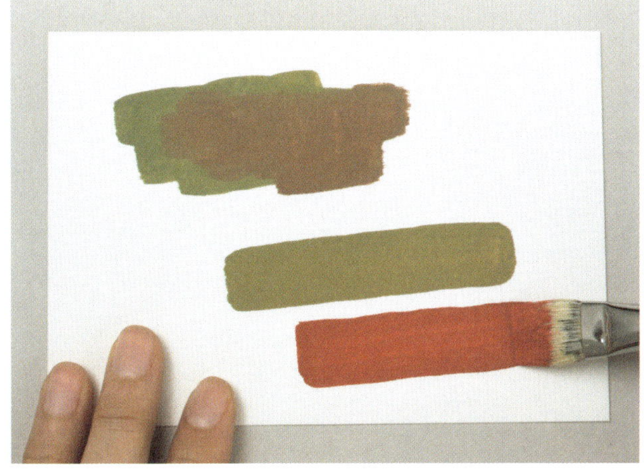

Try to apply the paint in one pass

If you layer or brush over acrylic paint before it dries, the colors can become muddy. Once you've mixed your color, aim to apply it cleanly in a single stroke whenever possible.

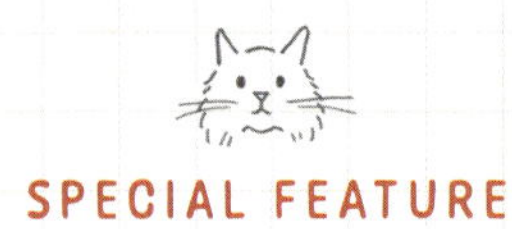

My family's beloved cats from the past

I first started living with a cat when I was thirteen years old. Ever since then—for several decades now—I've lived with cats almost continuously. Even the three cats I live with now came into my life thanks to the ones who came before them. When I was very young, I was a huge dog lover and dreamed only of owning a dog. But then I met a kitten born in an abandoned house behind ours, and my whole family and I became completely enchanted by cats. That's how Ikura-chan and Tara-chan came into our lives. Watching them gradually become our cats—moving from the yard to the living room, and eventually into my own room—was an experience I found endlessly endearing.

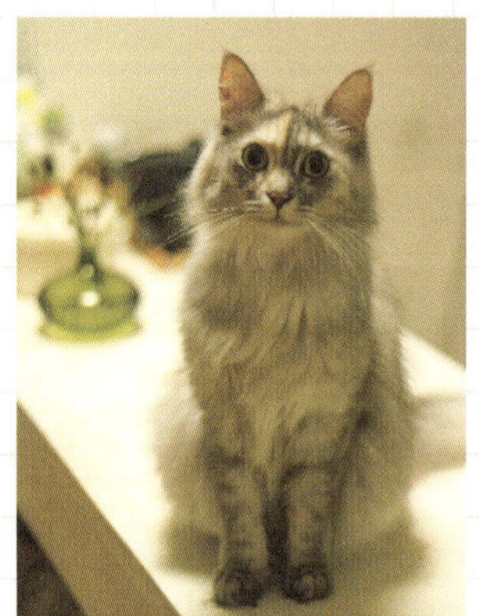

The dignified long-hair, Raku

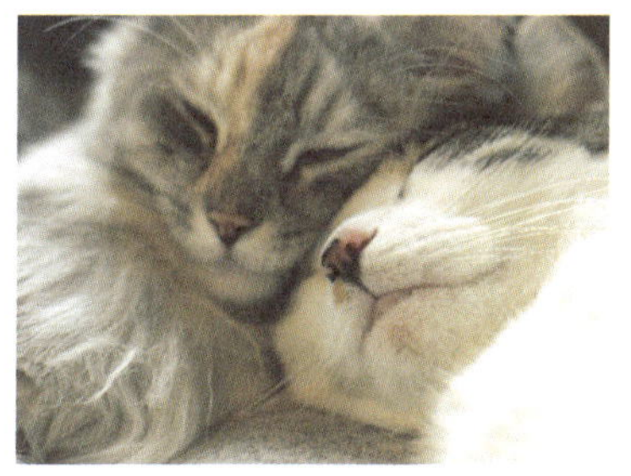

Close-knit siblings

Kuu, who was my partner's cat from a previous relationship, was a playful and affectionate girl. She loved being held, but would deliberately run away sometimes just to get my attention—an endearing and very cat-appropriate behavior. After Kuu passed away, Chōjirō and Raku, a brother and sister pair I received from an older neighbor, came into my life. I've written about the days I spent with them many times in my books, and I wouldn't exchange those experiences for anything. The joy of having something so precious close by adds rich color to everyday life. And those easygoing little creatures always seemed to be teaching me how to live in the moment, quietly suggesting, "Why not just relax a little more?"

Chōjirō was a very gentle cat

PART 4

Finishing Your Cat Art

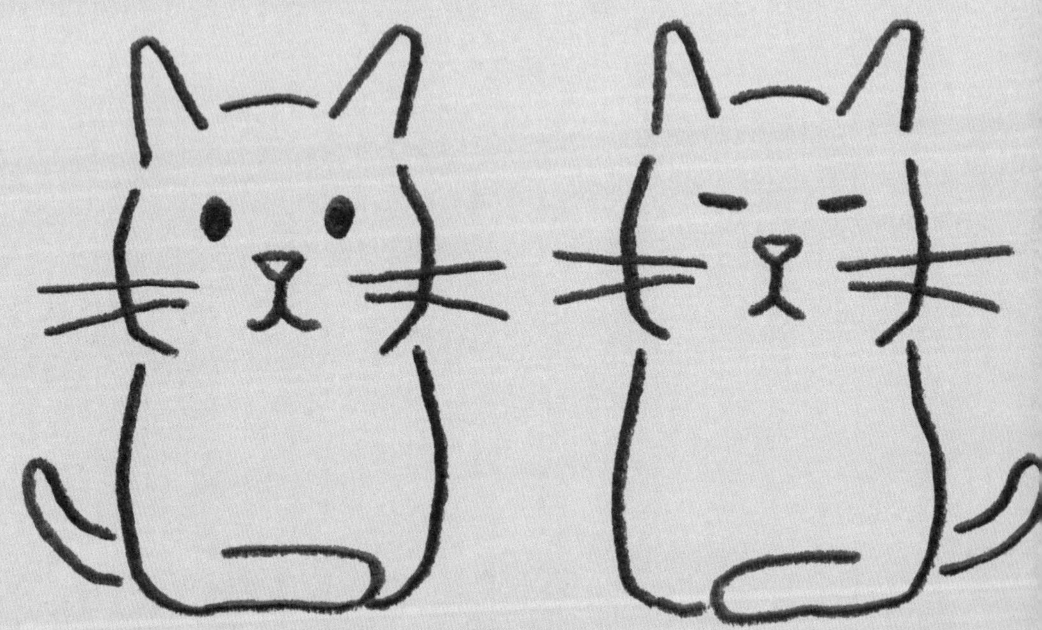

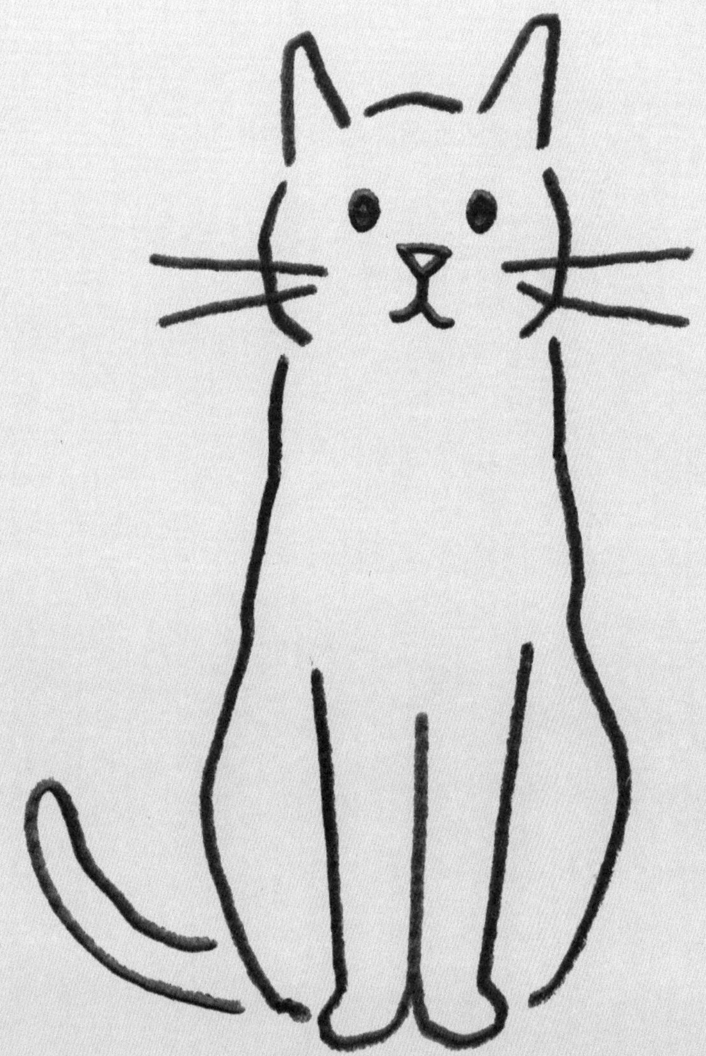

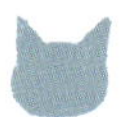 # Try drawing various backgrounds

Drawings of cats are cute on their own, but adding a background can make them feel more like finished works of art. Concrete elements like plants are lovely, but simply using blocks of color or abstract shapes also works well. Try different approaches to match the mood of your drawing.

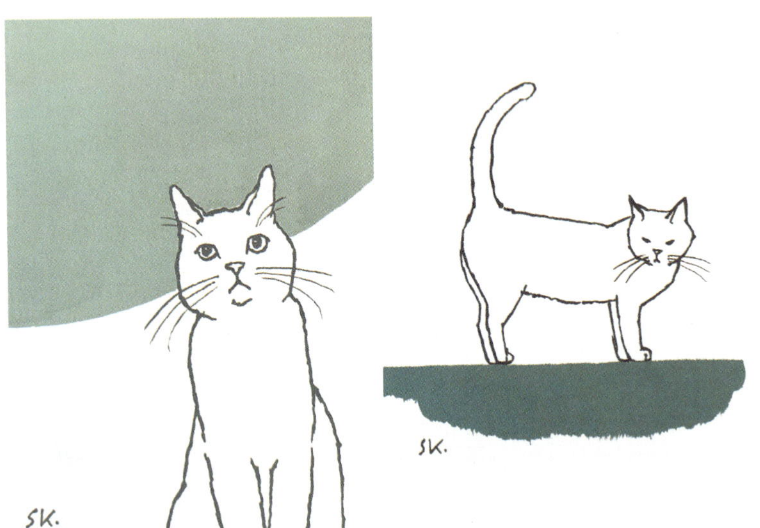

Pair a simple outline illustration of a cat with abstract shapes.
(Medium: acrylic paint)

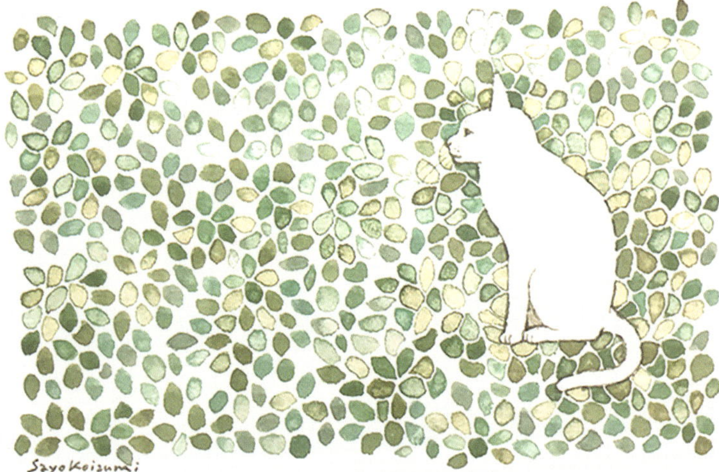

Fill the background with clusters of tree leaves.
(Medium: transparent watercolor paint)

82

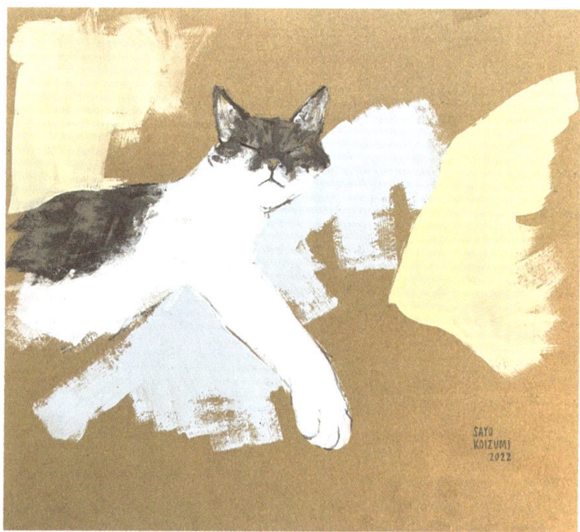

Paint roughly and boldly on cardboard.
(Medium: acrylic paint)

Even just painting the background your favorite color makes it pop and look amazing.
(Medium: acrylic paint)

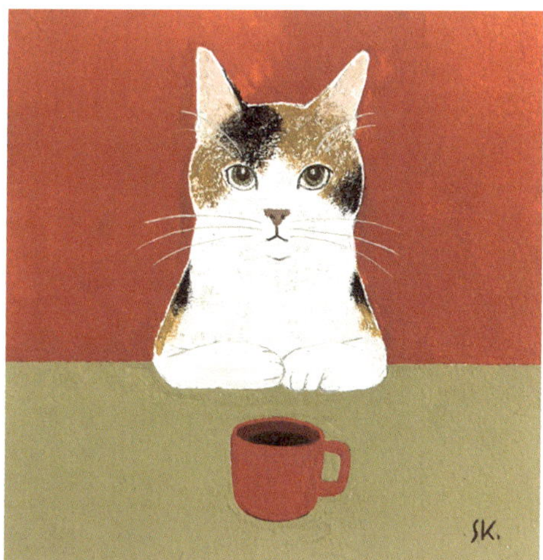

An image of a cat at the window, seen from outside.
(Medium: acrylic paint)

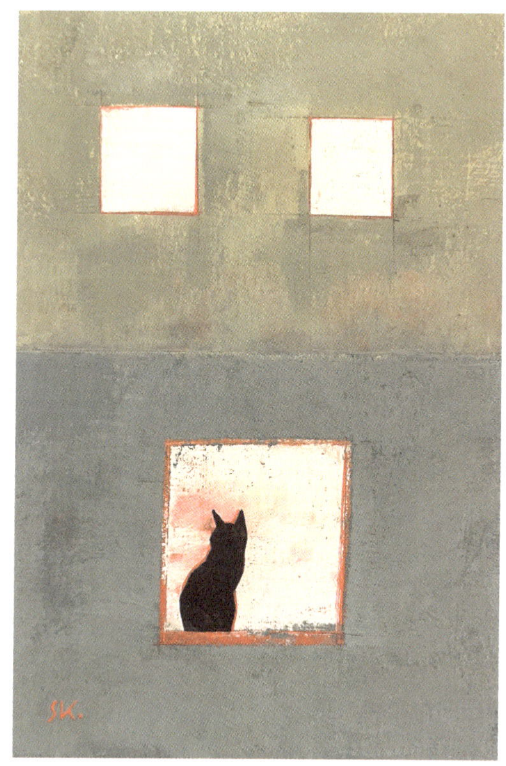

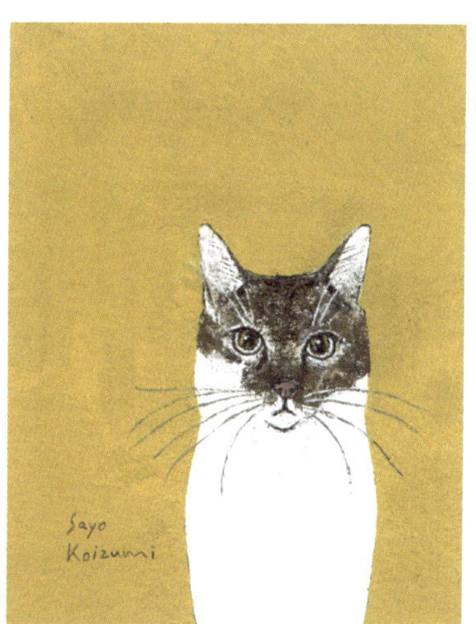

Have fun freely expressing ideas through collage

Using materials you have at home or can easily obtain is also a fun way to make collages. Play around with leftover newspapers, magazines, colored paper and wrapping paper.

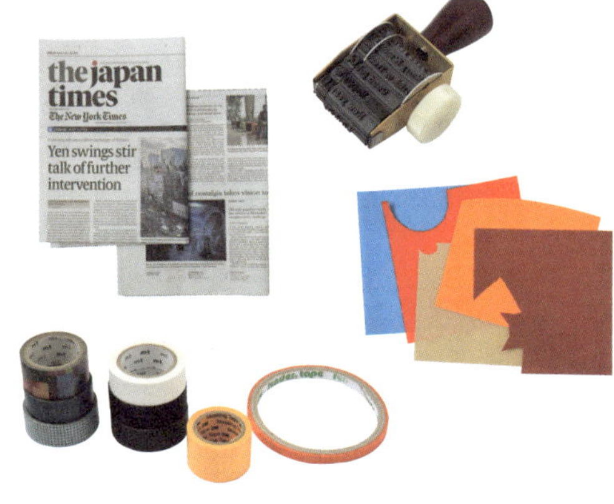

Gather materials like newspapers, magazines, colored paper, washi tape and other collage supplies from dollar stores.

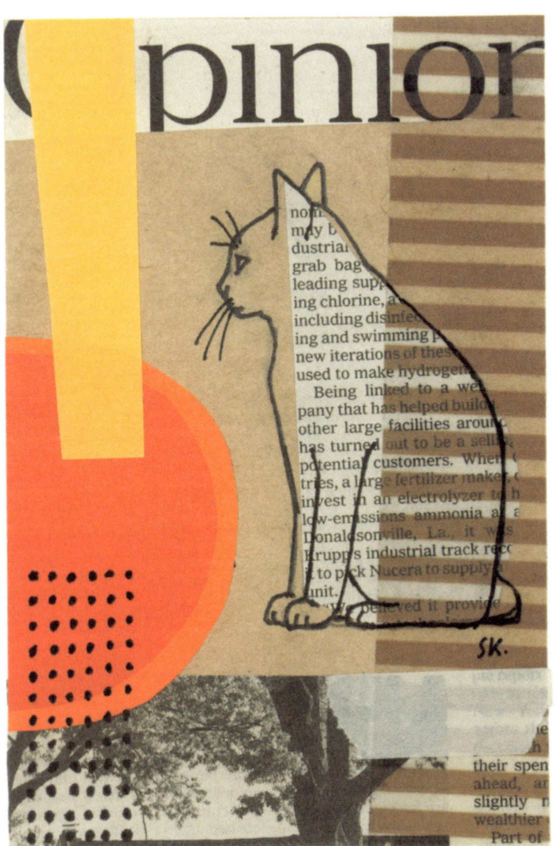

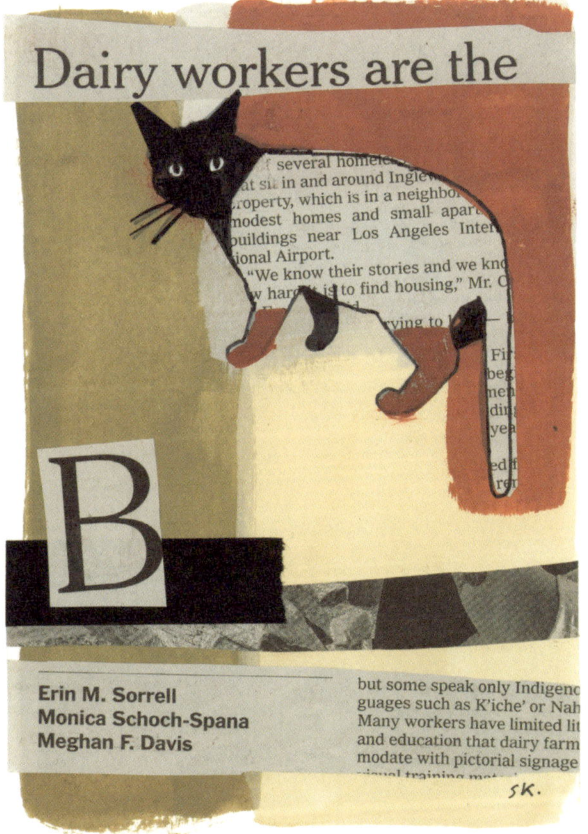

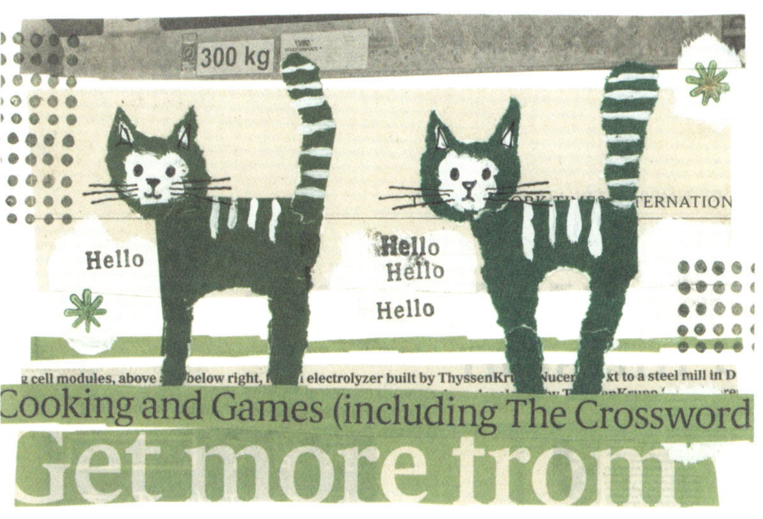

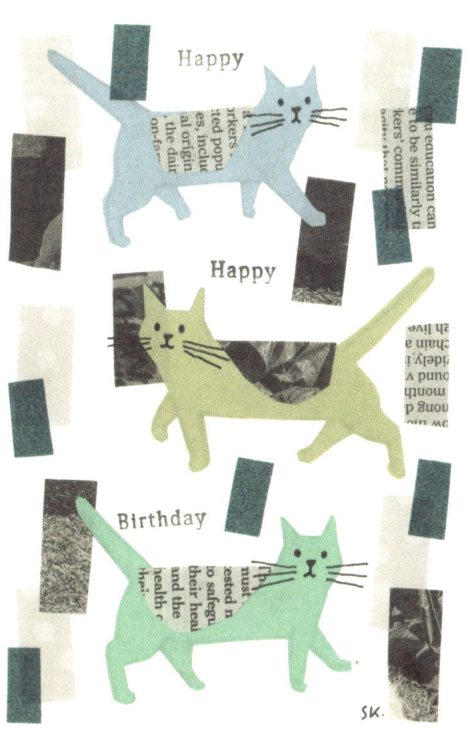

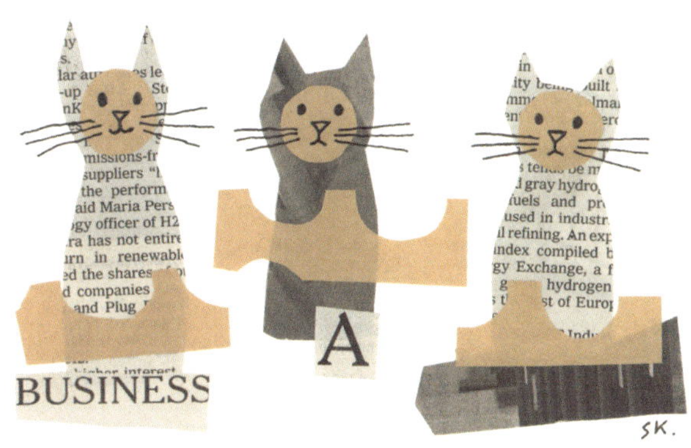

N O T E

Draw a cat and then affix various materials, or glue things down first and then draw a cat on top. It doesn't have to be perfect—explore and enjoy spontaneous cutting and pasting.

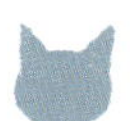 # Draw while observing a reference photo

If you have photos of your pet cat or a beloved cat from your past, using those to create a drawing is also a great idea. Unlike an active cat, you can observe a photo carefully and take your time focusing while drawing.

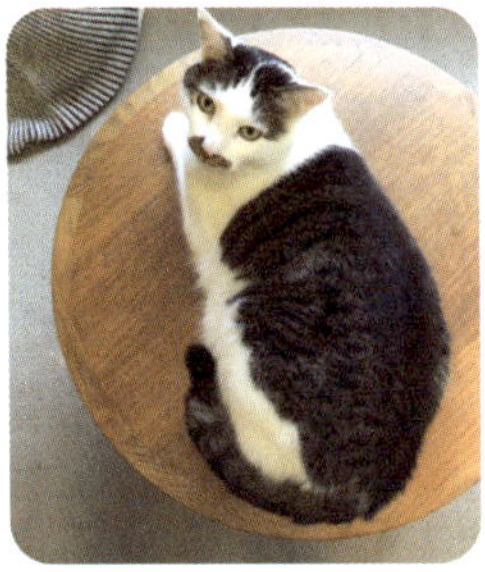

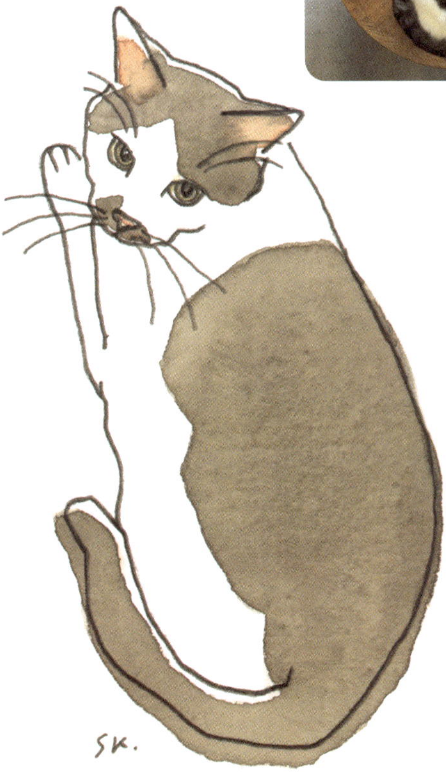

Media: pencil and transparent watercolor paint

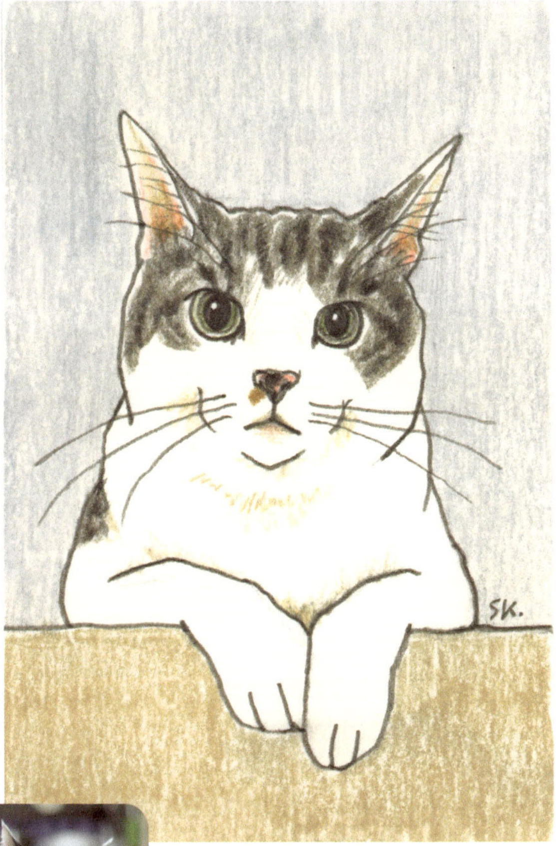

Media: pencil and colored pencil

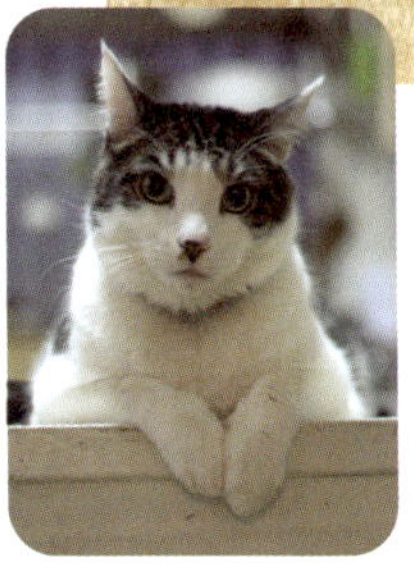

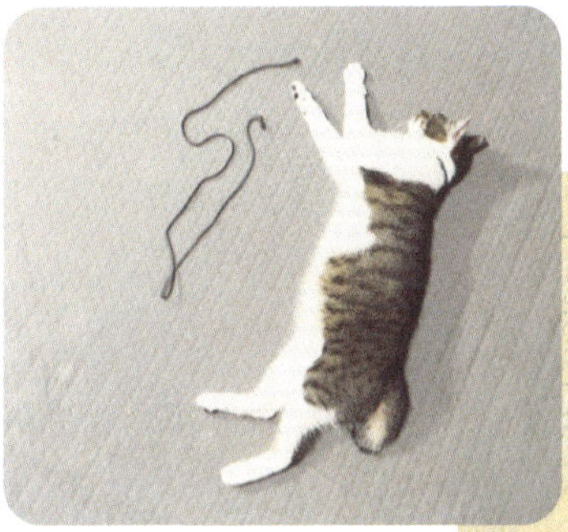

Medium: acrylic paint

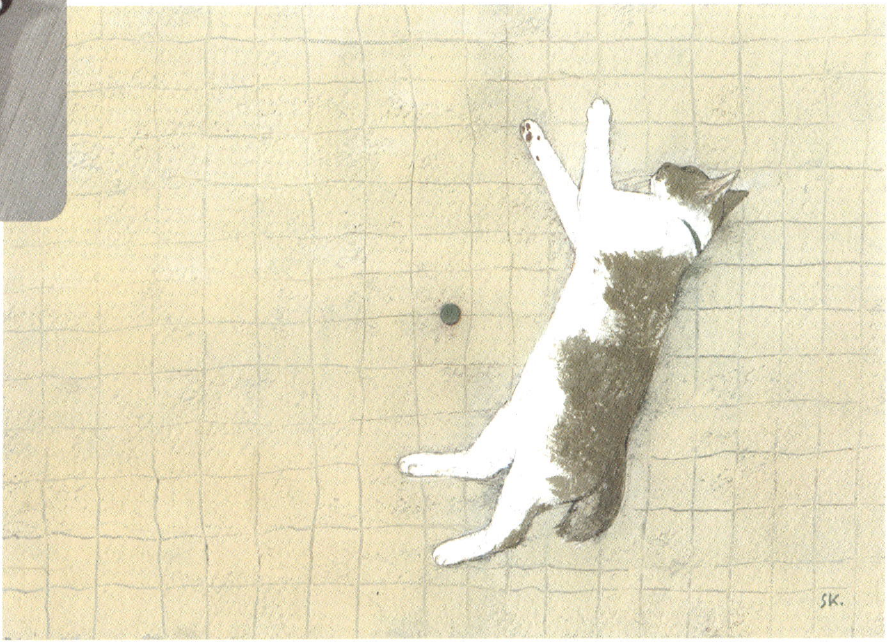

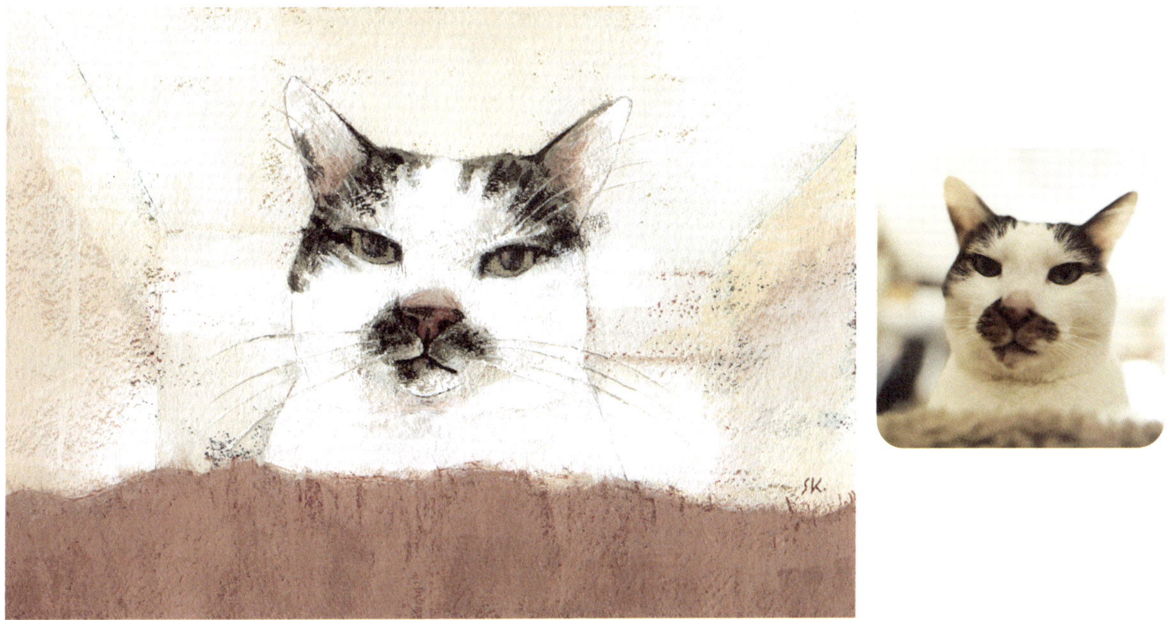

Medium: acrylic paint

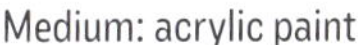

Add a signature to complete your original artwork!

Once your artwork is completed, add your signature. You can write it out in letters, or stamp it with a seal for an Asian flourish. It will give your piece a more polished look.

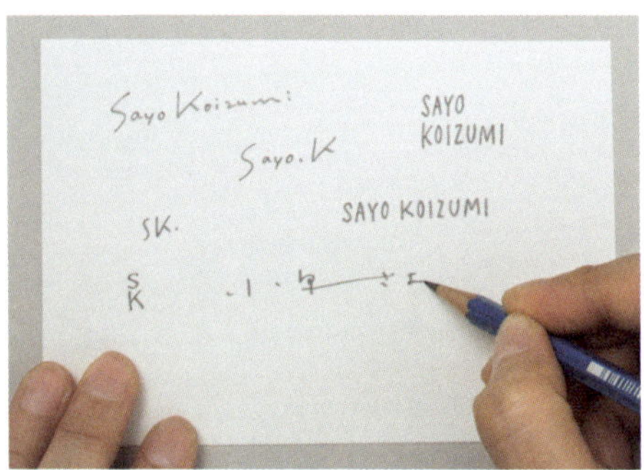

1 Think about your signature

Try out different formats—capital or lowercase letters, initials, etc. See what fits best: one line or two, printed or cursive. Experiment until it feels right.

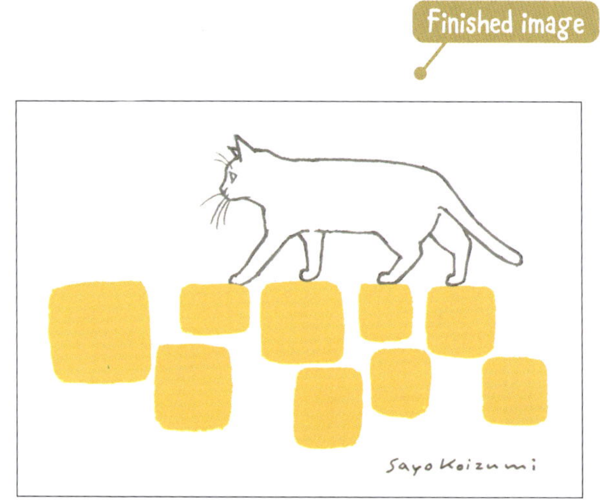

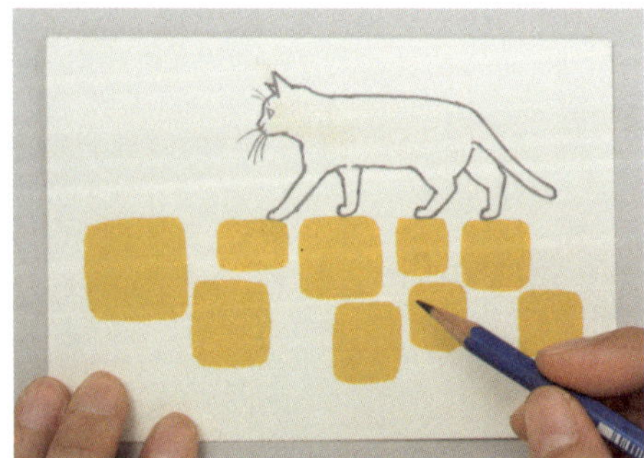

2 Decide where to place it

Choose where to place your signature. Look carefully at the composition. If you're unsure, go with the bottom right. Here, I'm signing with a pencil, but it's even better to sign in the same medium that was used for the artwork.

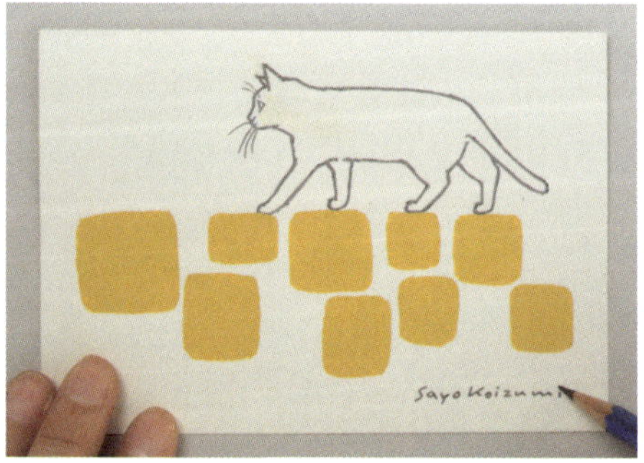

3 Add your signature

Your one-of-a-kind piece is now complete! You did it! Be sure to treasure it.

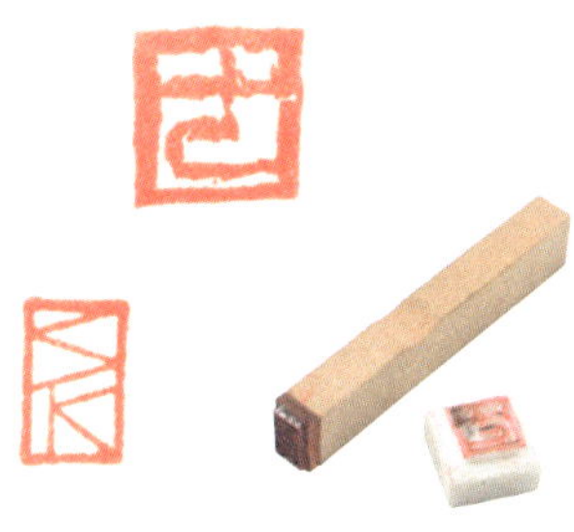

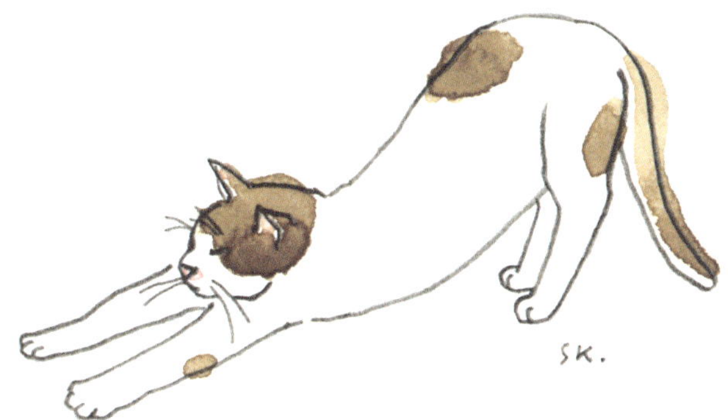

You can use a signature seal that you've purchased, or even try carving your own stamp from an eraser—which I highly recommend!

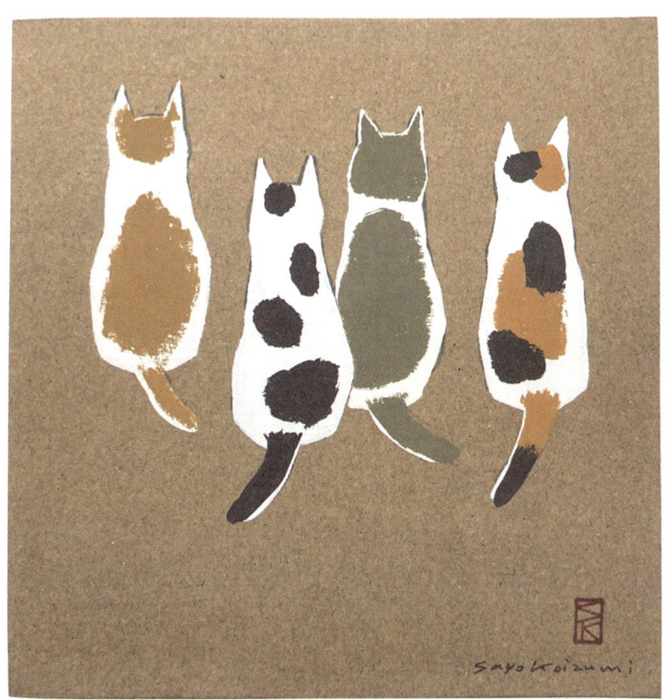

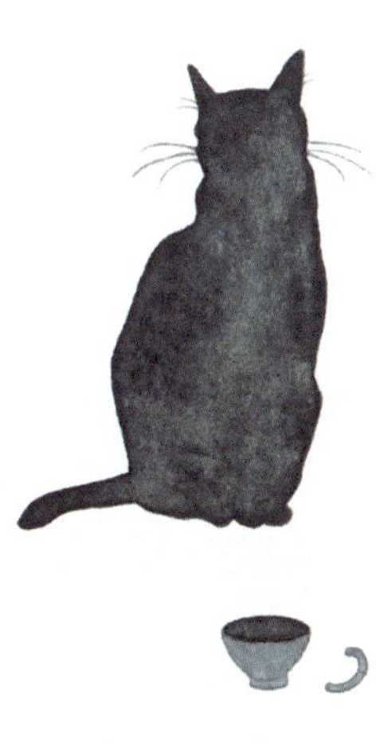

SAYO KOIZUMI

Spring motif illustration samples

Try adding a seasonal feel to your illustration. Draw seasonal flowers or small objects in the background, or combine cats with seasonal event motifs. Be sure to finish it in a colorful way!

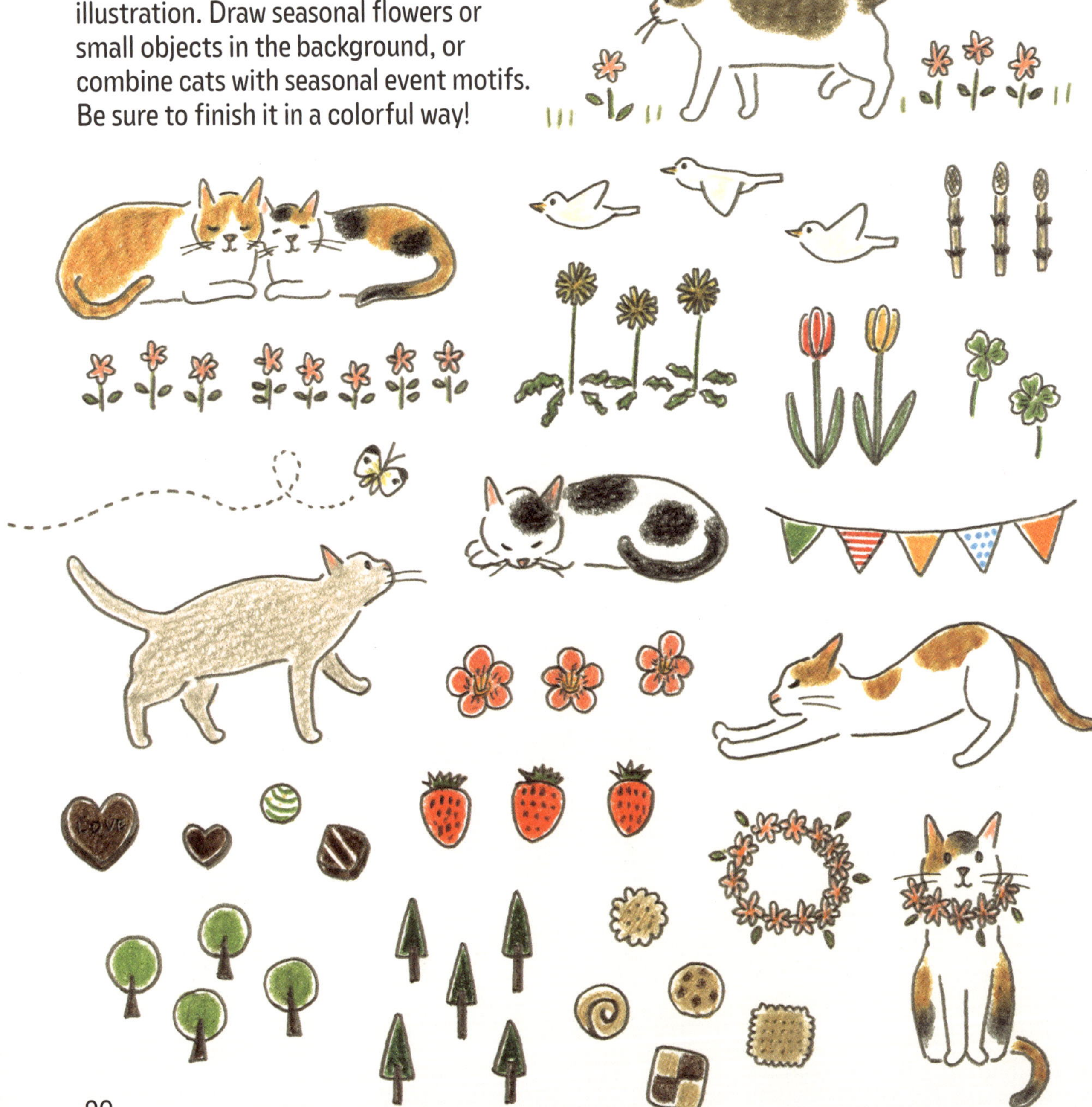

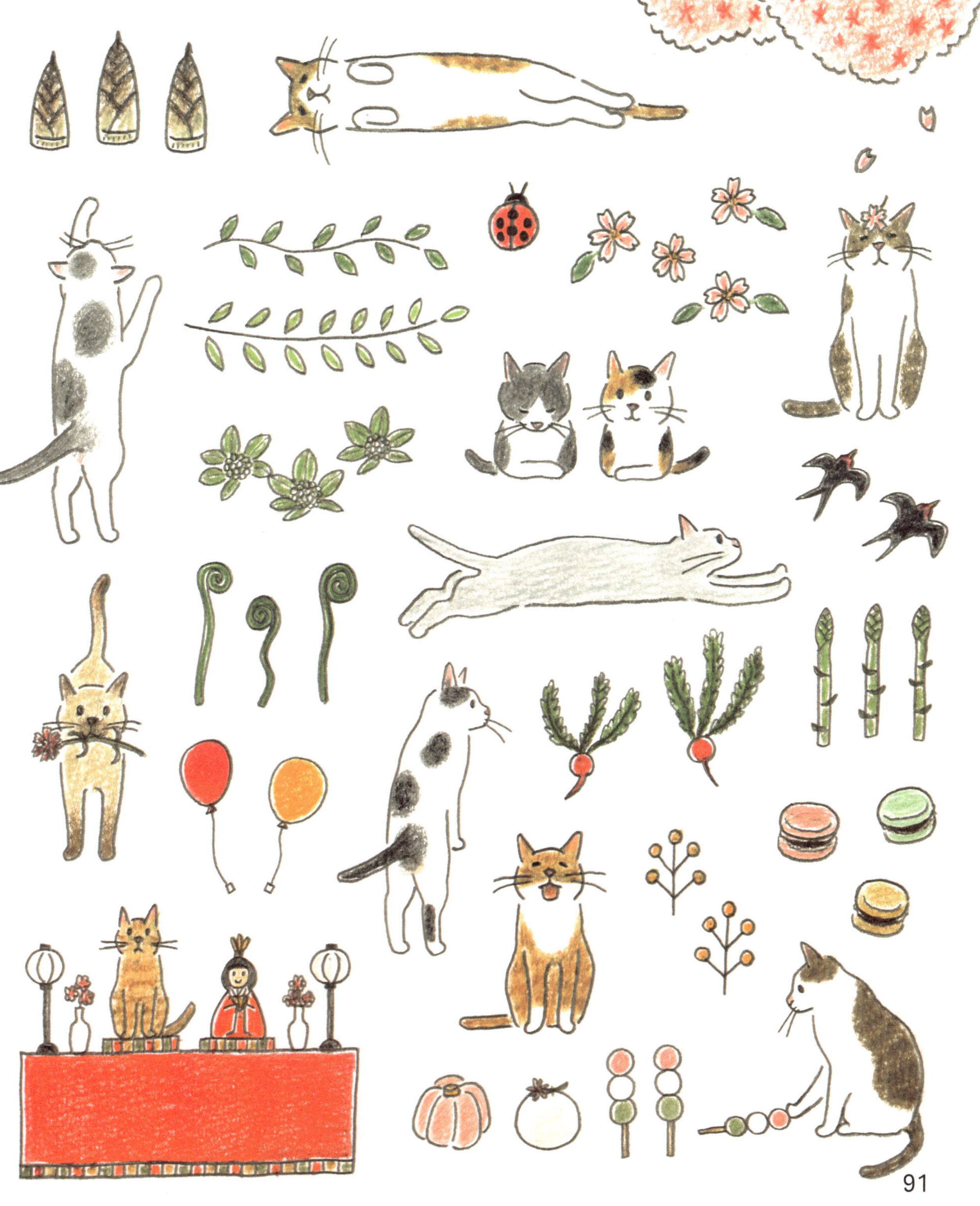

Summer motif illustration samples

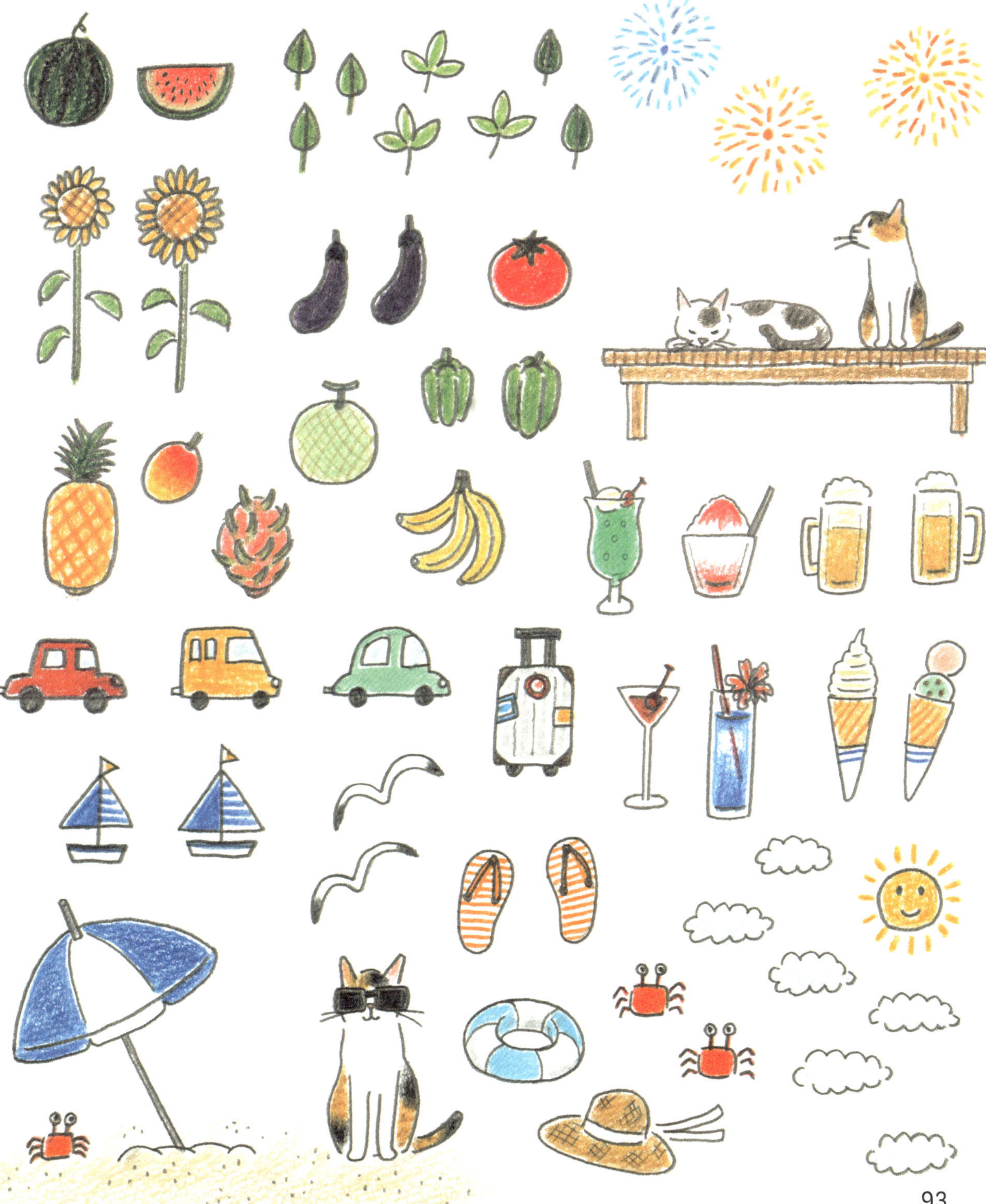

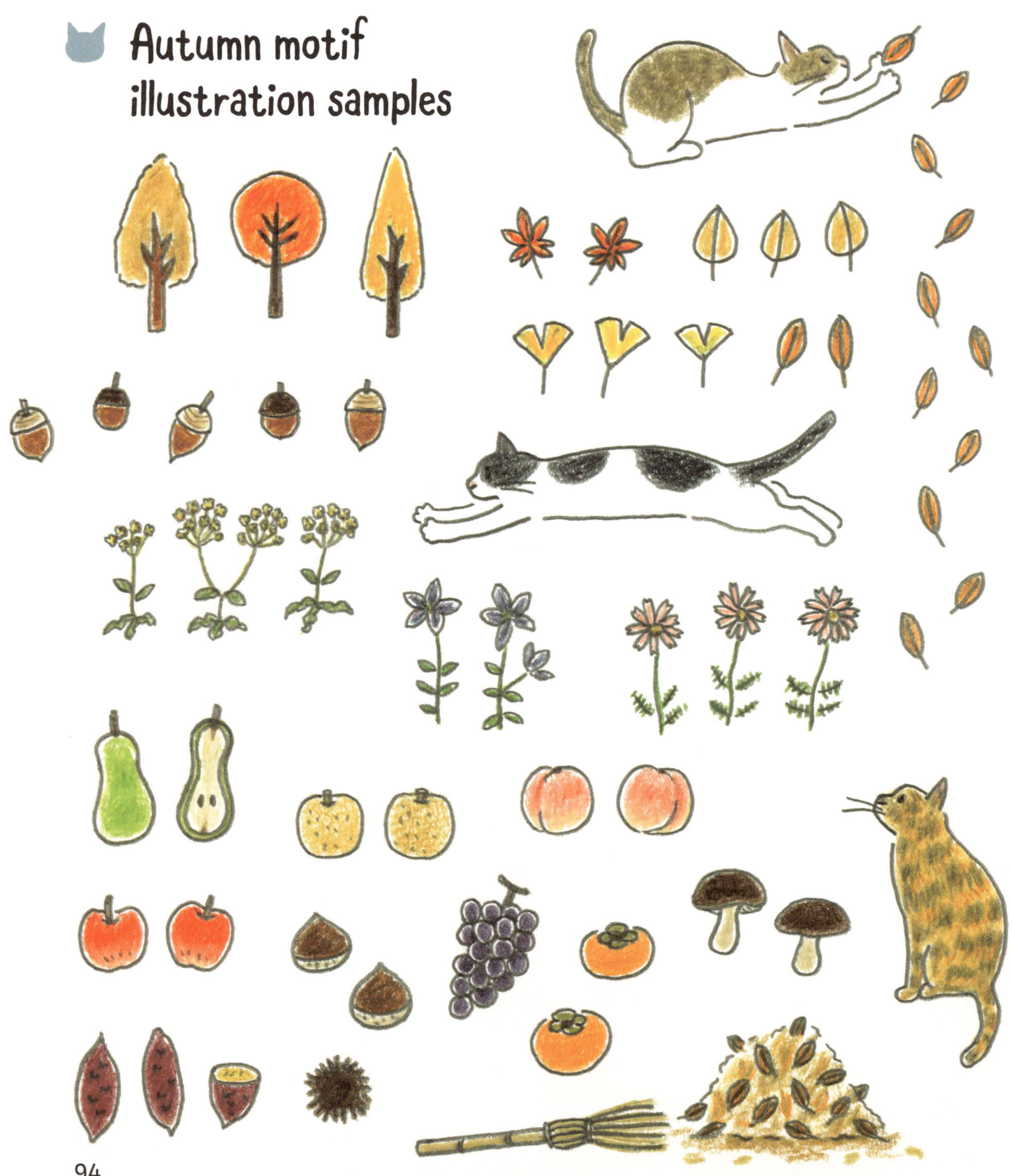

Autumn motif illustration samples

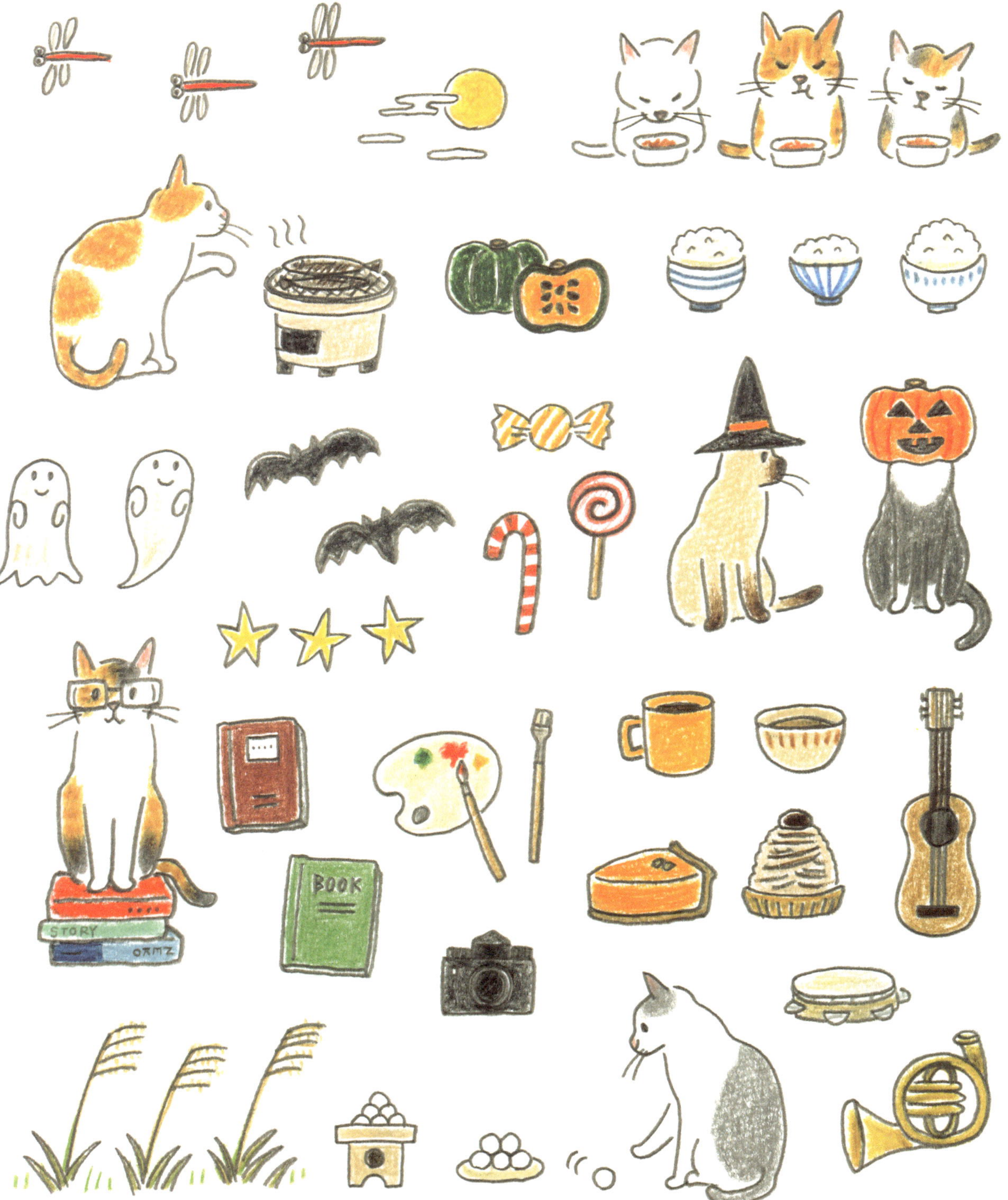

Winter motif illustration samples

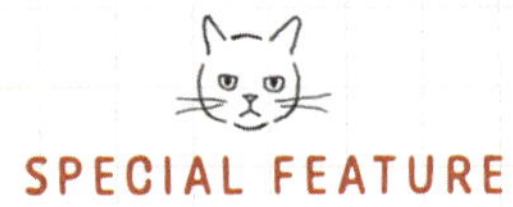

In praise of rescue cats

All the cats we've had in our home over the years have originally been strays, come from acquaintances or were adopted from rescue shelters. We never really considered buying a cat from a pet store to begin with, and I believe it's only natural that if there are cats in the community that need homes, and people there are wanting to care for cats, they should come together. Of course, wanting to help cats in need is part of it, but the biggest reason is really because rescue cats are just so charming! They might have a random spot in a funny place, or a face that looks like they just dove into mud, or suddenly one day you notice a pattern

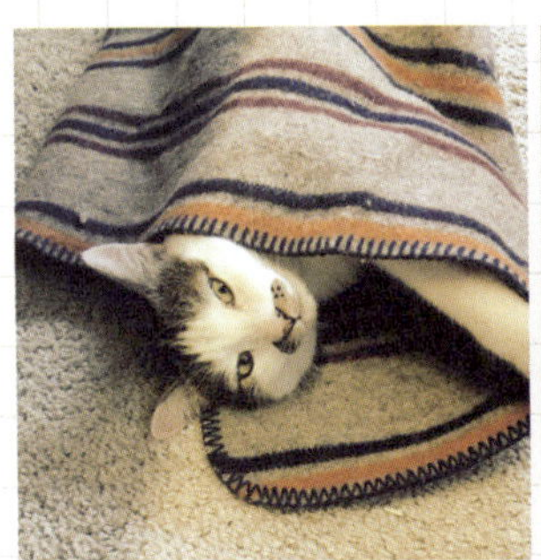
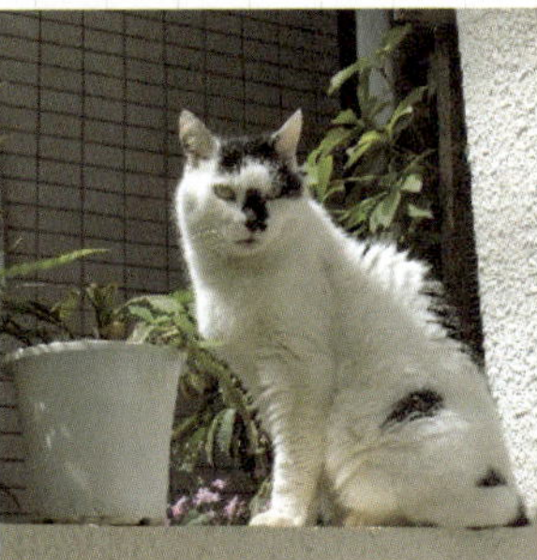
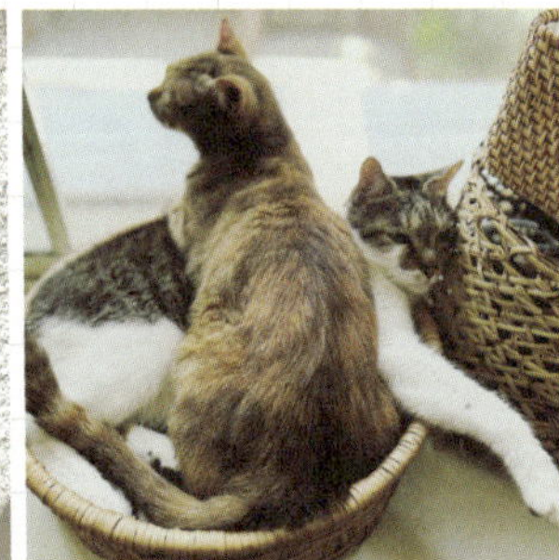

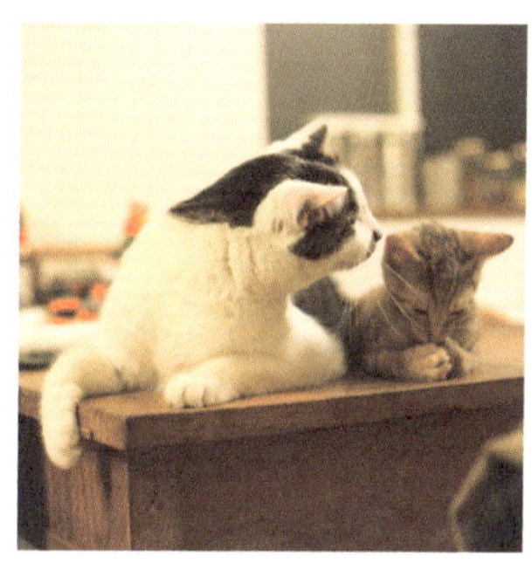

you'd overlooked—"Oh wow, there's a marking here too?" Each individual has unexpected, unique traits like no other cat in the world, and every day as I gaze at those quirky markings, I'm overwhelmed with affection. No matter what cat you meet, each one has its own charm, and somehow, you always end up falling in love with them. It doesn't matter what color or pattern they have, or what kind of personality. In the end, I guess what I'm saying is—cats are simply the best, aren't they?

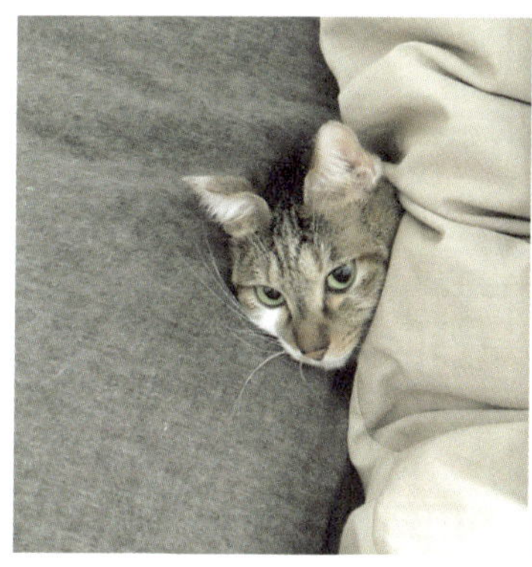

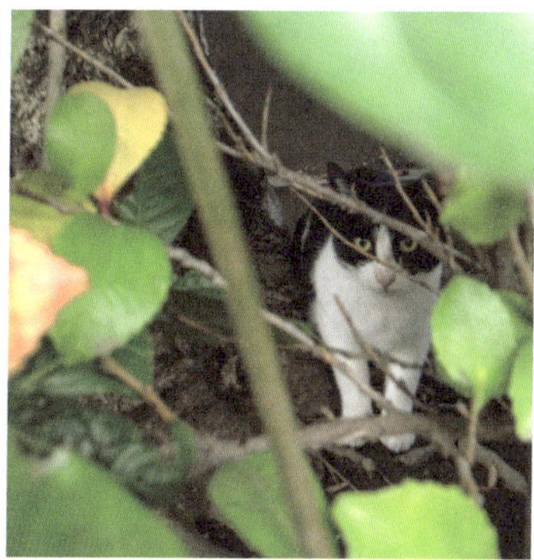

PART 5

Once You've Drawn a Cat...

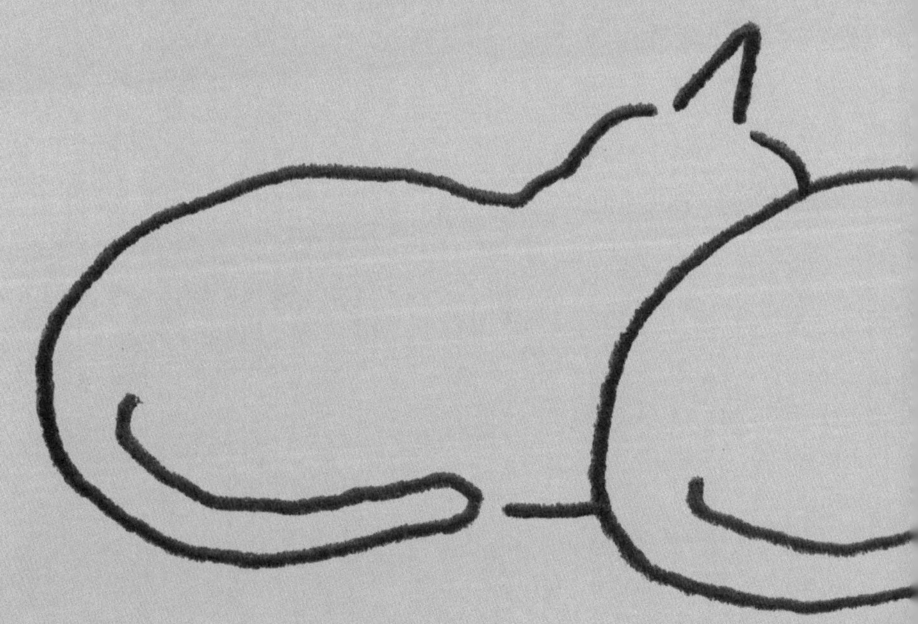

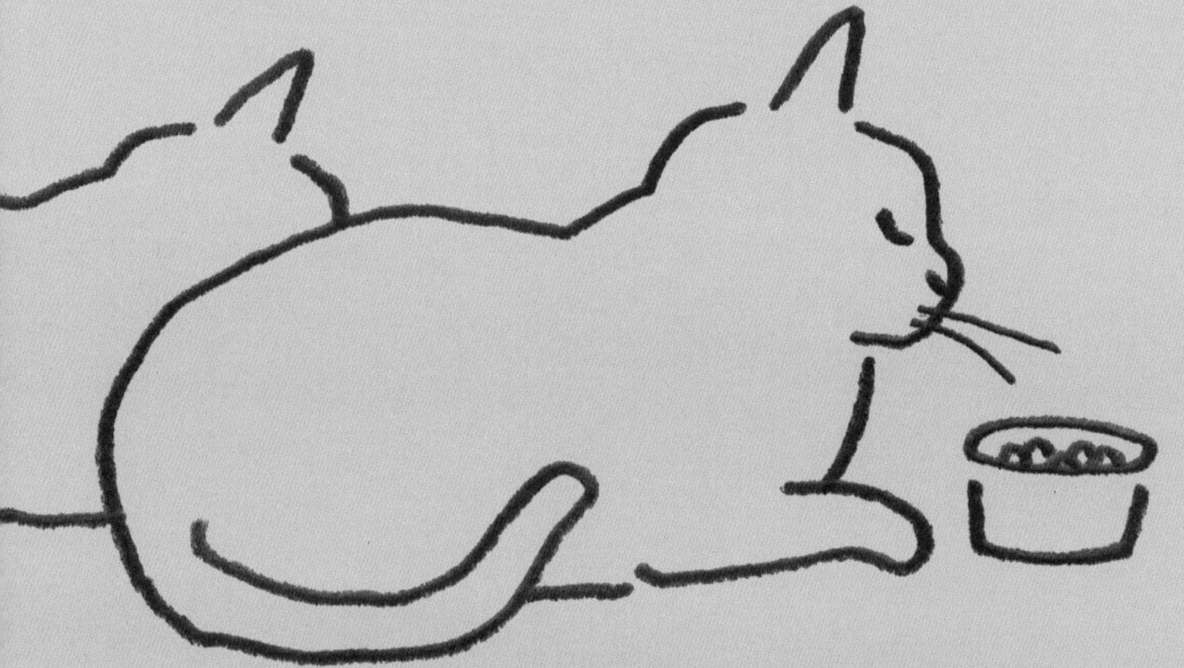

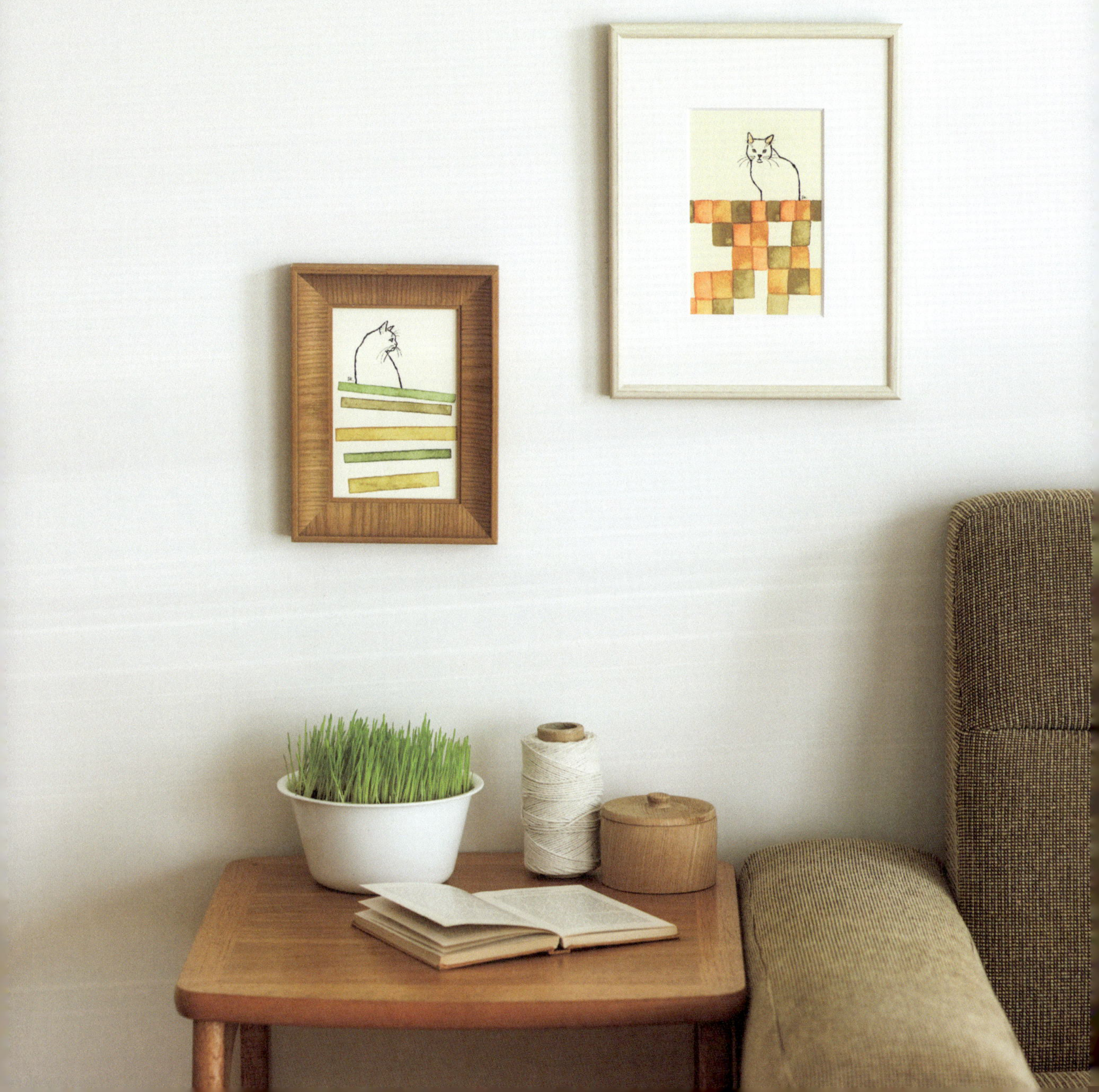

Once you've finished your cat drawing or painting,
why not put it in a frame to display it? It's a joyful
thing to display and admire a piece of art you made
yourself. You can buy frames at art supply stores or
home improvement centers.

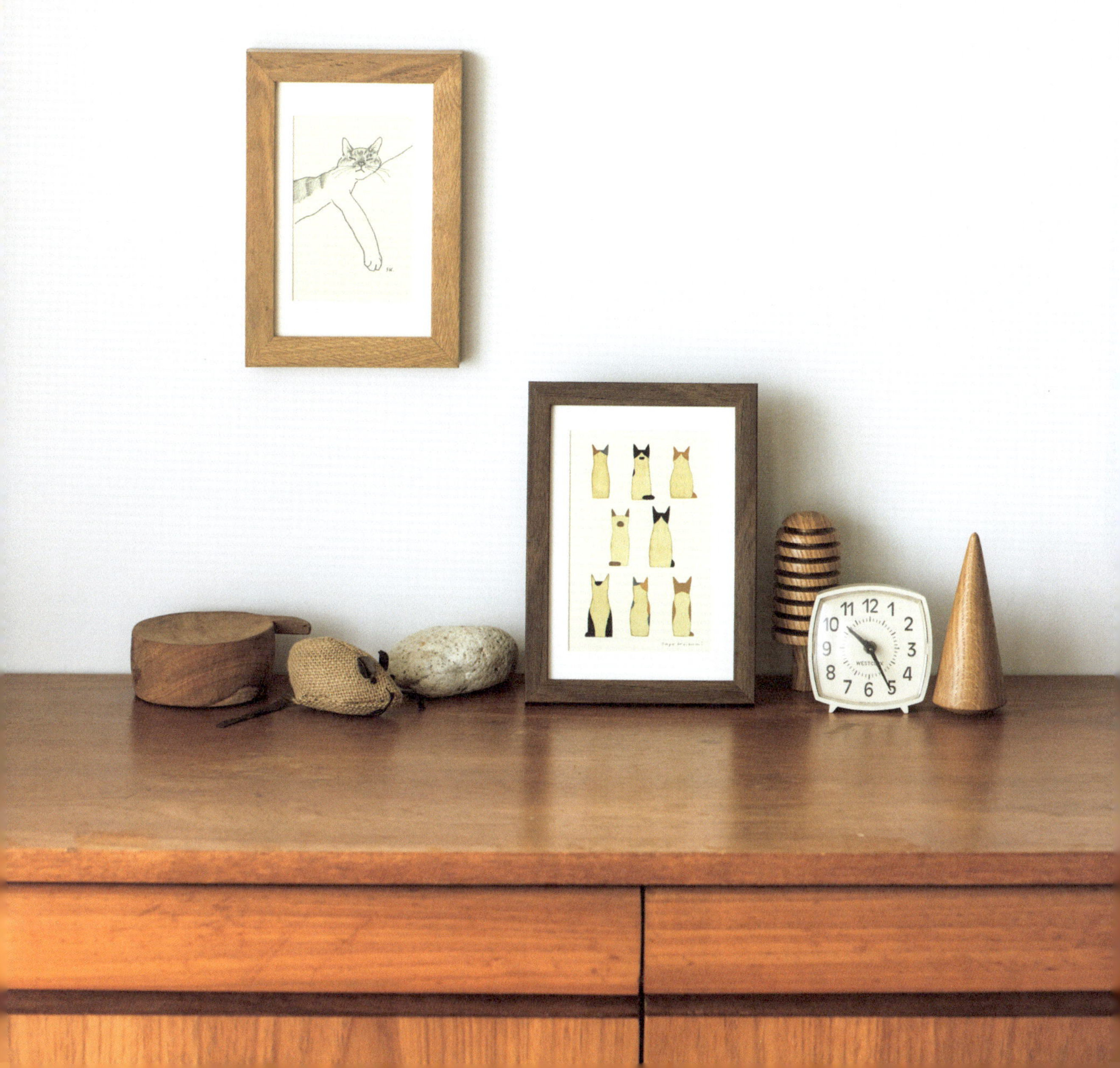

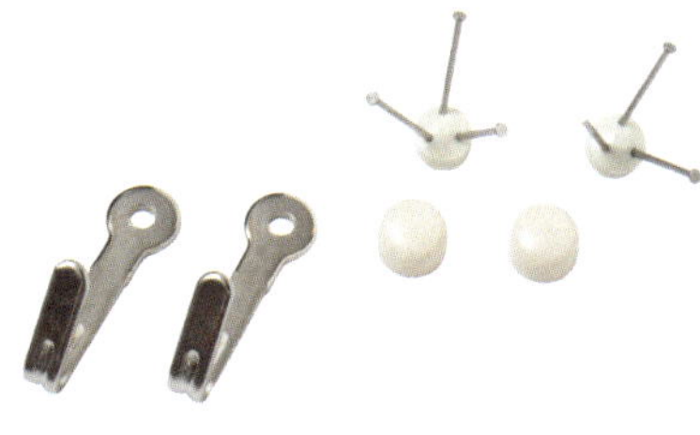 Various frames

Now, let's discuss the different types of frames and how to display them. There are many kinds to choose from, so use this as a guide to pick one that suits your artwork or personal taste.

When hanging artwork in your home, hardware designed for drywall is very convenient.

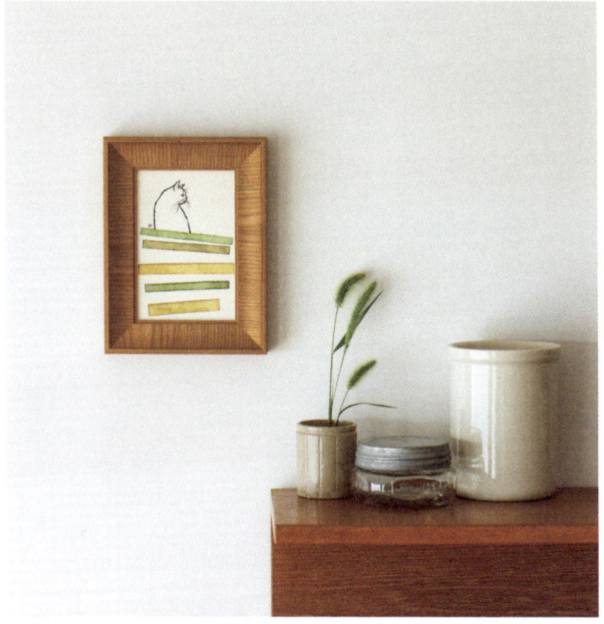

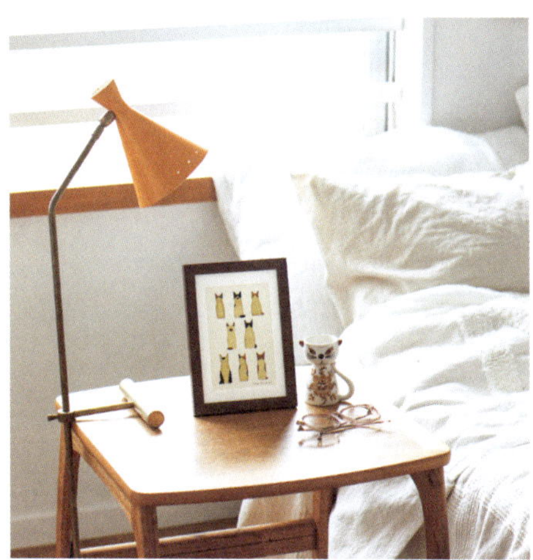

A classic wooden frame suits any type of painting.

A decorative frame is cute and attractive.

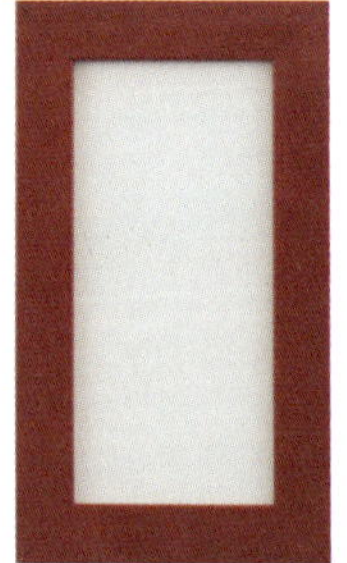

A vividly colored frame that matches the tones of your artwork is chic.

A simple acrylic picture frame gives a cool, modern impression.

🐾 Mat your artwork

When framing, adding a mat offers a more professional, finished look. A mat is a thick paper border placed inside the frame. By adding a border around your picture, it enhances the impression that it is a completed work of art!

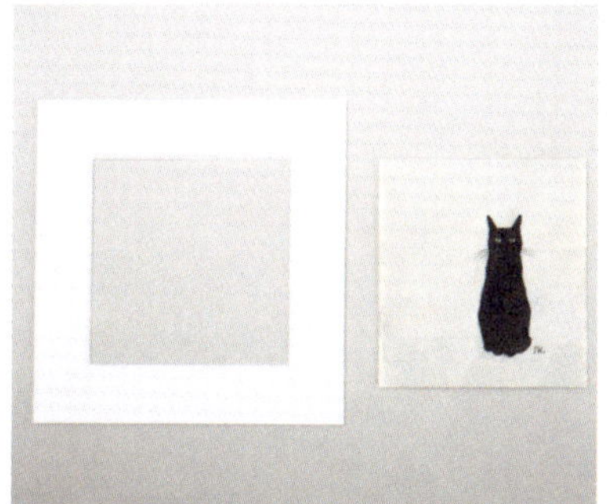

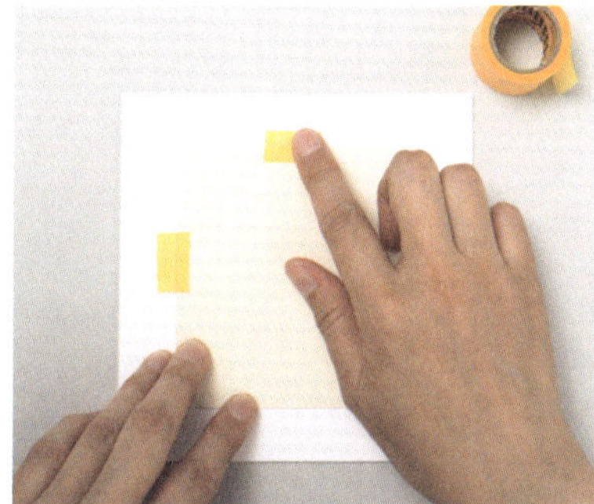

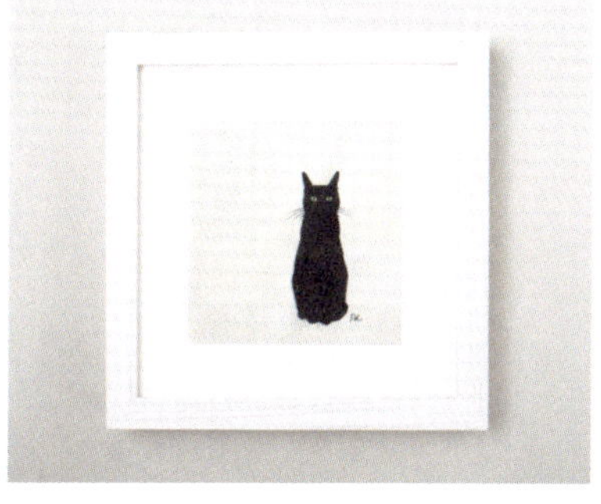

1 Purchase a mat in the correct dimensions for your piece at an art supply store. The outer size should match the frame, and the opening should be about 3/16–1/4 in (4–6 mm) smaller than the artwork size.

2 On the back of the mat, position the artwork face down so it extends 1/16–1/8 in (2–3 mm) past the edge of the opening underneath on each side, and secure it with masking tape.

3 Put the matted artwork in the frame, close up the back, and it's complete! Your artwork now looks even more refined!

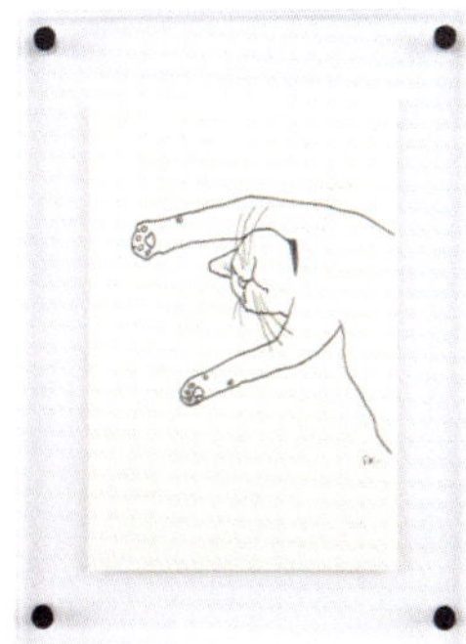

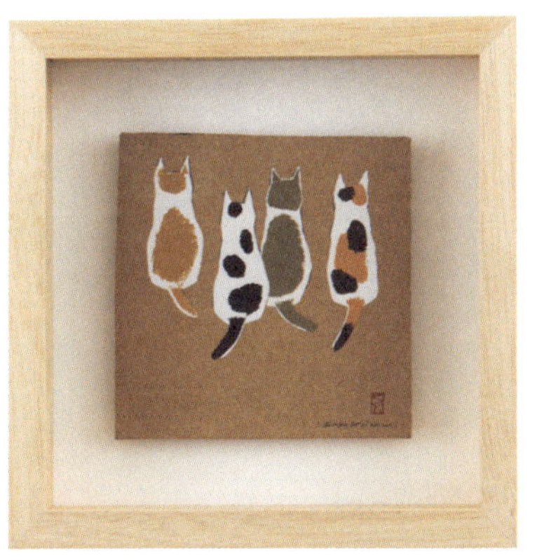

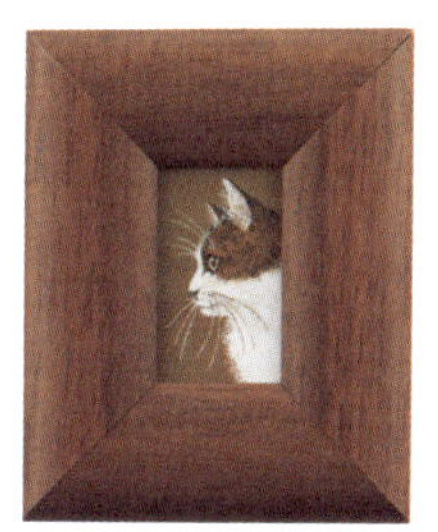

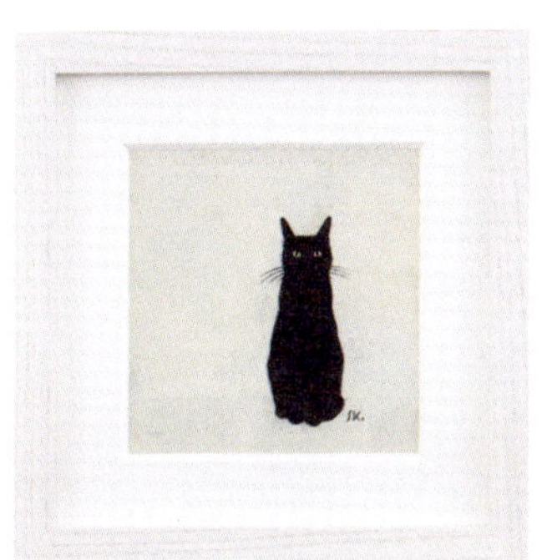

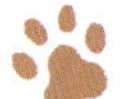 # Add a cat to a greeting card

If you draw or paint a cat, it's also a nice idea to give it as a gift to friends or acquaintances. Adding a small cat illustration to New Year's cards, greeting cards, letter paper or envelopes makes them really cute. The recipient will be delighted!

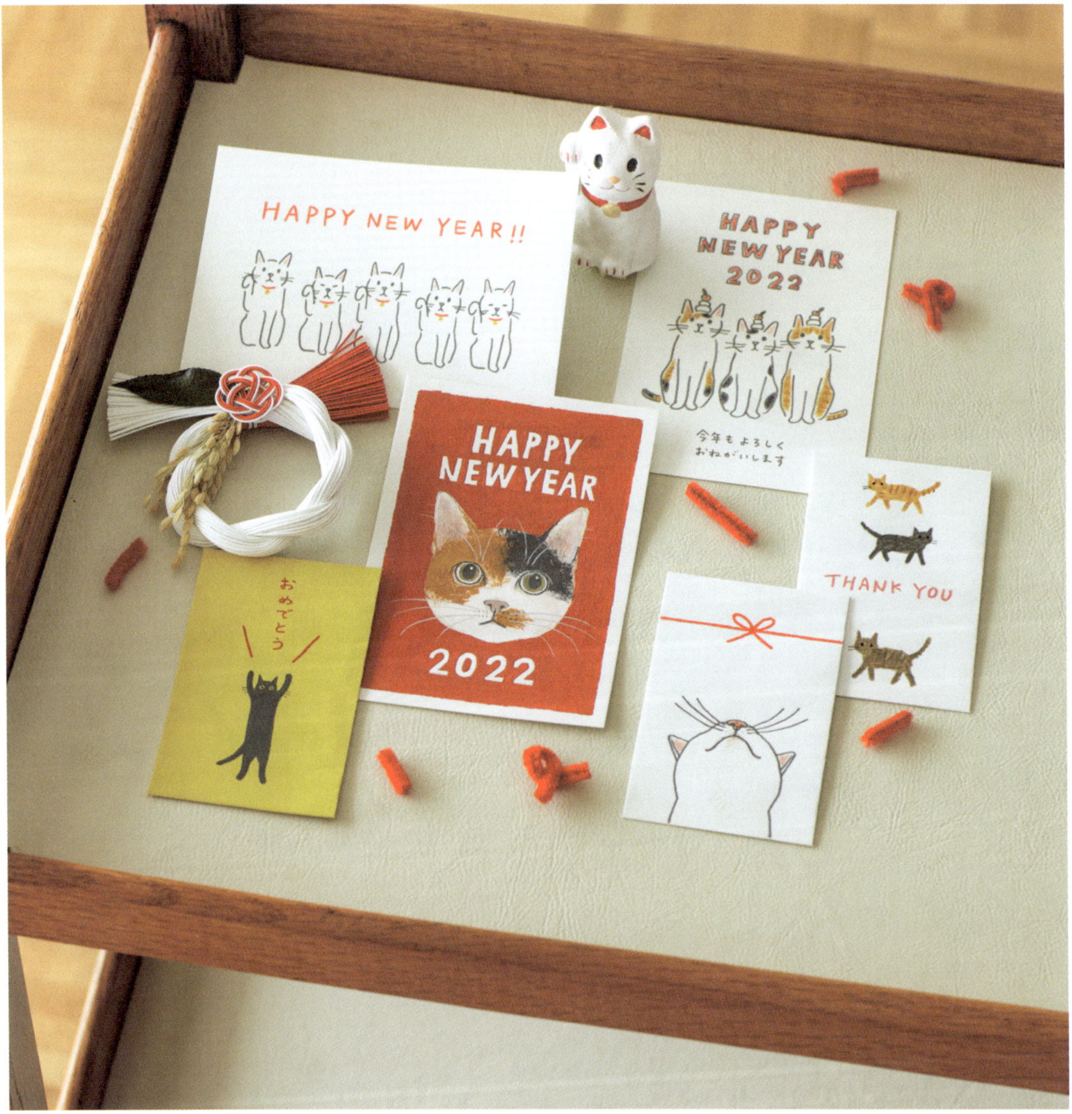

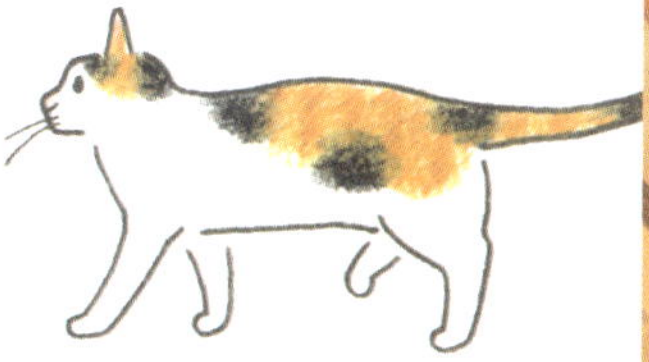

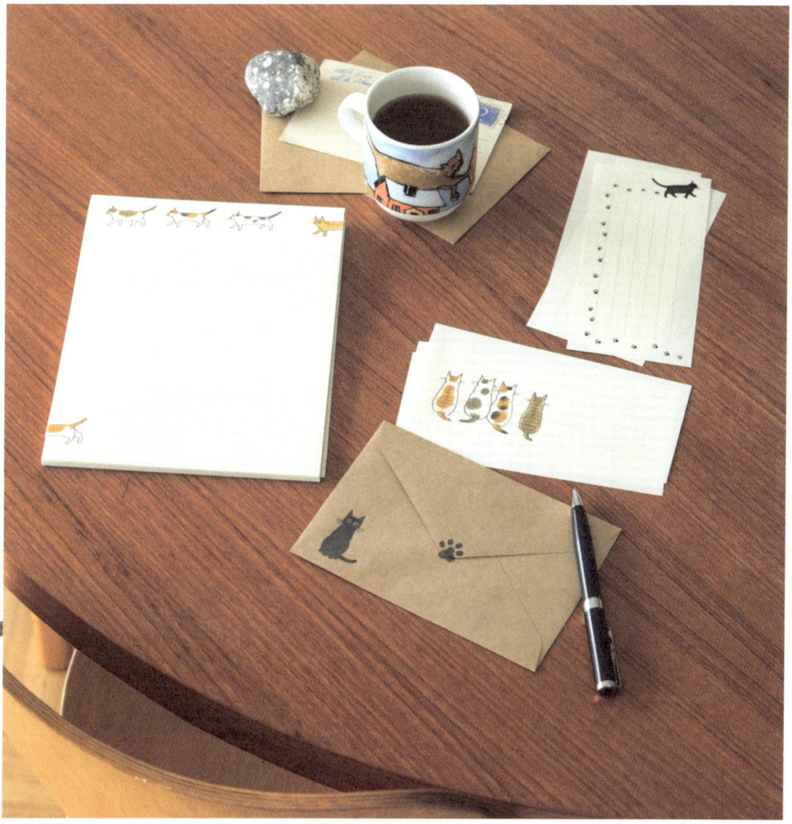

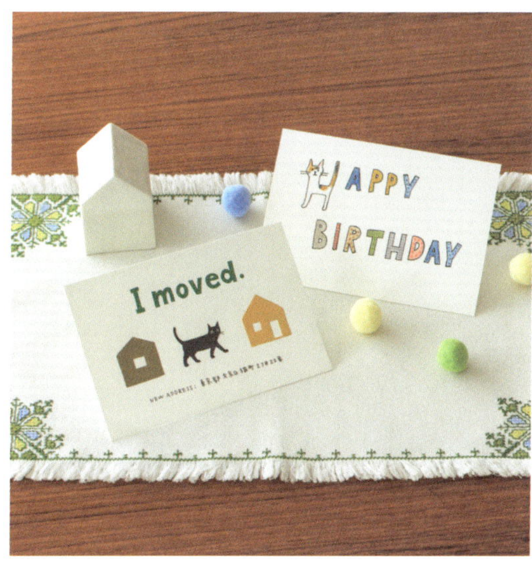

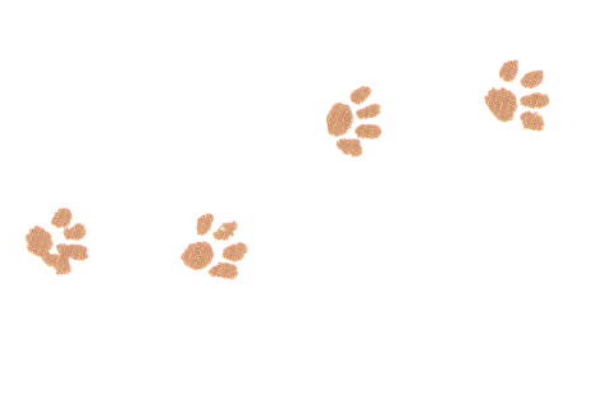

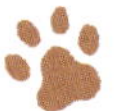 # Create cute cat correspondence

Try writing a cat-themed letter. Get plain postcards, letter paper or note cards. Thicker paper is recommended, as it's easier to draw on.

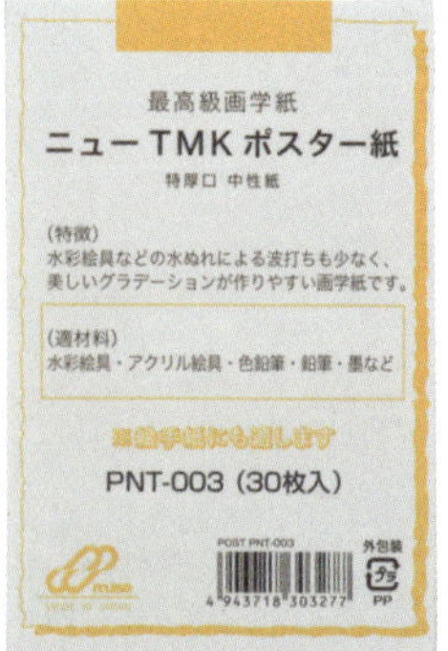

New TMK Poster Paper
Its smooth surface makes it easy to write and draw on.

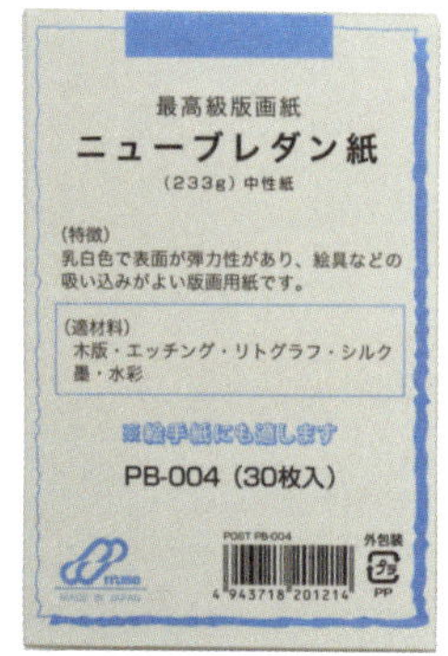

New Bredan Paper
It's actually printmaking paper, but works well with watercolors too. I use it often.

You don't need any special writing tools. Pencils, water-based pens and gel pens can all produce fine results.

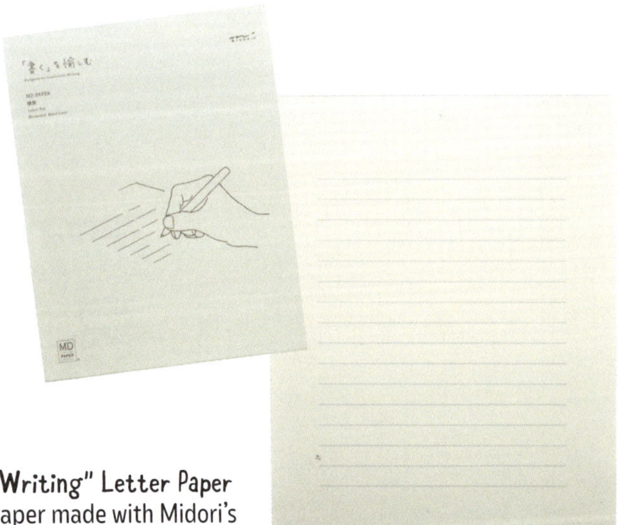

"Enjoy Writing" Letter Paper
Letter paper made with Midori's premium MD Paper.

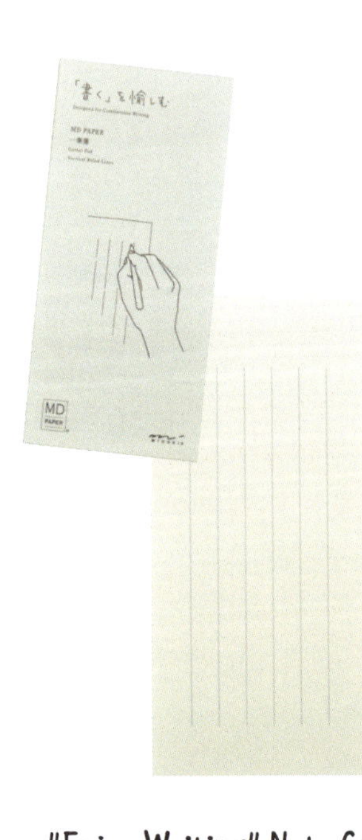

"Enjoy Writing" Note Cards
Note cards made with Midori's premium MD Paper. They feel amazing to write on!

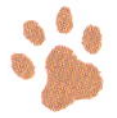 # Add a drawing to a postcard

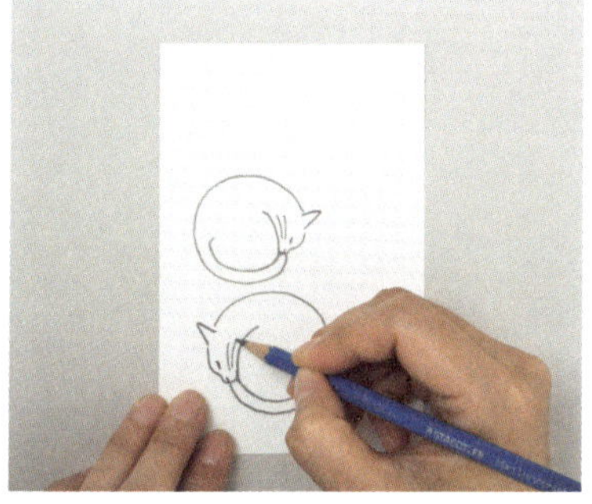

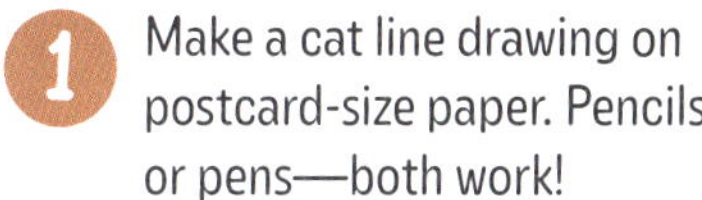

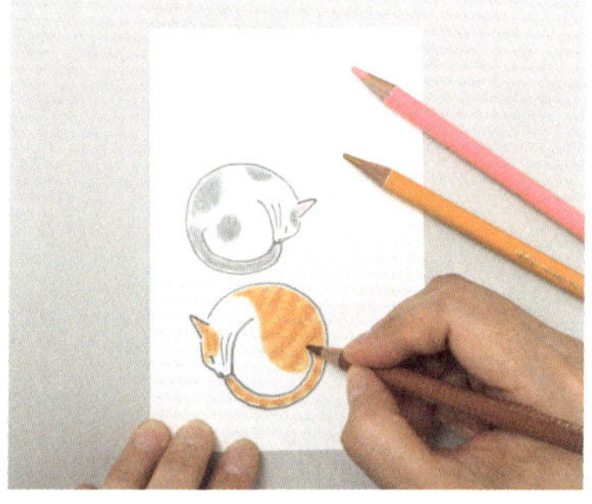

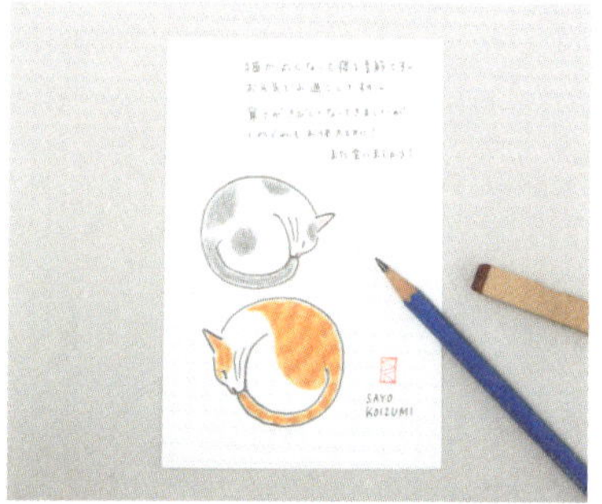

1 Make a cat line drawing on postcard-size paper. Pencils or pens—both work!

2 Color it in any way you like. This time, I'm using colored pencils.

3 Write your message. You can even add a personal stamp or seal.

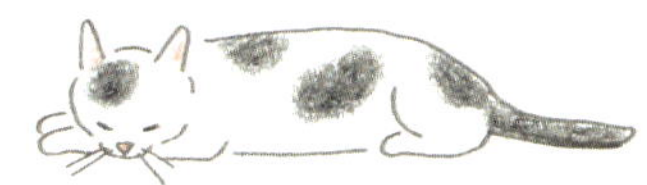 # Add a drawing to note paper

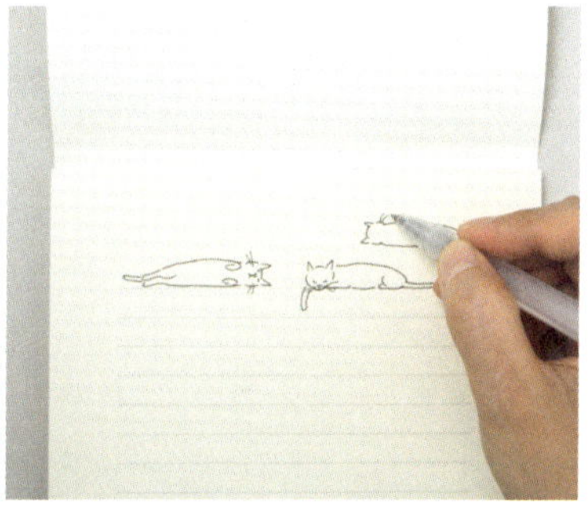

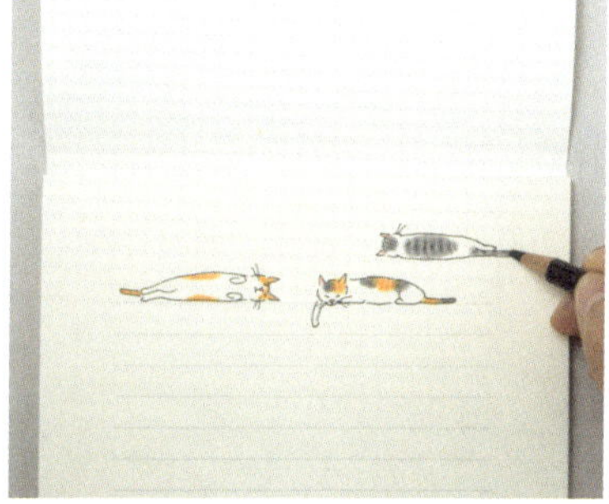

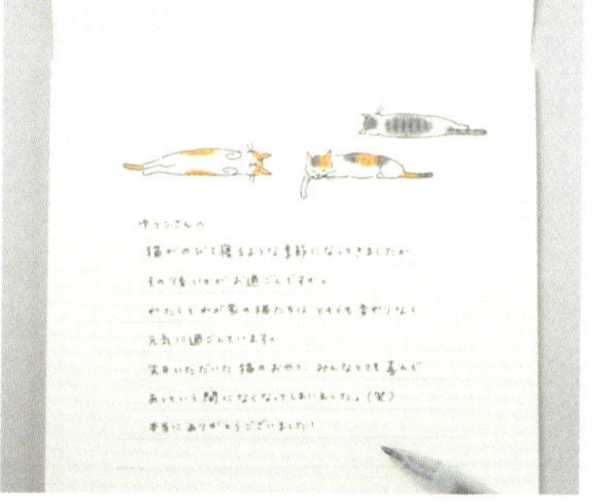

1 Because note paper is thinner than a postcard, draw gently with a pencil or fine pen. Using the same writing tool as your text gives a nice sense of cohesiveness.

2 Color gently. Watercolors may bleed through or warp the paper, so colored pencils are recommended.

3 Write your letter. Adding a touch of cat charm makes your sentiments even warmer.

Add feline finesse to your schedule

Adding cat motifs to your planner or calendar is sure to make your daily life more fun. Happy news and exciting plans—let the cat take care of your schedule!

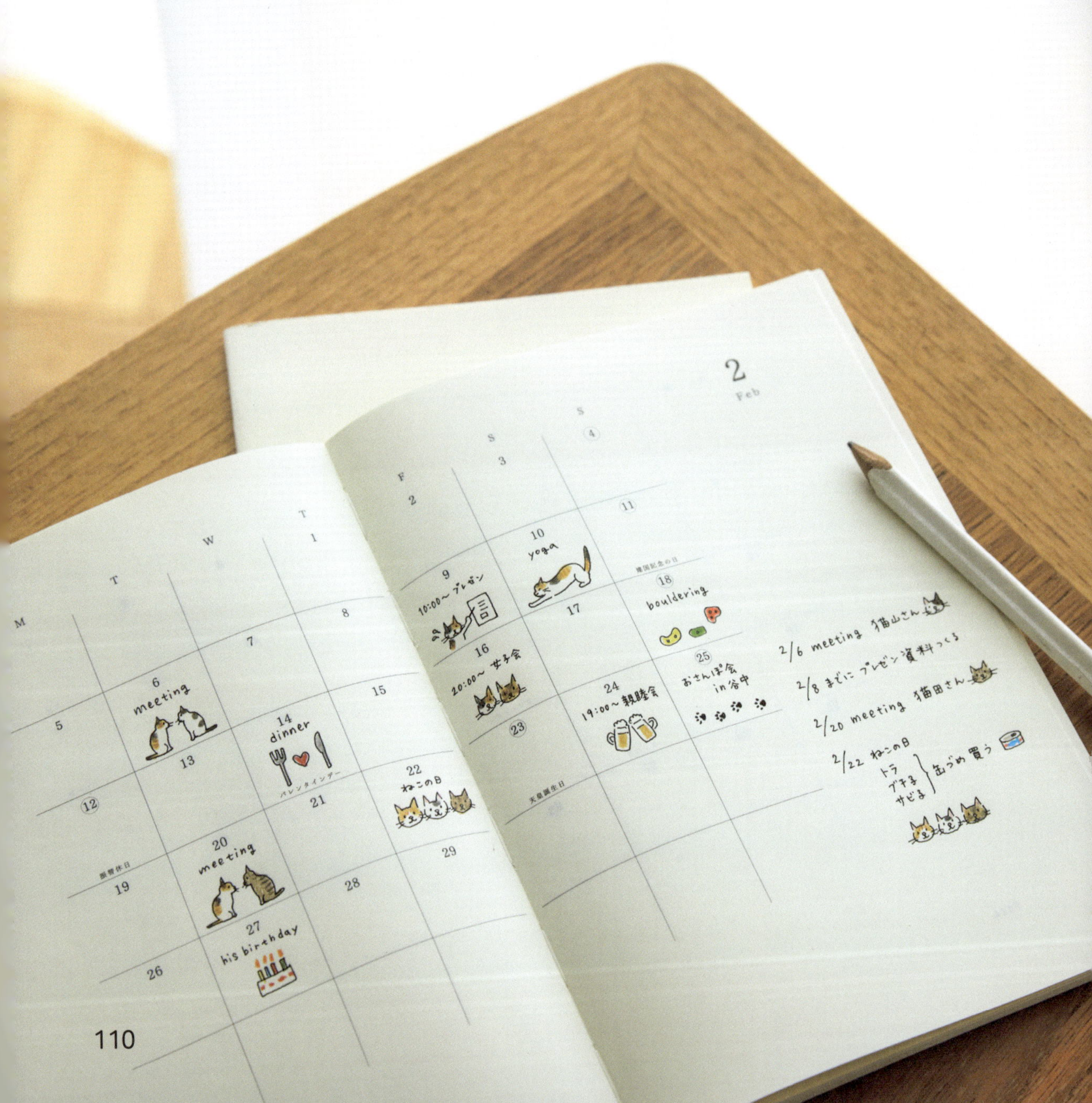

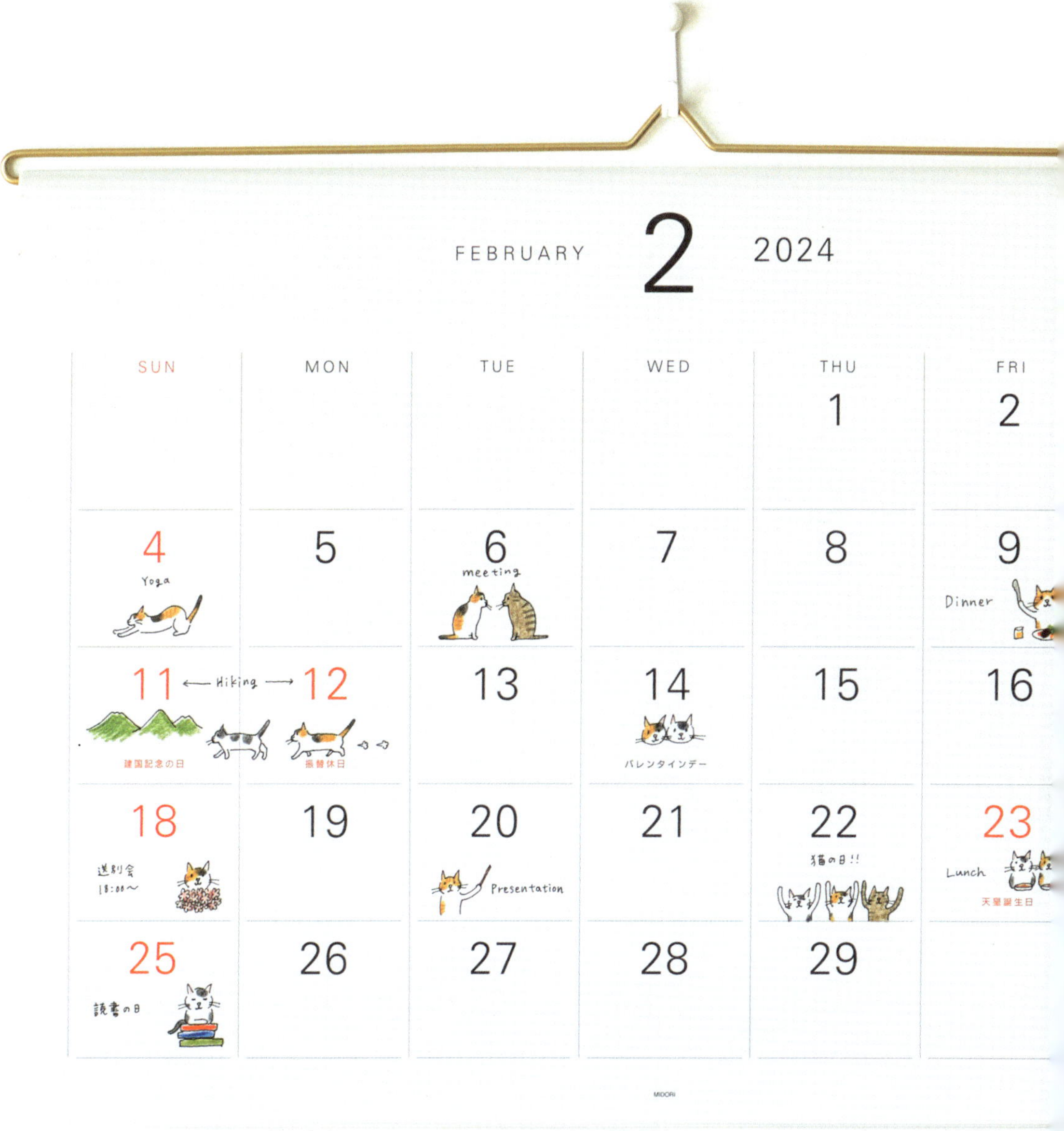

FEBRUARY 2 2024

SUN MON TUE WED THU FRI

1
2

4
Yoga
5
6
meeting
7
8
9
Dinner

11 ← Hiking → 12
建国記念の日 振替休日
13
14
バレンタインデー
15
16

18
送別会
18:00～
19
20
Presentation
21
22
猫の日!!
23
Lunch
天皇誕生日

25
読書の日
26
27
28
29

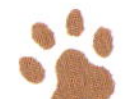 # Make a cat-themed schedule book or calendar

Because it's for everyday use, you don't need any special art materials. Just casually draw using your usual writing tools. You can also refer to the icons and motifs on the following page.

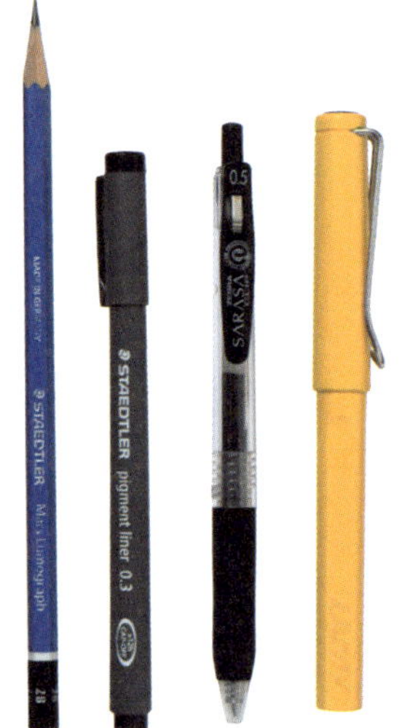

Pencils or pens—whatever writing tools you have handy are fine. Just choose something that's easy to draw with.

MD Wall Calendar (by Midori)
The simpler and larger the spaces, the easier it is to draw on.

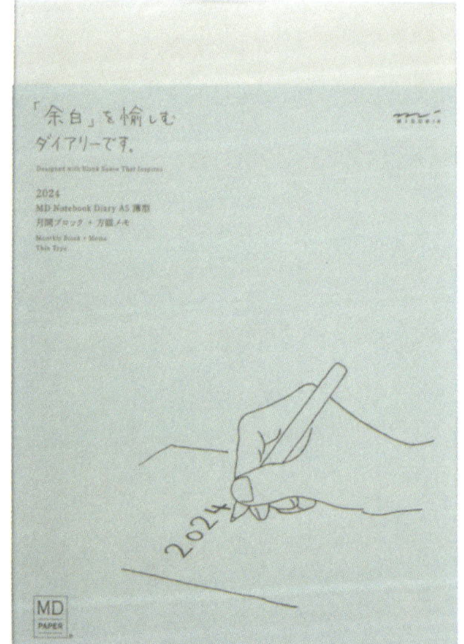

MD Notebook Diary (by Midori)
It has wide margins, so you can make lots of drawings—highly recommended!

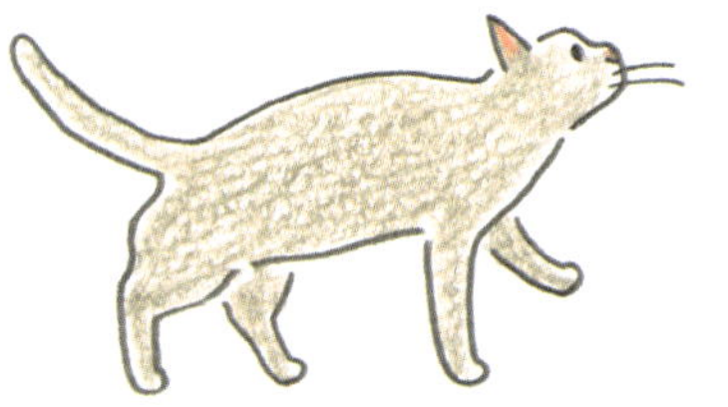

Fun motif and icon samples

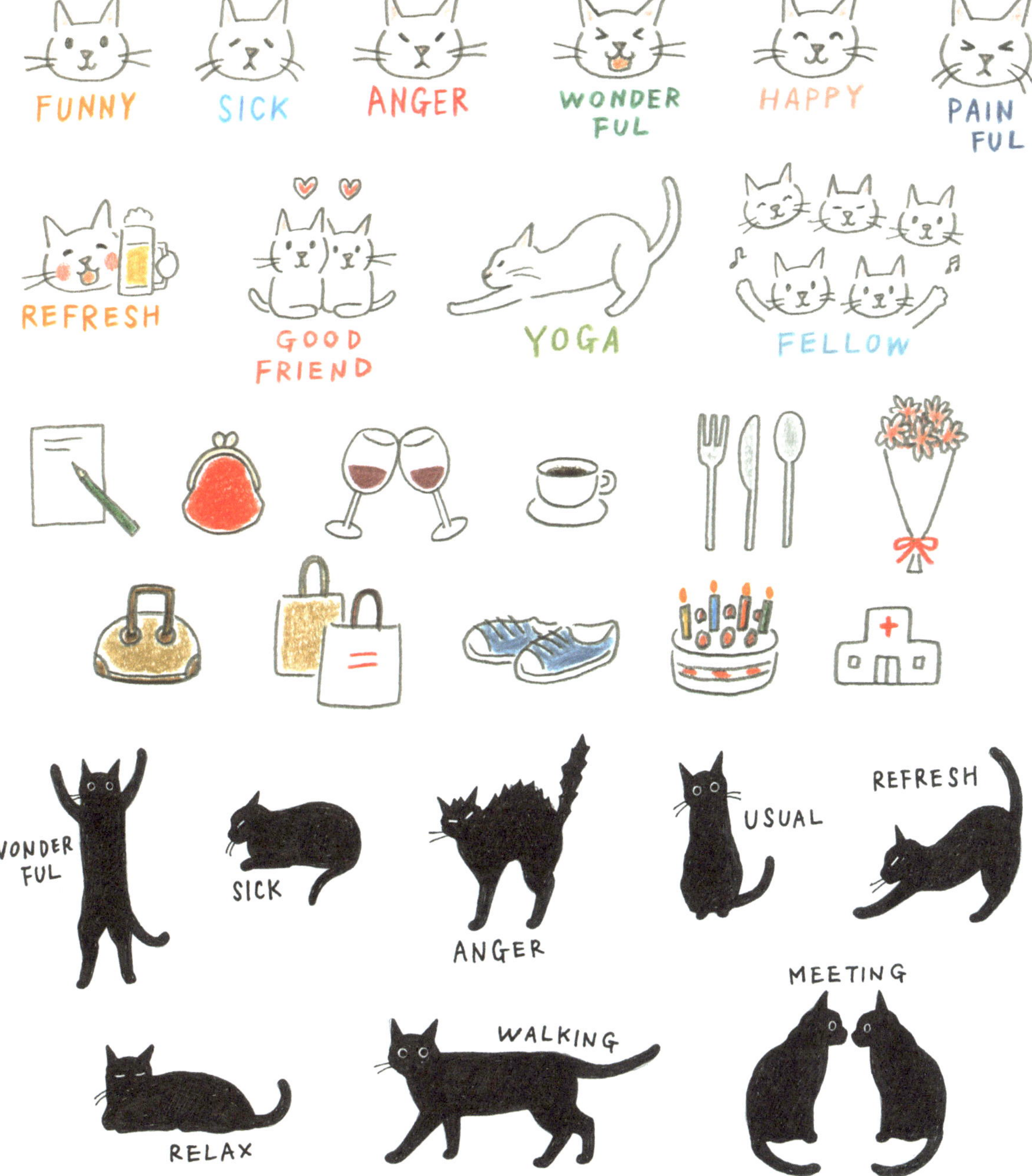

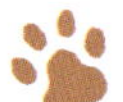 # Give cat art with a gift

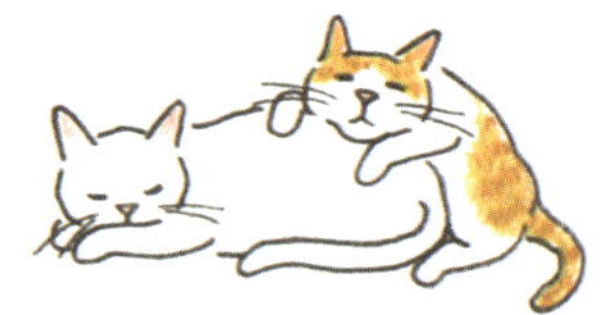

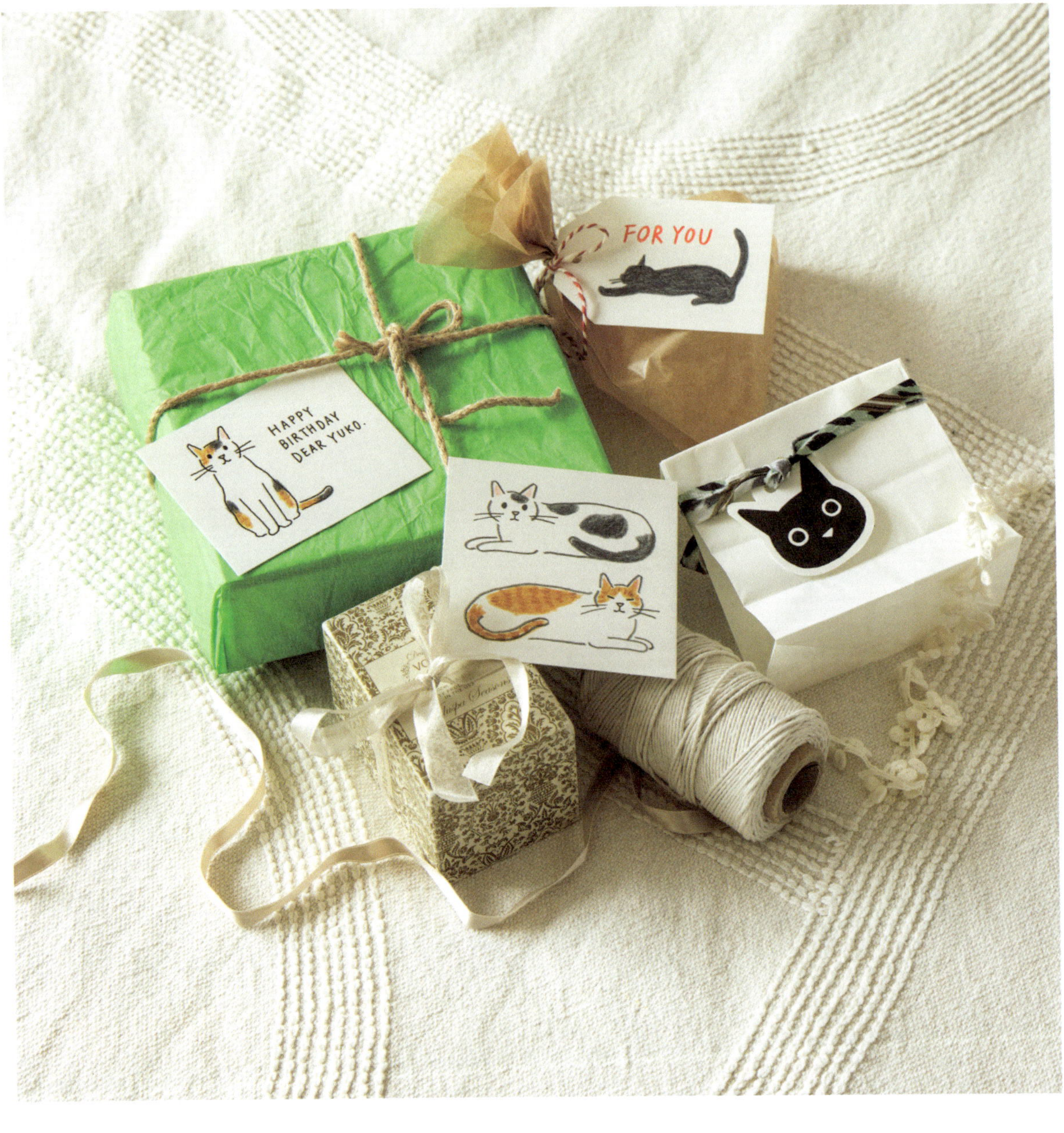

Try making a cat card to give along with a gift. If the gift is for someone who owns a cat, drawing their cat's fur pattern will be a lovely personal touch they're sure to appreciate!

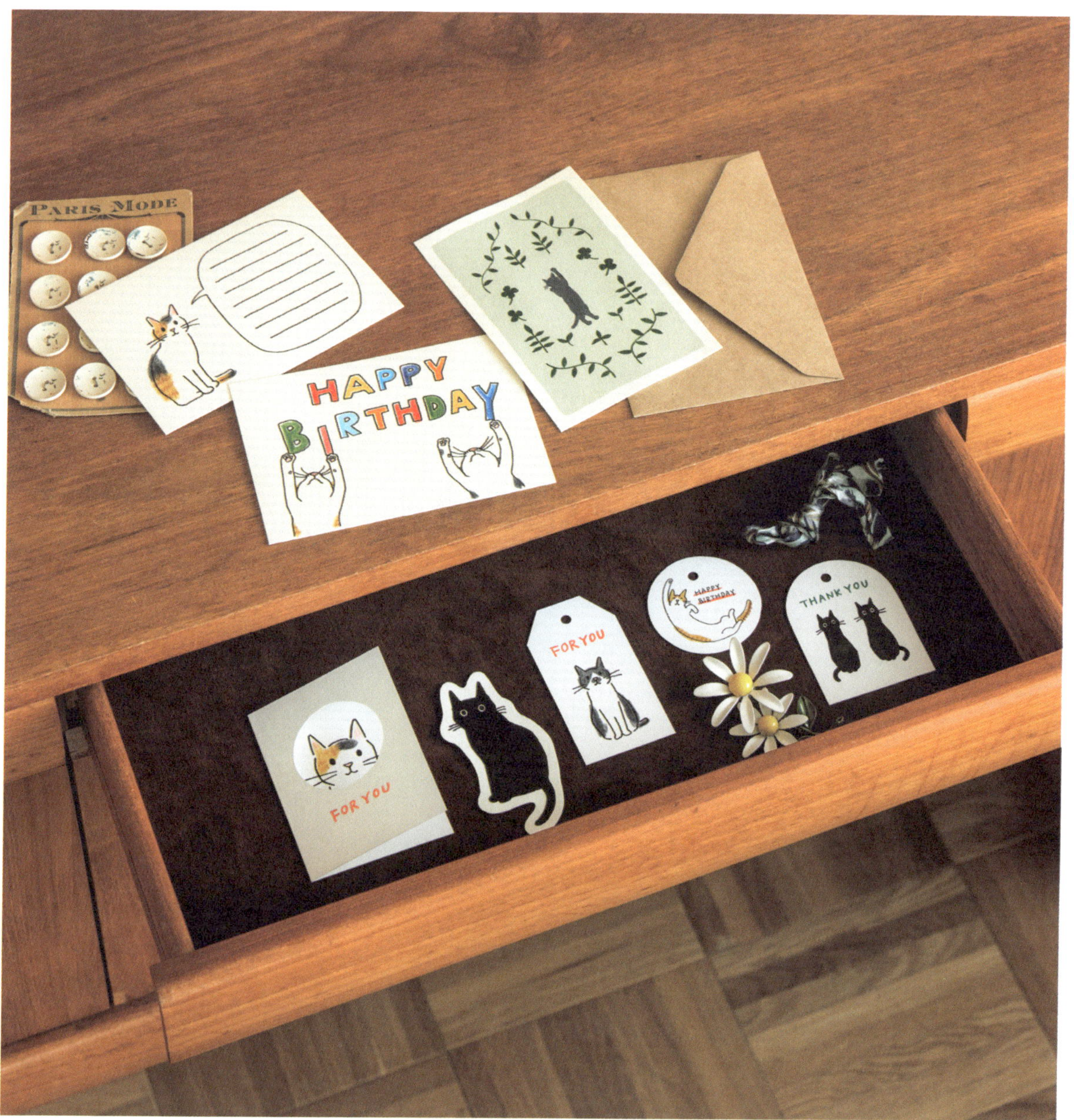

🐾 Make gift cards

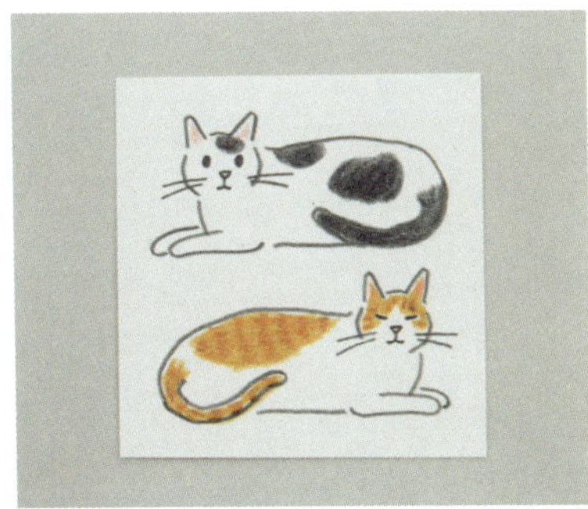

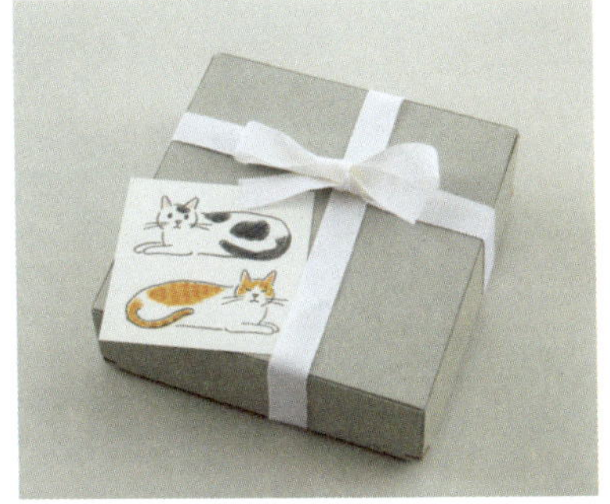

1 Trim paper to a size suitable for including with the gift. Because it's a card, thicker paper is better.

2 Draw a cat illustration.

3 Tuck it into the prepared gift, and it's done.

🐾 Make cards with windows

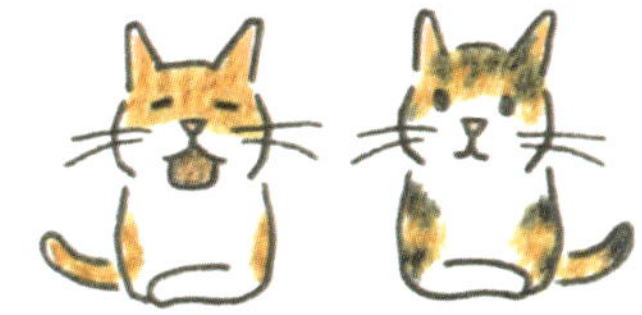

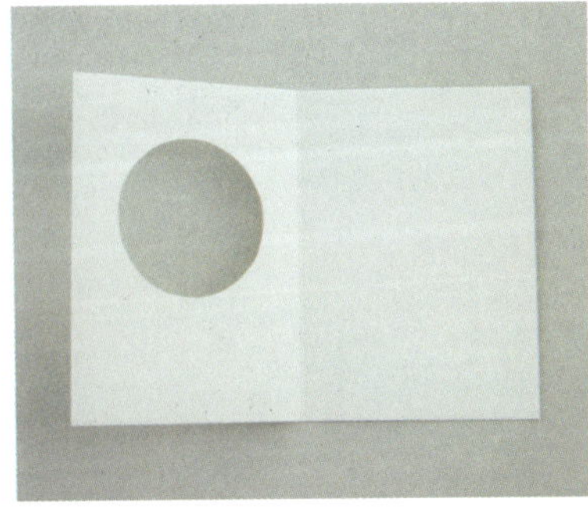

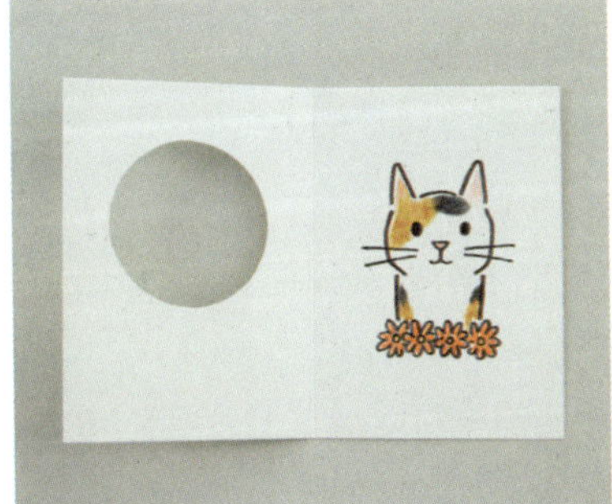

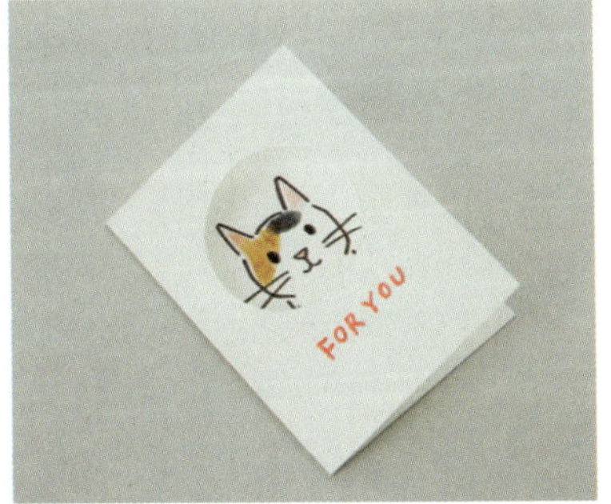

1 Fold postcard-size paper in half and cut a window on the left side with a cutter or punch.

2 On the right side, draw a cat illustration. Be sure to verify its position in the window in the early stages.

3 Close the card to finish. The cat's face is peeking through the window!

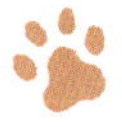 Make tag cards

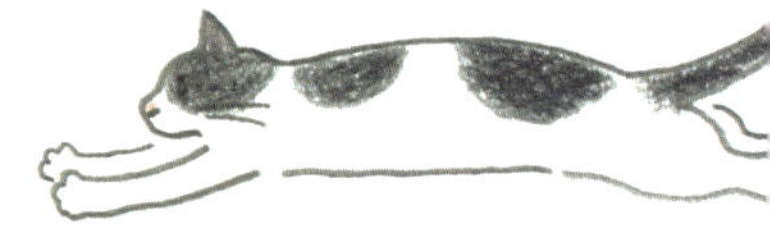

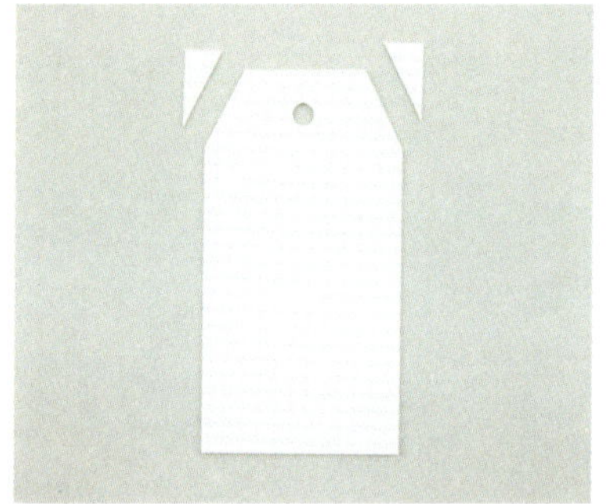

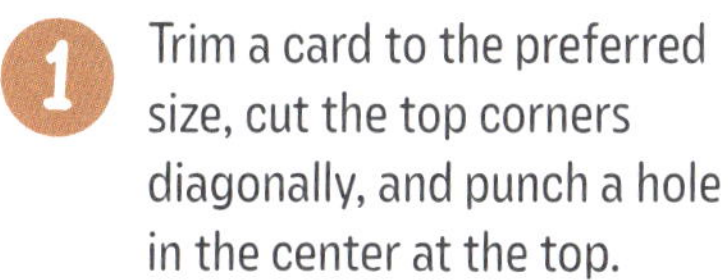

1 Trim a card to the preferred size, cut the top corners diagonally, and punch a hole in the center at the top.

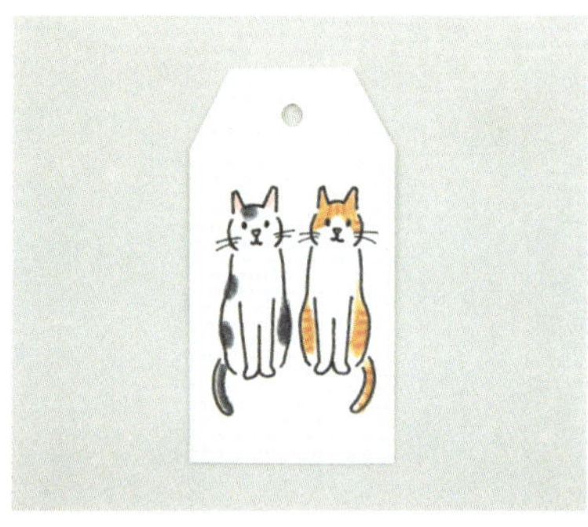

2 Draw a cat illustration.

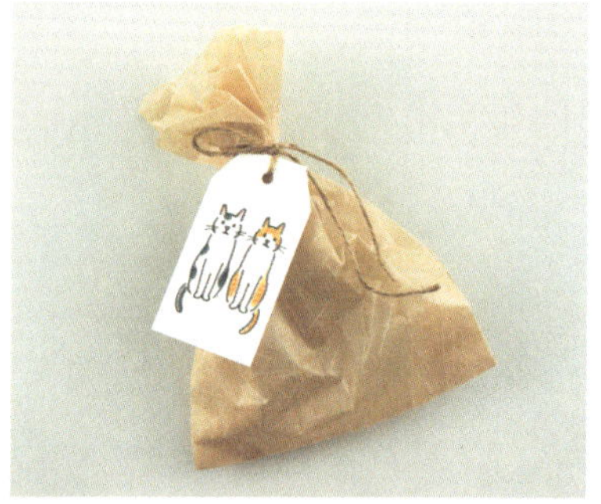

3 Thread cord or ribbon through the hole and attach it to your gift—it's completed.

Make shaped cards

1 Get some thick paper or cardstock that's slightly larger than the illustration you plan to draw.

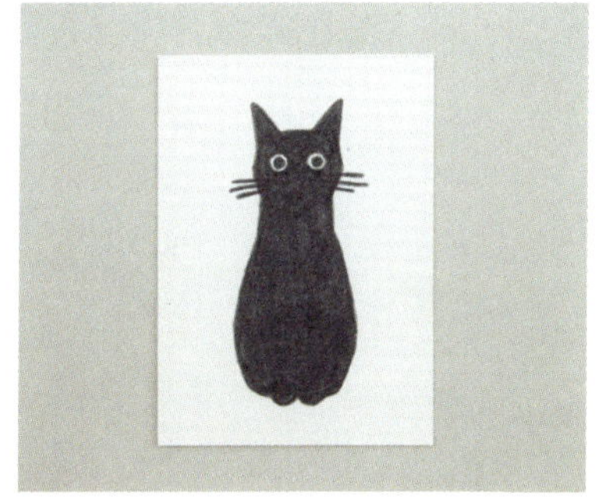

2 Draw the cat illustration while leaving room for the planned border.

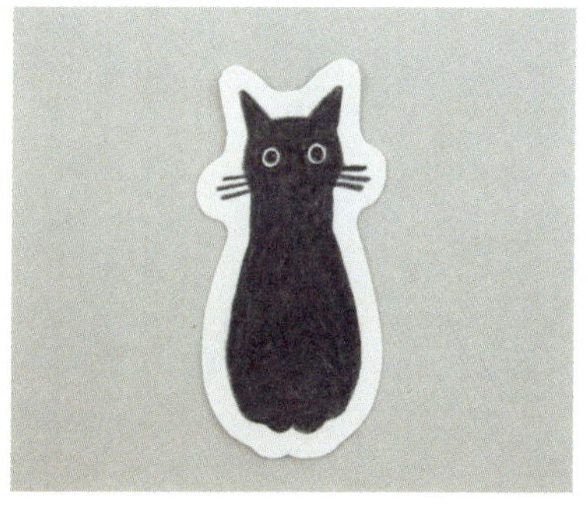

3 Use a cutter or scissors to cut your drawing out, leaving a consistent border all around the perimeter—and it's done.

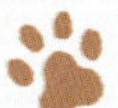 # Making personalized clothes and accessories

Use your cat illustrations to make your own unique items. You can draw directly on plain materials, or upload your artwork to a print-on-demand website—there are many ways to do it. It'll make the creative fun of drawing illustrations even more rewarding.

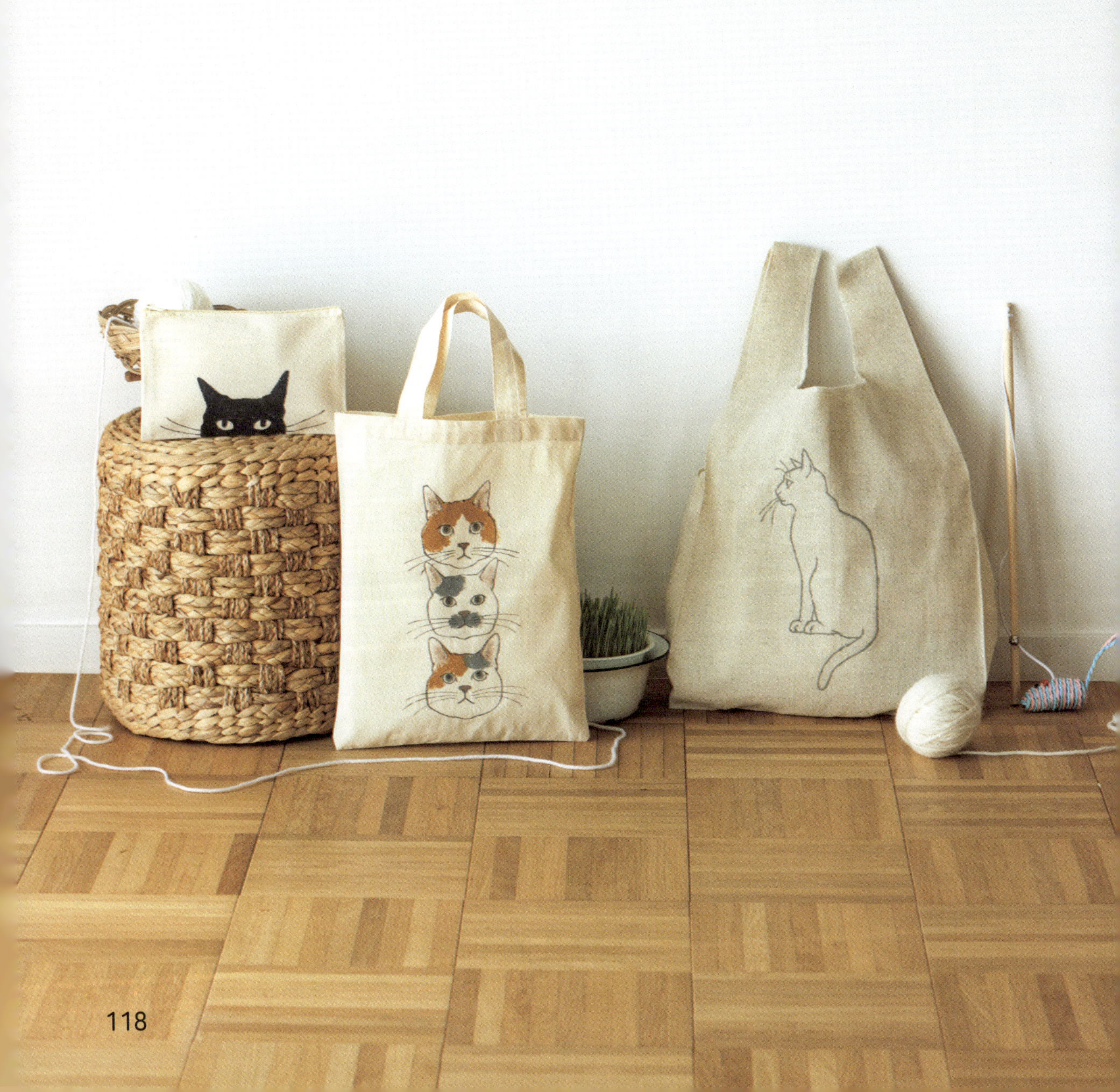

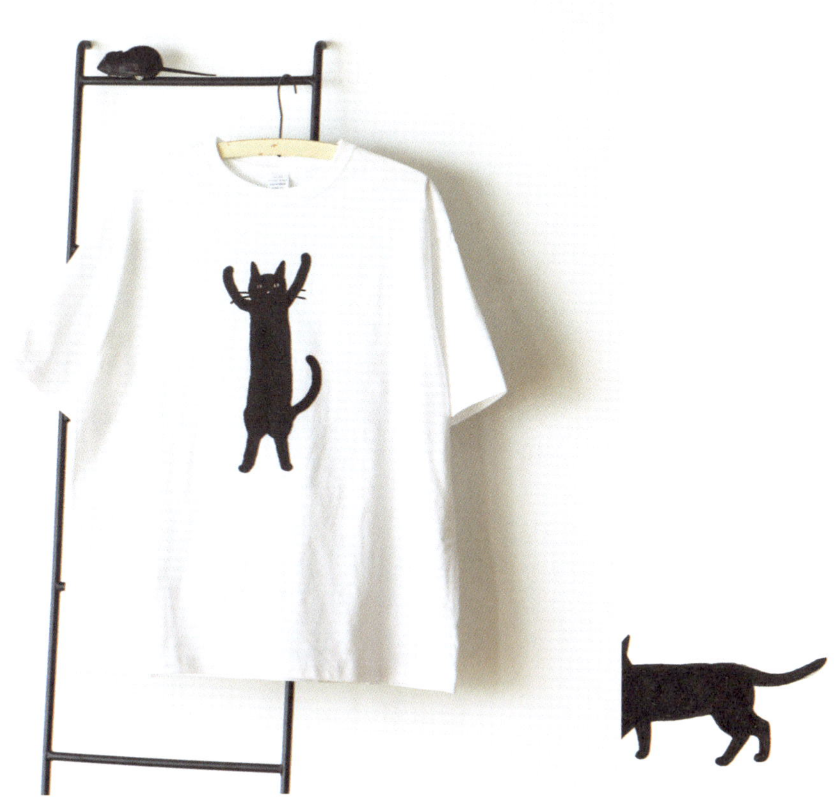

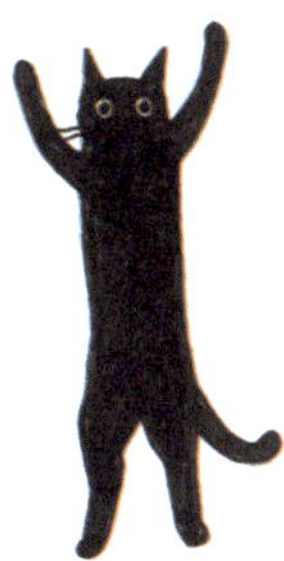

I decorated items with my original
artwork using the SUZURI website.

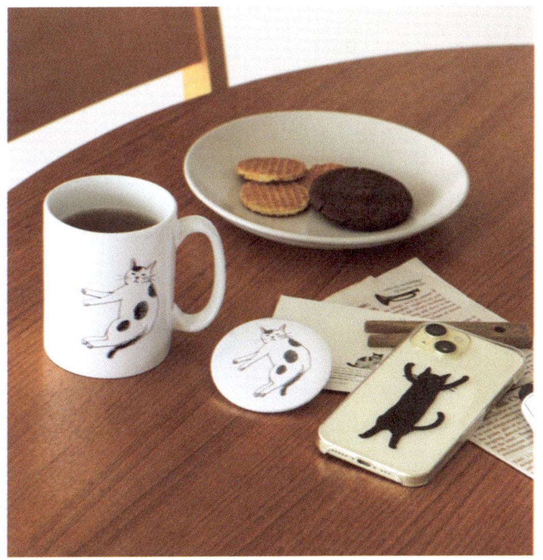

🐾 Paint directly on a fabric bag

Use a plain cotton bag and paint directly on it with acrylic paints. It can withstand getting wet, but the colors may fade or transfer, so handle it with care. Wash it gently by hand.

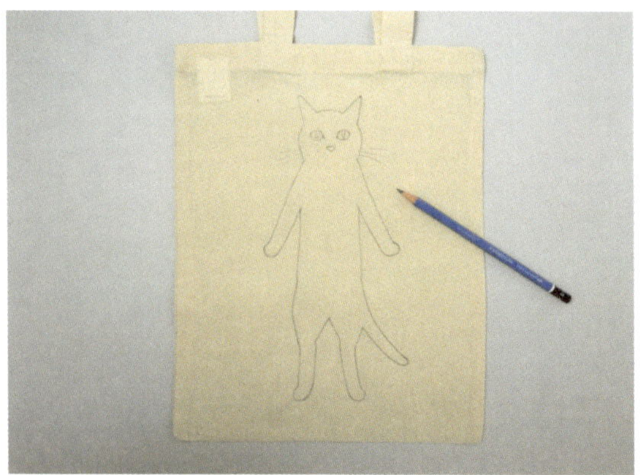

1 Smooth a plain cotton bag flat and lightly sketch a rough outline in pencil.

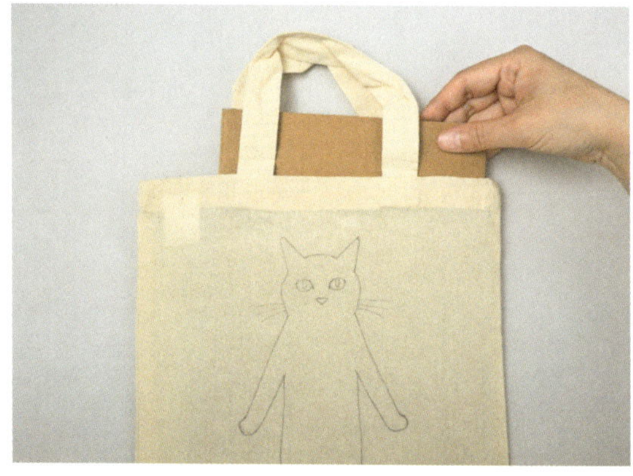

2 To prevent the paint from bleeding through to the back, insert cardboard or thick paper inside the bag.

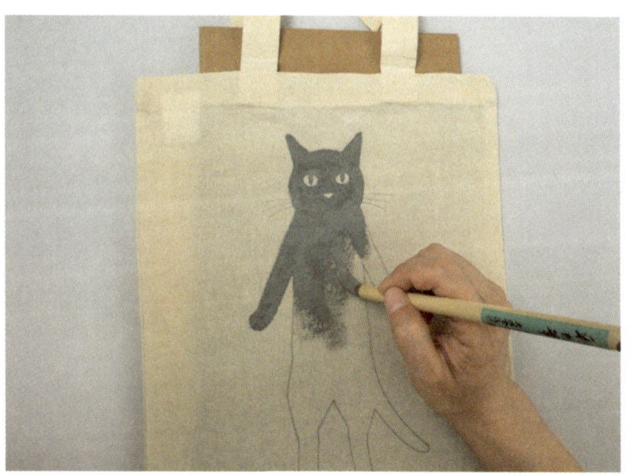

1 Paint over your sketch with acrylic paints. A bold touch works just right.

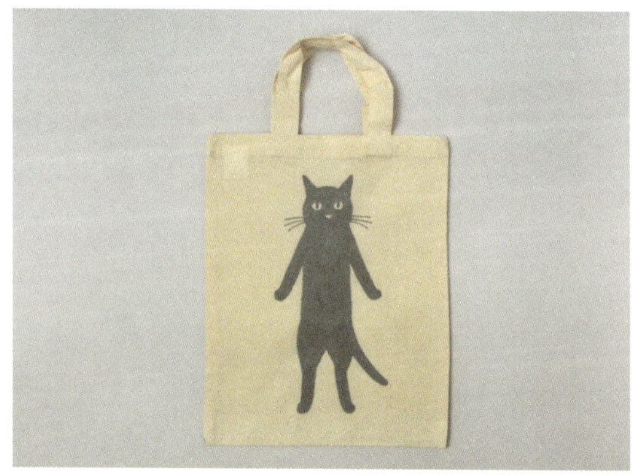

2 Once it's fully dry, your one-of-a-kind original bag is complete!

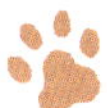 Create personalized items online

If you have a favorite drawing you've made, use an online service to print it on original apparel and accessories. You can create a variety of items and even sell them for extra income!

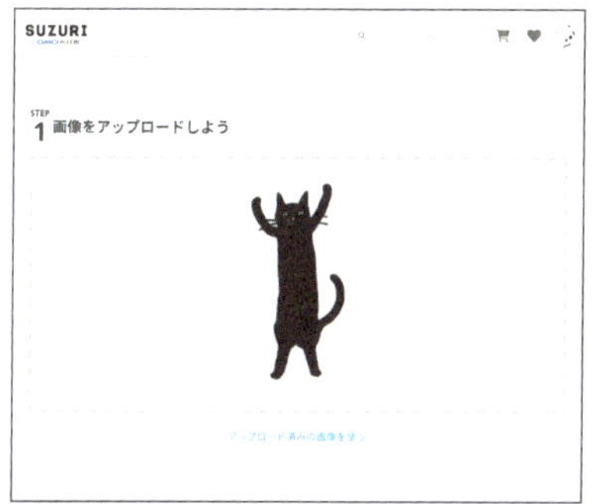

1 Prepare an image of the artwork you want to apply.* The image should be in .jpg or .png format and under 15 MB in size.

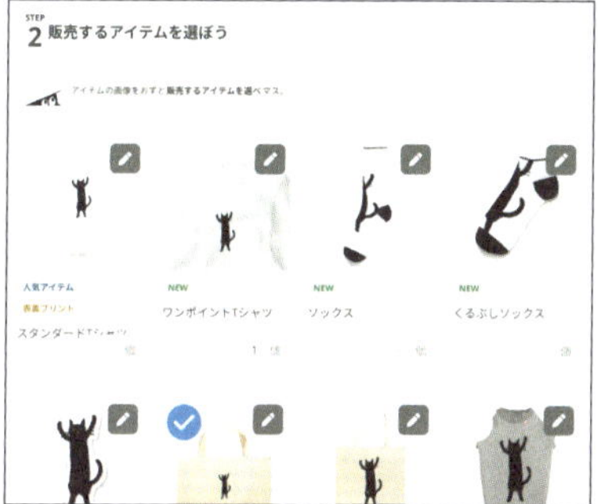

2 Create an account on the service's website. In this case, I'm using SUZURI. Choose the item you want to decorate and upload the prepared image.

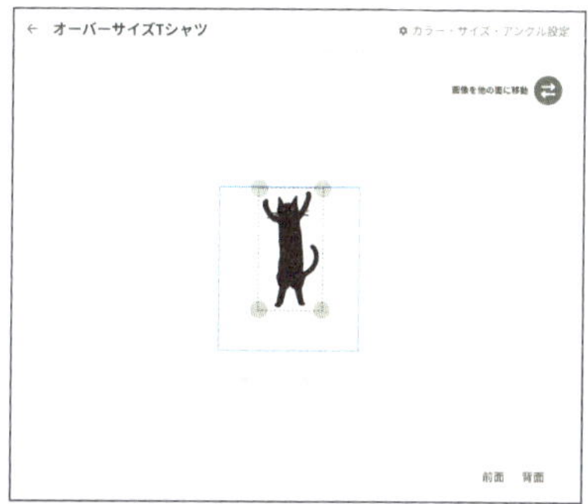

3 Review the size and position of your design on the article.

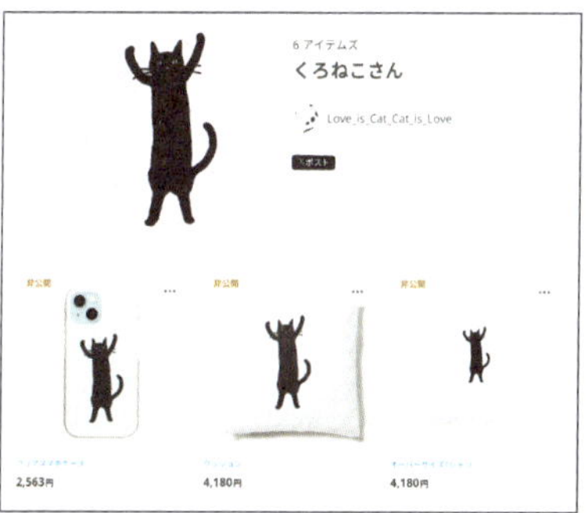

4 You can purchase a subscription to name your item and set your profit margin if you plan to offer it for sale. If it's just for you, buy the item at the base price.

5 Click "Sell" to start selling. If you're preparing the item for just yourself, set it to "private," so others won't be able to view or purchase it.

SUZURI
by GMOペパボ

SUZURI (suzuri.jp) is an easy-to-use Japanese website where you can create and sell custom merchandise decorated with your original artwork. (There are many others you could use, including: Printify, Printful, Amazon Merch On Demand, Teepublic, Redbubble, etc.) You can simply purchase the items yourself to easily get various personalized home goods, or offer them for sale. Because everything is printed on demand, there's no need to stock inventory. Why not make a little extra spending money?

*Using someone else's image may result in copyright infringement or violation of site rules, so only use your own original work. Please also refrain from using the illustrations from this book to create or sell merchandise.

🐾 Draw a four-panel comic strip

Once you can draw cats, making comics can be fun too! Get inspiration from your pet cat or come up with your own creative ideas. Drawing comics is a great mood-lifting activity.

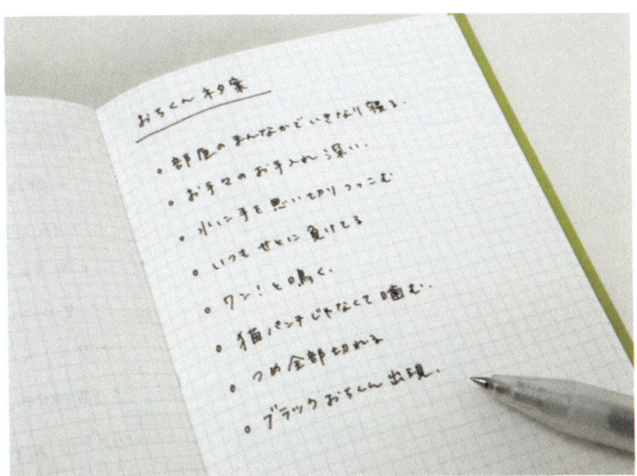

1 Keep a notebook of ideas where you jot down cute or funny observations from daily life.

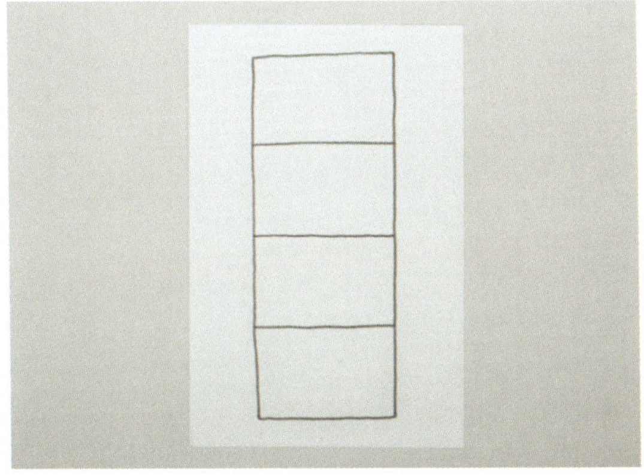

2 Draw panels on your favorite paper. Using a ruler for clean lines is fine, but loose freehand lines can look cute and lively too.

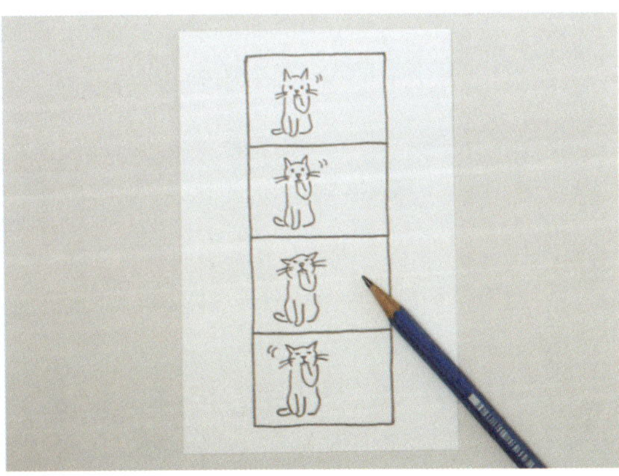

1 Draw your illustrations based on your ideas. Leave space in the panels for any text you plan to add.

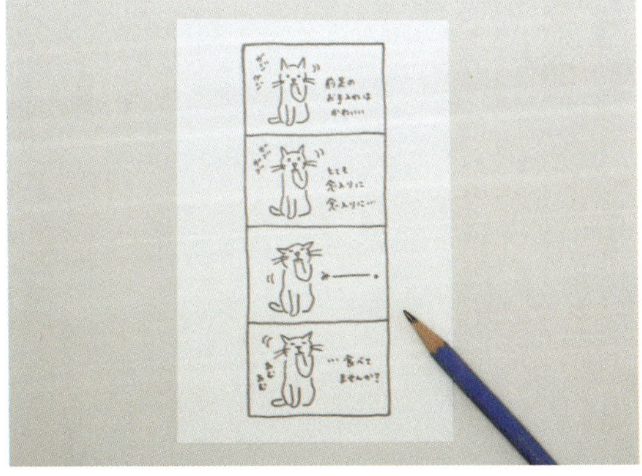

2 Add dialogue or text, and you're done! Did it turn out cute?

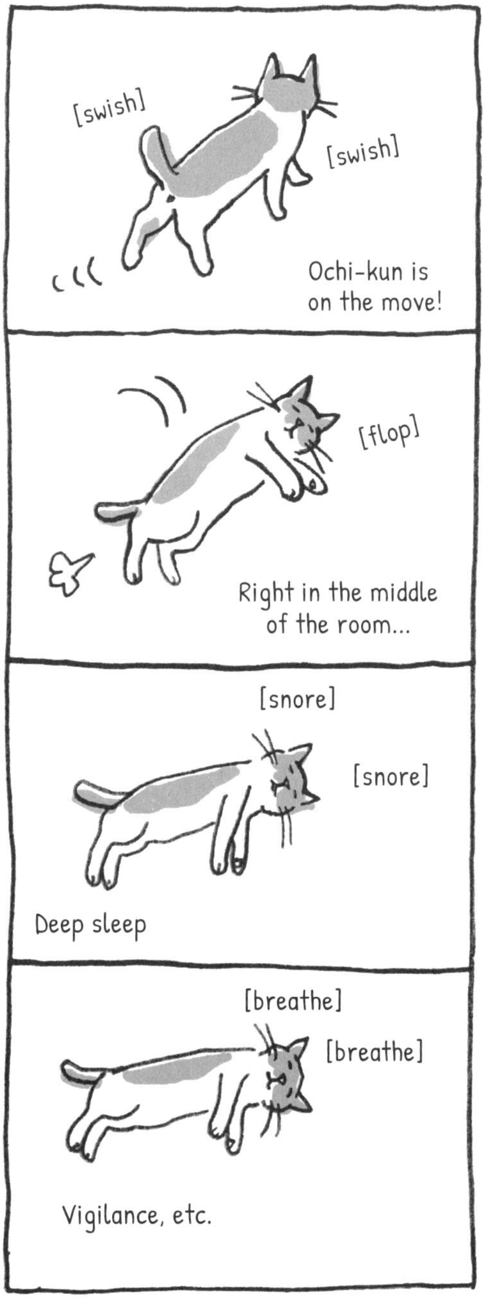

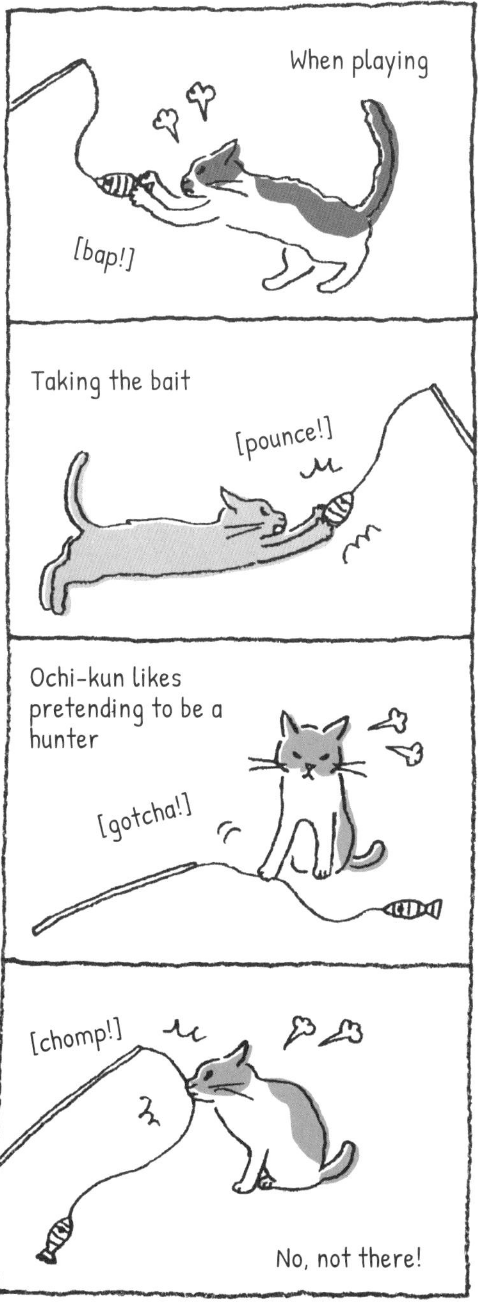

From *I'm Ochi-kun* (Tane LLC)

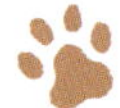 # Posting to Instagram

If you can draw cats, why not try posting your drawings on Instagram? You can easily upload photos taken with your smartphone, so check the image editing method on the following page and give it a try!

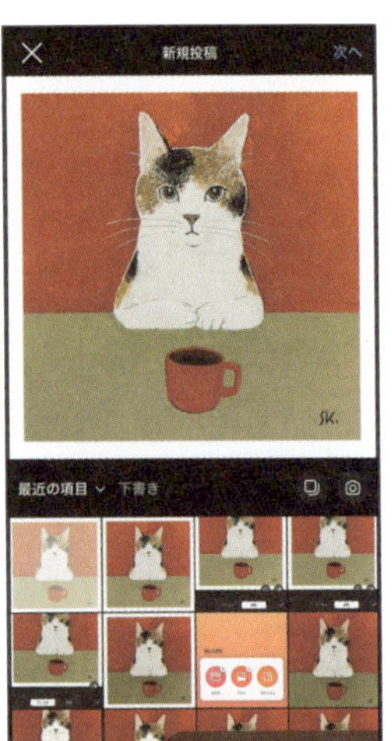

Take a picture of your cat drawing with your phone, open the Instagram app, and select the image from the "new post" (plus sign) button at the bottom. The edited version (see the following page) is ideal.

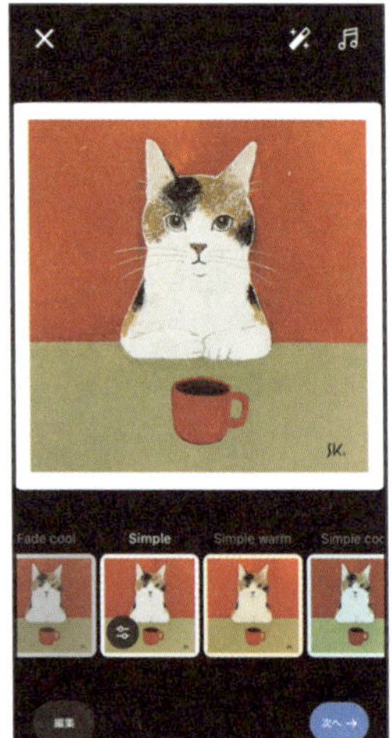

After selecting the image, press "Next" and choose your favorite filter or adjust brightness and color. If it's already edited, you don't need further adjustments.

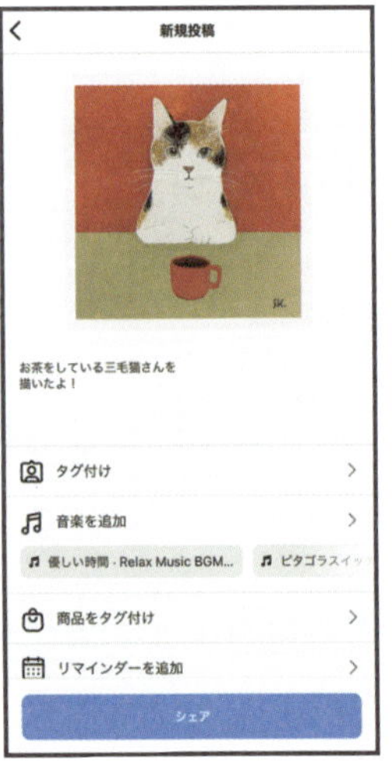

Press "Next" again and enter a caption. Write whatever you like—the title of your drawing or how you felt while drawing it.

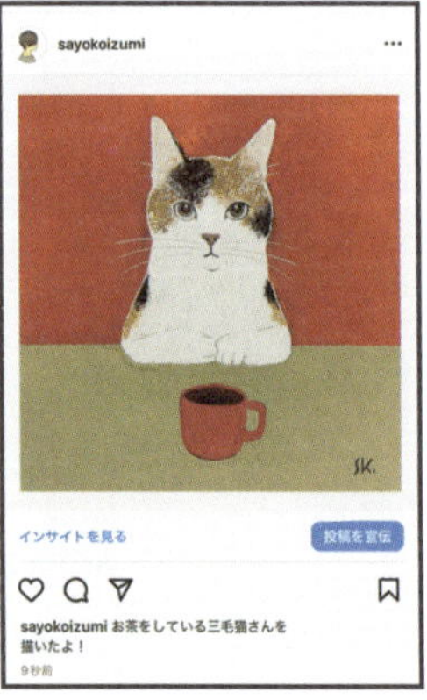

Press "Share" at the bottom and you're done! Getting likes and comments will make you feel great!

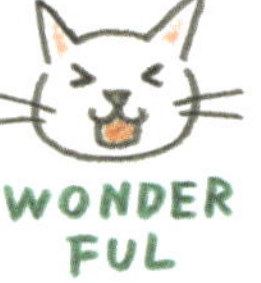

Editing images using an iPhone

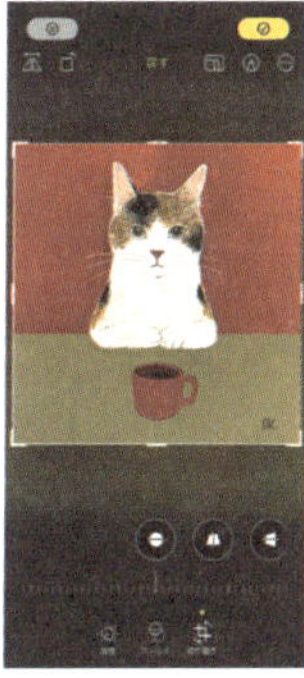 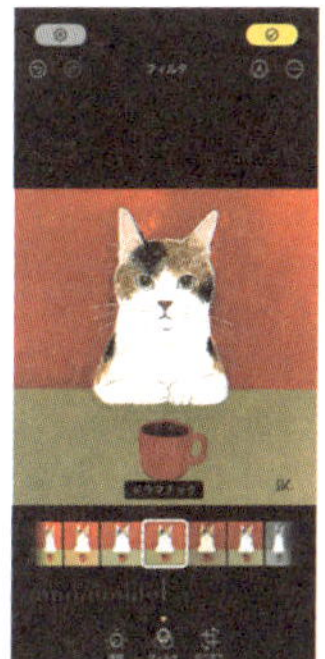 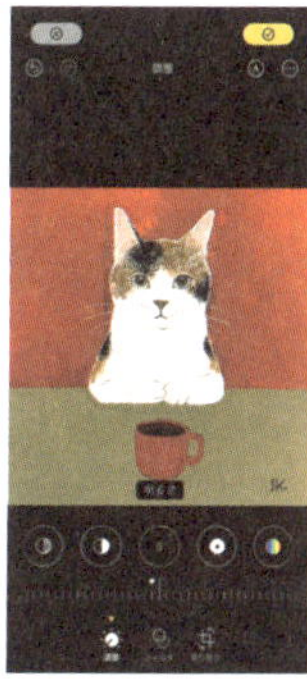

1 After selecting a photo from your smartphone, tap "Edit" in the upper right, then tap "Crop" in the lower right to set the size and crop the image.

2 Use "Filter" at the bottom center to choose a variation. You don't have to use one—comparing with the original image can make it easier to decide.

3 Use "Adjust" in the lower left to tweak brightness, contrast and other color settings. Once you're done, tap the yellow button in the upper right corner to save.

Using an image-editing app

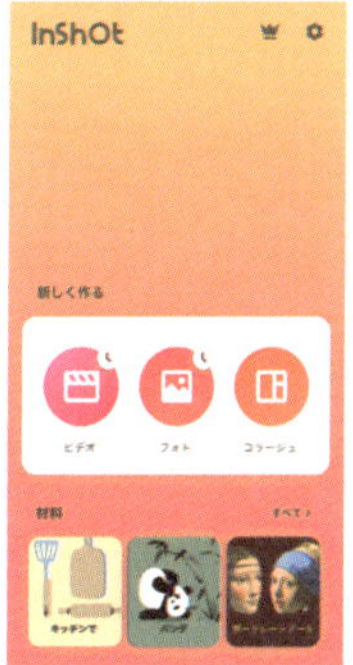 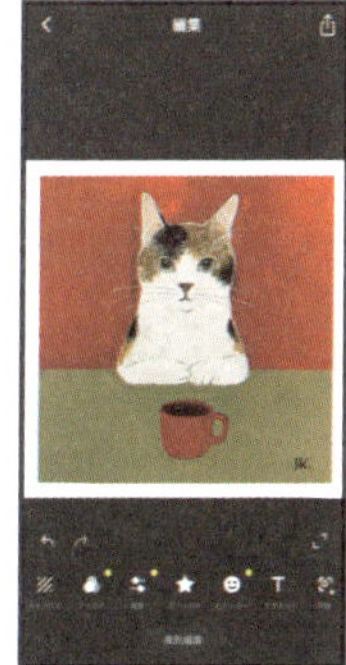 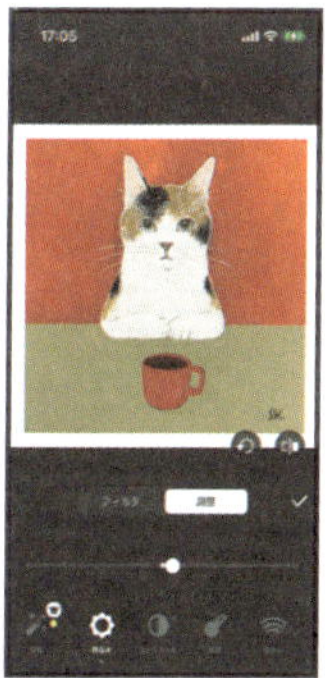

1 Download the app **InShot**.* When you open it, select "Photo" in the center.

2 Choose an image, then adjust the size under "Canvas." Adding a white border gives it a matted look, which is recommended.

3 Use "Filter" and "Adjust" to fine-tune the colors, then tap the checkmark icon to save.

*InShot is an application for editing photos and videos. Not only can you edit photos, but you can also work with videos and make collages, so there are lots of ways to have fun with it.

Afterword

Ever since I started living with cats, I've spent
every spare moment sketching them with complete
fascination. I've always loved drawing, so I poured my
affection for cats into my art, and before I knew it, I
was drawing nothing but cats! No matter how many I
draw, the cat—with its supple body always twisting—
seems to say, "Look, I can pose like this too," or "Here's
another expression for you." Their breathtaking beauty
is endlessly inspiring. Thanks to that, I never get tired
of drawing them. Of course, there are many ways to
express one's love for cats, but if you've picked up
this book, you're probably ready to add drawing and
painting as new ways to express that love. May your art
become one of the many bonds between you and your
beloved cat!

—**Sayo Koizumi**

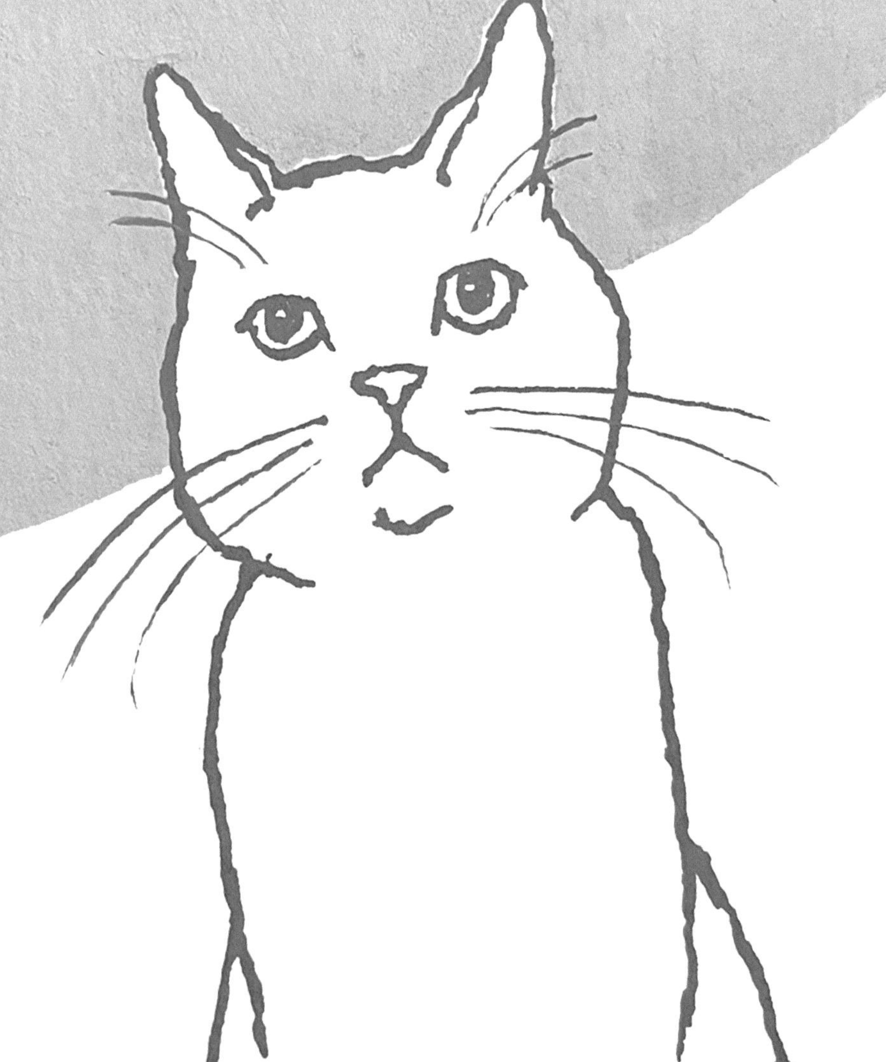

Sayo Koizumi is a talented illustrator and lifelong cat lover who has developed a successful career depicting cats in her native Japan. She graduated from Tokyo University of the Arts and completed her graduate studies there as well. She is the author of several books about cats in Japanese. She provides illustrations for the cat-themed magazine *Neko Biyori* (published by Takarajimasha), and illustrated *I Want to Go Home to a House with Cats* (ISBN: 9784777825318), a book containing short essays and poems by Tomosato Nio. Her work appears in many other books, magazines and publications, and she frequently holds solo exhibitions.

Website: sayokoizumi.com
Instagram: @sayokoizumi

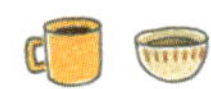

Published by Tuttle Publishing, an imprint of Periplus Editions (HK) Ltd.

www.tuttlepublishing.com

ISBN: 978-4-8053-2037-2

Neko no Kakikata Renshucho
Copyright © Koizumi Sayo
English translation rights arranged with Nitto Shoin Honsha Co., Ltd.
through Japan UNI Agency, Inc., Tokyo

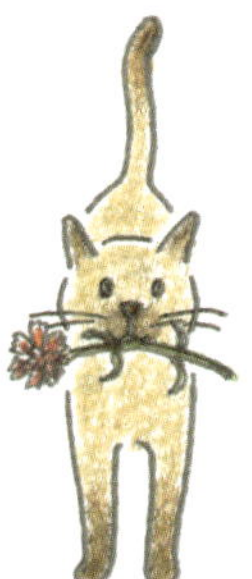

English translation © 2026 Periplus Editions (HK) Ltd

Distributed by:

North America, Latin America & Europe
Tuttle Publishing
364 Innovation Drive
North Clarendon
VT 05759-9436 U.S.A.
Tel: (802) 773-8930
Fax: (802) 773-6993
info@tuttlepublishing.com
www.tuttlepublishing.com

Japan
Tuttle Publishing
Yaekari Building 3rd Floor
5-4-12 Osaki Shinagawa-ku
Tokyo 141 0032
Tel: (81) 3 5437-0171
Fax: (81) 3 5437-0755
sales@tuttle.co.jp
www.tuttle.co.jp

Asia Pacific
Berkeley Books Pte. Ltd.
3 Kallang Sector, #04-01
Singapore 349278
Tel: (65) 6741-2178
Fax: (65) 6741-2179
inquiries@periplus.com.sg
www.tuttlepublishing.com

Printed in Malaysia   2601VP
30 29 28 27 26   10 9 8 7 6 5 4 3 2 1

GPSR Representative
Matt Parsons, matt.parsons@upi2mbooks.hr, UPI-2M PLUS d.o.o., Medulićeva 20, 10000, Zagreb, Croatia